Lost Indian Magic

BONUS CD!
AUTHENTIC NATIVE CHANTS FOR:
Prosperity! Good Luck!
To Harmonize
With The Spirits!

A Mystery Story of the Red Man as he Lived Before the White Men Came

BY GRACE AND CARL MOON
WITH ADDITIONAL MATERIAL BY DRAGONSTAR

GLOBAL COMMUNICATIONS

Lost Indian Magic

by Grace and Carl Moon
With Dragonstar

ISBN-10: 1-60611-085-3
ISBN-13: 978-1-60611-085-0

Nonfiction

Timothy Green Beckley: Editorial Director
Carol Rodriguez: Publishers Assistant
Tim Swartz: Associate Editor
Sean Casteel: Editorial Assistant
Cover Art: Tim R. Swartz

For free catalog write:
Global Communications
P.O. Box 753
New Brunswick, NJ 08903

Free Subscription to Conspiracy Journal E-Mail Newsletter
www.conspiracyjournal.com

Contents

Secret Magical Teachings Of Native Americans By Dragonstar - 7 -
Emerging From Within The Earth - 7 -
The Medicine Wheel - 9 -
Sacred Numbers - 11 -
Sacred Formulas Of The Cherokees - 11 -
Concerning Living Humanity - 14 -
Love Charm - 14 -
To Insure Constancy - 16 -
Those About To Be Slain - 17 -
This Tells About Going Into The Water - 17 -
Song For Painting - 18 -
To Attract And Fix The Affections - 19 -
For Separation Of Lovers - 20 -
To Shorten A Night-Goer On This Side - 20 -
I Have Lost Something - 22 -
This Is To Frighten A Storm - 23 -
What Those Who Have Been To War Did To Help Themselves - 24 -
Birth Totem - 27 -
Birth Totem Dates - 28 -
Budding Trees Moon: March 21 - April 19 - 29 -
Frogs Return Moon: April 20 - May 20 - 30 -
Corn Planting Moon: May 21 - June 20 - 31 -
Strong Sun Moon: June 21 - July 21 - 32 -
Ripe Berries Moon: July 22 - August 21 - 33 -
Harvest Moon: August 22 - September 21 - 33 -
Ducks Fly Moon: September 22 - October 22 - 34 -
Freeze Up Moon: October 23 - November 22 - 35 -
Long Snows Moon: November 23 - December 21 - 36 -
Earth Renewal Moon: December 22 - January 19 - 37 -

Rest & Cleansing Moon: January 20 - February 18 ... - 38 -
Big Winds Moon: February 19 - March 20 ... - 39 -
Cherokee Legend Of Crystals ... - 40 -
Sacred Herbs Of The Native Americans ... - 42 -
Northern White Cedar: ... - 42 -
White Sage Or Ghost Sage: ... - 42 -
Sweet Grass: ... - 42 -
Traditional Native American Prayer To Start The Day With Good Luck ... - 43 -

Lost Indian Magic: A Mystery Story Of The Red Man As He Lived Before The White Men Came. By Grace Purdie Moon & Carl Moon ... - 45 -

Foreword ... - 47 -
Prologue ... - 49 -
Chapter 1 The Theft ... - 51 -
Chapter 2 The Wrong Bag ... - 63 -
Chapter 3 Kay'-Yah At Ta-Pau'-Wee ... - 69 -
Chapter 4 The Hidden Passage ... - 83 -
Chapter 5 Dee-Nay's Narrative ... - 91 -
Chapter 6 The Cave Man ... - 101 -
Chapter 7 A Secret Council ... - 107 -
Chapter 8 The Mark Of The Bear-Witch ... - 115 -
Chapter 9 The Magic Sleep ... - 125 -
Chapter 10 Sah'-Ne In The "Eagle's Nest" ... - 135 -
Chapter 11 "Be'-Ta-Atsin!" ... - 143 -
Chapter 12 Kay'-Yah Tests The Bow ... - 153 -
Chapter 13 The Place Of The White Rock ... - 165 -
Chapter 14 Tag-A'-Mo Speaks ... - 175 -
Chapter 15 The Chin-Dog Howls ... - 181 -

ILLUSTRATIONS

Figure 1 Indian Totem Pole – Picture by Timothy Green Beckley ... - 6 -
Figure 2 Rock Hieroglyphics Of The Algonquians ... - 12 -
Figure 3 Native American Magic Symbols From Northern California ... - 13 -
Figure 4 Native American Petroglyphs Of Supernatural Beings ... - 26 -
Figure 5 Native American Magic Symbols ... - 44 -
Figure 6 Apache Mother and Children on Horseback, Painting by Carl Moon ... - 44 -
Figure 7 "He Raised His Arms In Salutation To The Great Light-Maker" ... - 46 -
Figure 8 Navajo Medicine Man, Pesothlanny (much money), Photo by Carl Moon ... - 47 -
Figure 9 Indian Totem Pole – Picture by Timothy Green Beckley ... - 48 -
Figure 10 Indian Totem Pole – Picture by Timothy Green Beckley ... - 50 -
Figure 11 "He Could Not Remember The Day When He Had Not Seen Sah'-Ne Pass With Her Water-Jar" ... - 57 -
Figure 12 Indian Chief, Painting by Carl Moon ... - 62 -
Figure 13 Daily Chores, Painting by Carl Moon ... - 68 -
Figure 14 "Stepping Quickly Backward, His Foot Went Into Empty Space, And He Felt Himself Falling Through The Air" ... - 80 -
Figure 15 Indian Totem Pole – Picture by Timothy Green Beckley ... - 82 -
Figure 16 Publisher of Lost Indian Magic. Timothy Beckley. is photographed in the Land of Enchantment by Charla Gene' ... - 90 -
Figure 17 Indian on Horseback, Painting by Carl Moon ... - 100 -
Figure 18 Tale of the Tribe, Relating the legends and magic by the oral tradition, Photo by Carl Moon ... - 124 -
Figure 19 "He Stopped In Front Of Kay'-Yah And, Shaking The Rattle And Prayer-Stick He Chanted His Song" ... - 131 -
Figure 20 Navajo Medicine Man, Meguelito, Photo by Carl Moon ... - 133 -
Figure 21 Native American cultures believe everyone has a birth totem that incorporates elements of their personality and individual characteristics. Photo by Timothy Beckley." ... - 134 -
Figure 22 The pottery maker, Nampeyo (painting pottery). (1904?-1910) Gelatin Print by Carl Moon ... - 142 -
Figure 23 Publisher of Lost Indian Magic Timothy Beckley is photographed in the Land of Enchantment by Charla Gene' ... - 152 -
Figure 24 "He Extended His Right Hand As Far As Possible Toward The Rope That Hung From The Tree" ... - 157 -
Figure 25 "Let An Arrow Fly At The Fleeing Figure That Was Now Running Swiftly" ... - 160 -
Figure 26 "He Drew It Out, Tight-Clasped In His Hand. . . . Sah'-Ne Watched Him With Growing Amazement" ... - 172 -
Figure 27 The Dancing Lesson – A Taos boy learning the Corn Dance, Photo by Carl Moon ... - 173 -
Figure 28 Publisher of Lost Indian Magic Timothy Beckley is photographed in the Land of Enchantment by Charla Gene' ... - 174 -
Figure 29 Home from the Hunt, Taos Hunter, Photo by Carl Moon ... - 174 -
Figure 30 1904 Gelatin Print Photo by Carl Moon ... - 180 -
Figure 31 "And The Song Was The To-To'-Me Death Chant" ... - 188 -

Figure 1
Indian Totem Pole – Picture by Timothy Green Beckley

Secret Magical Teachings Of Native Americans By Dragonstar

Over the last few decades there has been little attention paid to the magical traditions of the Native American tribes. This could be partly due to the overwhelming influence of the magical teachings originating from Europe and the Middle East. Another reason is that there is, and has been for centuries, a bias towards aboriginal cultures and their "animism" world-view.

The idea that souls, or spirits, exist not only in humans but also in animals, plants, rocks, and natural phenomena, predominated when humans were chiefly hunter-gatherers. However, this view shifted as people transitioned from nomadic to agricultural civilizations. This shift, from wandering hunter-gatherers to stationary farmers, created a schism that exists to this day.

Native American spirituality can also be described as panentheism (deity/spirit present in, as well as beyond, everything). Such a worldview assumes the existence of Spirit beyond the visible world, but also dwelling in all that is. The Lakota concept of Wakan Tanka (most frequently translated as Great Spirit) illustrates panentheism well: Wakan Tanka is the Spirit over, under, and throughout the entire physical world, its guiding principle, present in individual phenomena yet not confined to it, not strictly singular or plural, neither truly personal nor impersonal. Manitou/manitos of the Algonkians is a similar concept.

Once there was a time when mankind was in tune with nature and everyone easily communed with the spirits. However, this was replaced by priest-chaste wherein it was taught that only a select few could understand the secret rites and rituals to communicate with the spirits and access the magical energies. Natives to North and South America, at least those who maintained a hunter-gatherer lifestyle, retained their original spiritual beliefs with the help of shamans, or medicinemen.

Emerging From Within The Earth

Part of the unique spirituality that made up the Native American tribes was their creation narratives. Often these migration accounts related amazing tales of a group's emergence from within the Earth to populate the surface world. In *Legends & Lore of the American Indians* (1993) edited by Terri Harden we find: "Several tribes claim to have emerged from the interior of the Earth. The Oneidas point to a hill near the falls of Oswego River, N.Y. as their birthplace; the Witchitas rose from the rocks around Red River; the Creeks from a knoll in the valley of Big Black River in the

Natchez area, where dwelt the Master of Breath; the Aztecs were one of seven tribes that came out from the seven caverns of Aztlan, and the Navajos believe that they emerged at a place known to them in the Navajo Mountains."

Harden also writes that "The Mandan tribes of the Sioux suppose that their nation lived in a subterranean village near a vast lake. The Zuni believe that in the old days all men lived in caves in the center of the Earth. There were four caves, one over the other. Men first lived in the lowest cave. It was dark. There was no light, and the cave was crowded. All men were full of sorrow. Through several misadventures they finally reached the exterior of the Earth."

According to the Pawnee story of creation: "All living things were under the ground in confusion and asked one another what each was; but one day as the mole was digging around, he broke a hole through, so that the light steamed in, and he drew back frightened. He has never had any eyes since; the light put them out. The mole did not want to come out, but all the others came out on to the earth through the hole the mole had made."

Another good source of this ancient knowledge is *Native American Legends* (1987) compiled and edited by George E. Lankford. On page 113 he relates:

"What Chekilli, the head chief of the lower and upper Creeks [Indian tribes] said in a talk held in Savannah [Georgia] in 1735, and which was handed over by the interpreter word for word, as follows: 'At a certain time the Earth opened in the west, where it's mouth is. The Earth opened and the Kasihtas [Creeks] came out.'"

The Hopis believe there has been a succession of four worlds. The first world was destroyed by fire, the second by earthquake, and the third by flooding. Some chosen people were saved from the disasters that destroyed the first two worlds by taking refuge underground, and some survived the destruction of the third world by being sealed inside hollow reeds. The Pima Indians speak of the emergence into our world through a spiral hole that was bored up to the Earth's surface.

All Native American tribes generally believed in a great spirit and the animal spirits were considered elders. Humans were seen as young in the world, but to their view animals were spirits, not necessarily confined to looking as they seem to obviously, and the line between human and animal wasn't drawn. So they might speak of Grandfather Coyote, and they would mean it believing that their people had descended from the time of creation from the spirit coyote.

They perceived themselves as part of the natural order and not separate from it as is the common "western" approach. They had a tradition of prayer, but it wasn't really the practice of supplication to a higher power like it was in Europe. If a hunter brought down a deer he would pray, thanking his brother or sister for giving their life so the tribe could eat. Because they believed that the deer spirit gave its flesh willingly, being an ancestor and that if they disrespected the deer it could speak with its kin and have all deer avoid the tribe's hunters.

Spirit of animal, plant, or human, all kin, that was a universal belief across the American tribes and is part of why they had funerary rites, like returning fish skin and bones to the water, or enshrining bear remains in a cave. That was their territory, and they believed that they had to respect the remains. Even if they took something like deer antlers, it was believed that the deer was still connected to that, and that the power of what they made from the antler came from the deer's cooperation.

The tribes Shamans differed in their view of the power of each spirit, so they didn't see them all as relating the same way. In one tribe Grandmother Spider was the one who put order to the living things in their culture. In another Corn Woman governed the cycle of life in that land and the other spirits needed to respect her. In yet another, Buffalo Woman either spoke for or against the tribe not only to her own kind but to the other native spirits as well.

Often one spirit was seen as especially influential, and even the ancestor spirits, the former Shamans who passed on, or the great war chiefs that are still remembered in stories to the tribe, were said to keep a closer connection to the ancestor spirits than they did to their human descendants. So if a tribe's Shaman went on a spirit journey to ask the grandfathers of the tribe for intercession, they could very likely get: "You offended the great salmon, you screwed up so say you're sorry or stay hungry."

Human or not, the spirit world was a big community and like the Chinese belief that Earth needed to coincide with the celestial kingdom, they felt they had to remember the traditions and respect the spirits though they weren't visible. The idea that the invisible wasn't real was more or less meaningless in Native American culture.

The Medicine Wheel

Native American magicians generally considered achieving inner and outer harmony by balancing all aspects of one's being an ultimate, life goal. The Medicine Wheel is a symbolic representation of this balance and harmony in all aspects of one's being. Implicit in the symbolism of the Medicine Wheel is the idea that each individual aspect within the totality of one's being is itself an infinity of aspects that must be balanced before the whole can be brought into balance.

The Medicine Wheel symbolizes the individual journey we each must take to find our own path. Within the Medicine Wheel are The Four Cardinal Directions and the Four Sacred Colors. The Circle represents the Circle of Life and the Center of the Circle, the Eternal Fire. The Eagle, flying toward the East, is a symbol of strength, endurance and vision. East signifies the renewal of life and the rebirth of unity.

East = Red = success; triumph
North = Blue = defeat; trouble
West = Black = death
South = White = peace; happiness

There are three additional sacred directions:
Up Above = Yellow
Down Below = Brown
Here in the Center = Green

Winter=go-la
The color for North is Blue which represents sadness, defeat.
It is a season of survival and waiting.
The Cherokee word for North means "cold" u-yv-tlv.

Spring=gi-la-go-ge
The color for East is Red which represents victory, power.
Spring is the re-awakening after a long sleep,
victory over winter; the power of new life.
The Cherokee word for East is ka-lv-gv

Summer=go-ga
The color for South is White for peace, happiness & serenity.
Summer is a time of plenty.
The Cherokee word for South means "warm" u-ga-no-wa.

Autumn=u-la-go-hv-s-di
The color for West is Black which represents death.
Autumn is the final harvest; the end of Life's Cycle.
The Cherokee word for West is wu-de-li-gv.

RED was symbolic of success. It was the color of the war club used to strike an enemy in battle as well as the other club used by the warrior to shield himself. Red beads were used to conjure the red spirit to insure long life, recovery from sickness, success in love and ball play or any other undertaking where the benefit of the magic spell was wrought.

BLACK was always typical of death. The soul of the enemy was continually beaten about by black war clubs and enveloped in a black fog. In conjuring to destroy an enemy, the priest used black beads and invoked the black spirits, which always lived in the West, bidding them to tear out the man's soul and carry it to the West, and put it into the black coffin deep in the black mud, with a black serpent coiled above it.

BLUE symbolized failure, disappointment, or unsatisfied desire. To say "they shall never become blue" expressed the belief that they would never fail in anything they undertook. In love charms, the lover figuratively covered himself with red and prayed that his rival would become entirely blue and walk in a blue path. "He is entirely blue," approximates meaning of the common English phrase, "He feels blue." The blue spirits lived in the North.

WHITE denoted peace and happiness. In ceremonial addresses, as the Green Corn Dance and ball play, the people symbolically partook of white food and, after the dance or game, returned along the white trail to their white houses. In love charms, the man, to induce the woman to cast her lost with his, boasted, "I am a white man," implying that all was happiness where he was. White beads had the same meaning in bead conjuring, and white was the color of the stone pipe anciently used in ratifying peace treaties. The White spirits lived in the South.

Sacred Numbers

Two numbers are sacred to the Cherokee. Four is one number; it represented the four primary directions. At the center of their paths lays the sacred fire. Seven is the other and most sacred number. Seven is represented in the seven directions: north, south, east, west, above, bellow, and "here in the center" the place of the sacred fire. Seven also represented the seven ancient ceremonies that formed the yearly Cherokee religious cycle.

The whole being is made up of an indefinite number of individual selves. The Medicine Wheel abstracts from all these individual selves a whole made up of only four, archetypal selves: the illuminated self, the introspective self, the innocent self, and the wise (or knowledgeable) self. Although the whole being is made up of a multiplicity of selves, in Native American traditions these four, archetypal selves are thought to be the most important to re-manifest in order to bring the whole into balance and harmony. The Native American author, Hyemeyohsts Storm, describes this concept in the following passage from Seven Arrows.

> At birth, each of us is given a particular Beginning Place within these Four Great Directions on the Medicine Wheel. This Starting Place gives us our first way of perceiving things, which will then be our easiest and most natural way throughout our lives. But any person who perceives from only one of these Four Great Directions will remain just a partial man. For example, a man who possesses only the Gift of the North will be wise. But he will be a cold man, a man without feeling. And the man who lives only in the East will have the clear, far sighted vision of the Eagle, but he will never be close to things. This man will feel separated, high above life, and will never understand or believe that he can be touched by anything. A man or woman who perceives only from the West will go over the same thought again and again in their mind, and will always be undecided. And if a person has only the Gift of the South, he will see everything with the eyes of a Mouse. He will be too close to the ground and too near sighted to see anything except whatever is right in front of him, touching his whiskers.

Sacred Formulas Of The Cherokees

With the Native Americans magic was sung, and songs had magic power. Both were accompanied by appropriate bodily movement, so that a Native American will say indifferently, "I cannot sing that dance, or I cannot dance that song." Words, melody and movement were as much mixed as the water of a river with its own ripples and its rate of flowing.

Lost Indian Magic

Tiráwa, Wokonda, The Friend of the Soul of Man, is in everything; in the field we plant, the stone we grind with, the bear we kill. By singing, the soul of the singer is put in harmony with the essential Essence of Things. There are songs for every possible adventure of tribal life; songs for setting out on a journey, a song for the first sight of your destination, and a song to be sung by your wife for your safe return. Many of these songs occur detached from everything but the occasion from which they sprang, such as the women's grinding song, measured to the beat of the mealing stone, or the Paddle Song which follows the swift rhythm of the stroke. Others, less descriptive and retaining always something of a sacred character, occur originally as numbers in the song sequences by which are celebrated the tribal mysteries.

The first stage of Native American magic is the rise of the singer on his own song to a plane of power; only while he is in this plane is he able to bring the wish of his client to pass. It is a natural process of deterioration which leads to the song being thought of as having potency in itself.

Figure 2
Rock Hieroglyphics Of The Algonquians

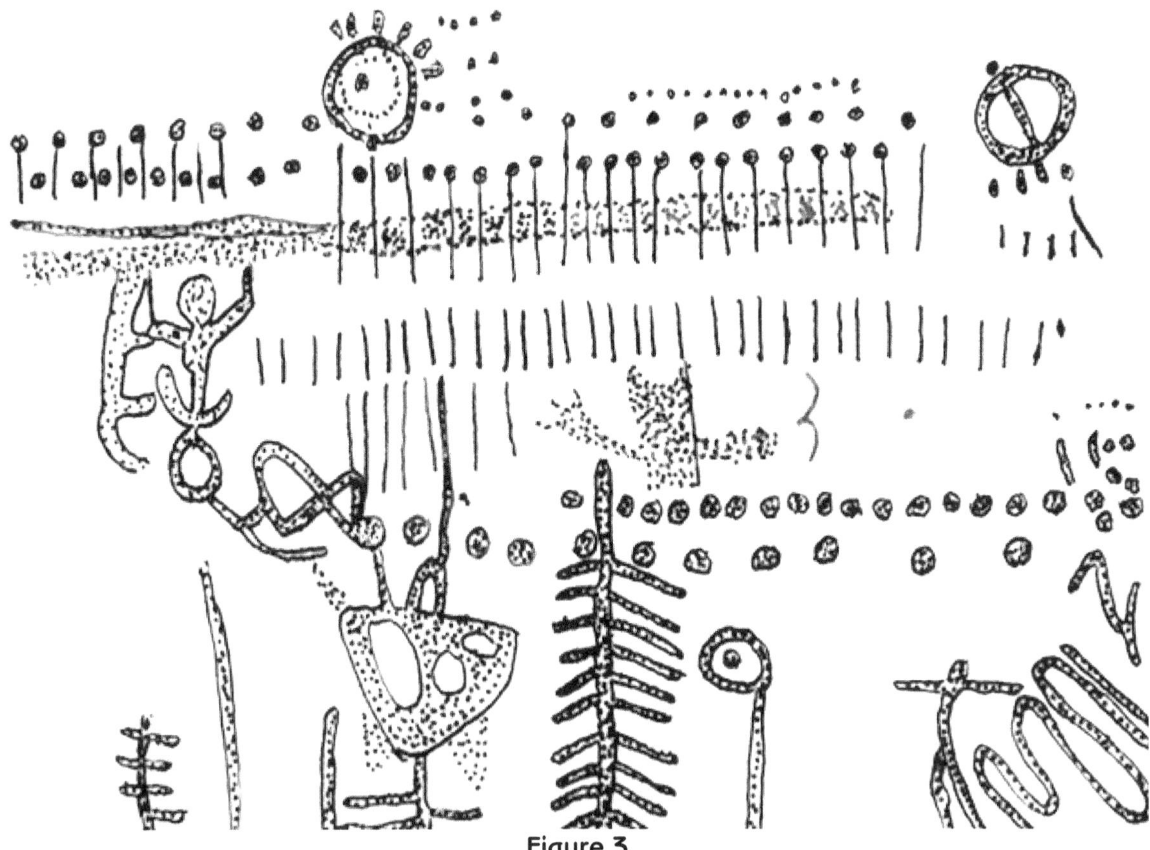

Figure 3
Native American Magic Symbols From Northern California

Magic songs can generally be recognized by the form of affirmation in which they are cast, as in the Winnebago Love Song, which is not really a song of love, but a song to secure success in love:

Whosoe'r I look upon
He becomes love crazed.

Or the Cherokee formula to insure the constancy of the beloved, and the Micmac vengeance song:

Death I make,
Singing.

Among the Navajo the magic effect is made certain by the fourfold repetition of the affirming phrase, four being a sacred number. These are all items which have to be taken into account in interpreting Native American Indian magic. It is in the very nature of primitive verse that it should require interpretation, even among the audiences for whom it is originally intended.

For verse is to the Red singer but a shorthand note to his emotions, a sentence or two, a phrase out of the heart of the situation. It is the "inside song" alone which is important. Says the Medicine Man, explaining these matters, "You see Injun man singin' an' cryin' while he sing. It ain't what he singin' make him cry; iss what the song make him think, thass what he cryin' about."

Concerning Living Humanity

Love Charm

Hû! Listen! In Alahí yi you repose, O Terrible Woman,
O you have drawn near to hearken.
There in Elahiyi you are at rest, a White Woman.
No one, is ever lonely when with you.
You are most beautiful.
Instantly and at once you have rendered me a white man.
No one is ever lonely when with me.
Now you have made the path white for me.
It shall never be dreary.
Now you have put me into it.
It shall never become blue.
You have brought down to me from above the white road.
There in mid-earth you have placed me.
I shall stand erect upon the earth.
No one is ever lonely when with me.
I am very handsome.
You have put me into the white house.
I shall be in it as it moves about and no one with me shall ever be lonely.
Verily, I shall never become blue.
Instantly you have caused it to be so with me.

And now there in Elahiyi you have rendered the woman blue.
Now you have made the path blue for her.
Let her be completely veiled in loneliness.
Put her into the blue road.
And now bring her down.

Place her standing upon the earth.
Where her feet are now and wherever she may go, let loneliness leave its mark upon her.
Let her be marked out for loneliness where she stands.

Ha! I belong to the Wolf clan, that one alone which was allotted into for you.
No one is ever lonely with me.
I am handsome.
Let her put her soul in the very center of my soul, never to turn away.
Grant that, in the midst of men she shall never think of them.
I belong to the one clan alone which was allotted for you when the seven clans were established.

Lost Indian Magic

Where other men live it is lonely.
They are very loathsome.
The common polecat has made them so like himself that they are fit only for his company.
They have become mere refuse.
They are very loathsome.
The common opossum has made them so like himself that they are fit only to be with him.
They are very loathsome.
Even the crow has made them so like himself that they are fit only for his company.
They are very loathsome.
The miserable rain-crow has made them so like himself that they are fit only for his company.

The seven clans all alike make one feel very lonely in their company.
They are not even good looking.
They go about clothed with mere refuse.
They even go about covered with dung.
But I—I was ordained to be a white man.

I stand with my face toward the Sun Land.
No one is ever lonely with me.
I am very handsome.
I shall certainly never become blue.
I am covered by the everlasting white house wherever I go.
No one is ever lonely with me.
Your soul has come into the center of my soul, never to turn away.
I, Gatigwan asti—I take your soul.
Sge!

To Insure Constancy

Listen! O, now you have drawn near to harken, O, Ancient One.
This woman's soul has come to rest at the edge of your body.
You are never to let go your hold upon it.
It is ordained that you shall do just as you are requested to do.
Let her never think upon any other place.
Her soul has faded within her.
She is bound by the black threads.

Listen! "Ha! Now the souls have met, never to part," you have said, O Ancient One above.
O Black Spider, you have brought down from on high.
You have let down your web.
She is of the Deer clan; her name is Ayâsta.
Her soul you have wrapped up in your web.
Listen! Ha! But now you have covered her with loneliness.
Her eyes have faded.
Whither can her soul escape?
Let her be sorrowing as she goes along, and not for one night alone.

Let her become an aimless wanderer, whose trail may never be followed.
O Black Spider, may you hold her soul in your web so that it shall never get through the meshes.
What is the name of the soul?
They two have come together.
It is mine!

Listen! Ha! And now you have harkened,
O Ancient Red.
Your grandchildren have come to the edge of your body.
You hold them yet more firmly in your grasp, never to let go your hold.
O Ancient One, we have become as one.
The woman has put her soul into our hands.
We shall never let it go!
Yu!

Those About To Be Slain

Ha yi! Yû! Listen!
Now instantly we have lifted up the red war club.
Quickly his soul shall be without motion.
There under the earth, where the black war clubs shall be moving about like ball sticks in the game, there his soul shall be, never to reappear.
We cause it to be so.
He shall never go and lift up the war club.
We cause it to be so.
There under the earth the black war club and the black fog have come together as one for their covering.
The black fog shall never be lifted from them.
We cause it to be so.

This Tells About Going Into The Water

This formula is repeated by the lover when about to bathe in the stream preparatory to painting himself for the dance. The services of a shaman are not required, neither is any special ceremony observed. The technical word used in the heading, ä'tawasti'yï, signifies plunging or going entirely into a liquid. The expression used for the ordinary "going to water," where the water is simply dipped up with the hand, is ämâ'yï dita`ti'yï, "taking them to water."

The prayer is addressed to Agë'`yaguga, a formulistic name for the moon, which is supposed to exert a great influence in love affairs, because the dances, which give such opportunities for love making, always take place at night. The shamans can not explain the meaning of the term, which plainly contains the word agë'`ya, "woman," and may refer to the moon's supposed influence over women. In Cherokee mythology the moon is a man. The ordinary name is nû'ndâ, or more fully, nû'ndâ sûnnâyë'hï, "the sun living in the night," while the sun itself is designated as nû'nndâ igë'hï, "the sun living in the day."

By the red spittle of Agë'`yagu'ga and the red dress with which the lover is clothed are meant the red paint which he puts upon himself. This in former days was procured from a deep red clay known as ela-wâ'tï, or "reddish brown clay." The word red as used in the formula is emblematic of success in attaining his object, besides being the actual color of the paint. Red, in connection with dress or ornamentation, has always been a favorite color with Indians throughout America, and there is some evidence that among the Cherokees it was regarded also as having a mysterious protective power. In all these formulas the lover renders the woman blue or disconsolate and uneasy in mind as a preliminary to fixing her thoughts upon himself.

Listen! O, now instantly, you have drawn near to hearken, O Agë'`yagu'ga. You have come to put your red spittle upon my body. My name is (Gatigwanasti.) The blue had affected me. You have come and clothed me with a red dress. She is of the (Deer) clan. She has become blue. You have directed her paths straight to where I have my feet, and I shall feel exultant. Listen!

Song For Painting

This formula immediately follows the one last given. The expressions used have been already explained. The one using the formula first bathes in the running stream, reciting at the same time the previous formula "Amâ'yï Ä'tawasti'yï." He then repairs to some convenient spot with his paint, beads, and other paraphernalia and proceeds to adorn himself for the dance, which usually begins about an hour after dark, but is not fairly under way until nearly midnight. The refrain, yû'nwëhï, is probably sung while mixing the paint, and the other portion is recited while applying the pigment, or vice versa. Although these formulas are still in use, the painting is now obsolete, beyond an occasional daubing of the face, without any plan or pattern, on the occasion of a dance or ball play.

Yû'nwëhï, yû'nwëhï, yû'nwëhï, yû'nwëhï.
I am come from above--Yû'nwëhï, yû'nwëhï, yû'nwëhï, yû'nwëhï.
I am come down from the Sun Land--yû'nwëhï.

O Red Agë`yagu'ga. you have come and put your red spittle upon my body--Yû'nwëhï, yû'nwëhï, yû'nwëhï!.

To Attract And Fix The Affections

This formula is said by the young husband, who has just married an especially engaging wife, who is liable to be attracted by other men. The same formula may also be used by the woman to fix her husband's affections. On the first night that they are together the husband watches until his wife is asleep, when, sitting up by her side, he recites the first words: *Sgë! Ha-nâ'gwa hatû'ngani'ga nihï'*, and then sings the next four words: *Tsawatsi'lû tsïkï' tsïkû' ayû'*, "Your spittle, I take it, I eat it," repeating the words four times. While singing he moistens his fingers with spittle, which he rubs upon the breast of the woman.

The next night he repeats the operation, this time singing the words, "I take your body." The third night, in the same way, he sings, "I take your flesh," and the fourth and last night, he sings "I take your heart," after which he repeats the prayer addressed to the Ancient One, by which is probably meant the Fire (the Ancient White).

The final sentences should be masculine, i.e., His soul has faded, etc., and refers to any would-be seducer. There is no gender distinction in the third person in Cherokee. He claimed that this ceremony was so effective that no husband need have any fears for his wife after performing it.

Listen! O, now you have drawn near to hearken--
--Your spittle, I take it, I eat it.
--Your body, I take it, I eat it.
--Your flesh, I take it, I eat it
--Your heart, I take it, I eat it
Each sung four times.

Listen! O, now you have drawn near to hearken, O, Ancient One. This man's (woman's) soul has come to rest at the edge of your body. You are never to let go your hold upon it. It is ordained that you shall do just as you are requested to do. Let her never think upon any other place. Her soul has faded within her. She is bound by the black threads.

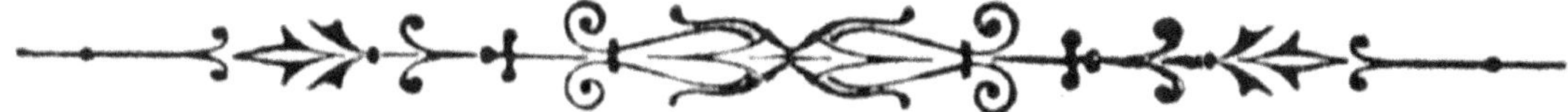

For Separation Of Lovers

This formula is used to separate two lovers or even a husband and wife, if the jealous rival so desires. In the latter case the preceding formula, from the same source, would be used to forestall this spell. No explanation of the ceremony is given, but the reference to tobacco may indicate that tobacco is smoked or thrown into the fire during the recitation. The particular hawk invoked (giya'giya') is a large species found in the coast region but seldom met with in the mountains. Blue indicates that it brings trouble with it, while white in the second paragraph indicates that the man is happy and attractive in manner.

In the first part of the formula the speaker calls upon the Blue Hawk to separate the lovers and spoil their souls, i.e., change their feeling toward each other. In the second paragraph he endeavors to attract the attention of the woman by eulogizing himself. The expression, "we shall turn her soul over," seems here to refer to turning her affections, but as generally used, to turn one's soul is equivalent to killing him.

Yû! On high you repose, O Blue Hawk, there at the far distant lake. The blue tobacco has come to be your recompense. Now you have arisen at once and come down. You have alighted midway between them where they two are standing. You have spoiled their souls immediately. They have at once become separated.

I am a white man; I stand at the sunrise. The good sperm shall never allow any feeling of loneliness. This white woman is of the Paint (iyustï) clan; she is called (iyustï) Wâyï'. We shall instantly turn her soul over. We shall turn it over as we go toward the Sun Land. I am a white man. Here where I stand it (her soul) has attached itself to (literally, "come against") mine. Let her eyes in their sockets be forever watching (for me). There is no loneliness where my body is.

To Shorten A Night-Goer On This Side

This formula is for the purpose of driving away a witch from the house of a sick person, and opens up a most interesting chapter of Cherokee beliefs. The witch is supposed to go about chiefly under cover of darkness, and hence is called sûnnâ'yï edâ'hï, "the night-goer." This is the term in common use; but there are a number of formulistic expressions to designate a witch, one of which, u'ya igawa'stï, occurs in the body of the formula and may be rendered "the imprecator," i.e., the sayer of evil things or curses. As the counteracting of a deadly spell always results in the death of its author, the formula is stated to be not merely to drive away the wizard, but to kill him, or, according to the formulistic expression, "to shorten him (his life) on this side."

When it becomes known that a man is dangerously sick the witches front far and near gather invisibly about his house after nightfall to worry him and even force their way in to his bedside unless prevented by the presence of a more powerful shaman within the house. They annoy the sick man and thus hasten his death by stamping upon the roof and beating upon the sides of the house; and if they can manage to get inside they raise up the dying sufferer from the bed and let him fall again or even drag him out upon the floor.

The object of the witch in doing this is to prolong his term of years by adding to his own life as much as he can take from that of the sick man. Thus it is that a witch who is successful in these practices lives to be very old. Without going into extended details, it may be sufficient to state that the one most dreaded, alike by the friends of the sick man and by the lesser witches, is the Kâ'lana-ayeli'skï or Raven Mocker, so called because he flies through the air at night in a shape of fire, uttering sounds like the harsh croak of a raven.

The formula here given is short and simple as compared with some others. There is evidently a mistake in regard to the Red Man, who is here placed in the north, instead of in the east, as it should be. The reference to the arrows will be explained further on. Purple, mentioned in the second paragraph, has nearly the same symbolic meaning as blue, viz: Trouble, vexation and defeat; hence the Purple Man is called upon to frustrate the designs of the witch.

To drive away the witch the shaman first prepares four sharpened sticks, which he drives down into the ground outside the house at each of the four corners, leaving the pointed ends projecting upward and outward. Then, about noontime he gets ready the Tsâl-agayû'nlï or "Old Tobacco" (Nicotiana rustica), with which he fills his pipe, repeating this formula during the operation, after which he wraps the pipe thus filled in a black cloth. This sacred tobacco is smoked only for this purpose.

He then goes out into the forest, and returns just before dark, about which time the witch may be expected to put in an appearance. Lighting his pipe, he goes slowly around the house, puffing the smoke in the direction of every trail by which the witch might be able to approach, and probably repeating the same or another formula the while. He then goes into the house and awaits results. When the witch approaches under cover of the darkness, whether in his own proper shape or in the form of some animal, the sharpened stick on that side of the house shoots up into the air and comes down like an arrow upon his head, inflicting such a wound as proves fatal within seven days.

This explains the words of the formula, "We have prepared your arrows for the soul of the Imprecator. He has them lying along the path". When wounded the witch utters a groan which is heard by those listening inside the house, even at the distance of half a mile. No one knows certainly who the witch is until a day or two afterward, when some old man or woman, perhaps in a remote settlement, is suddenly seized with a mysterious illness and before seven clays elapse is dead.

Listen! In the Frigid Land above you repose, O Red Man, quickly we two have prepared your arrows for the soul of the Imprecator. He has them lying along the path. Quickly we two will take his soul as we go along.

*Listen! In the Frigid Land above you repose, O Purple Man, * * * *. Ha! Quickly now we two have prepared your arrows for the soul of the Imprecator. He has them lying along the path. Quickly we two will cut his soul in two.*

I Have Lost Something

This formula, for finding anything lost, is so simple as to need but little explanation. Brown in this instance has probably no mythological significance, but refers to the color of the stone used in the ceremony. This is a small rounded water-worn pebble, in substance resembling quartz and of a reddish-brown color. It is suspended by a string held between the thumb and finger of the shaman, who is guided in his search by the swinging of the pebble, which, according to their theory, will swing farther in the direction of the lost article than in the contrary direction. The shaman, who is always fasting, repeats the formula, while closely watching the motions of the swinging pebble.

He usually begins early in the morning, making the first trial at the house of the owner of the lost article. After noting the general direction toward which it seems to lean he goes a considerable distance in that direction, perhaps half a mile or more, and makes a second trial. This time the pebble may swing off at an angle in another direction. He follows up in the direction indicated for perhaps another half mile, when on a third trial the stone may veer around toward the starting point, and a fourth attempt may complete the circuit.

Having thus arrived at the conclusion that the missing article is somewhere within a certain circumscribed area, he advances to the center of this space and marks out upon the ground a small circle inclosing a cross with arms pointing toward the four cardinal points. Holding the stone over the center of the cross he again repeats the formula and notes the direction in which the pebble swings.

This is the final trial and he now goes slowly and carefully over the whole surface in that direction, between the center of the circle and the limit of the circumscribed area until in theory, at least, the article is found. Should he fail, he is never at a loss for excuses, but the specialists in this line are generally very shrewd guessers well versed in the doctrine of probabilities.

There are many formulas for this purpose, some of them being long and elaborate. When there is reason to believe that the missing article has been stolen, the specialist first determines the clan or settlement to which the thief belongs and afterward the name of the individual. Straws, bread balls, and stones of various kinds are used in the different formulas, the ceremony differing according to the medium employed.

The stones are generally pointed crystals or antique arrowheads, and are suspended as already described, the point being supposed to turn finally in the direction of the missing object. Several of these stones have been obtained on the reservation and are now deposited in the National Museum. It need excite no surprise to find the hog mentioned in the formula, as this animal has been domesticated among the Cherokees for more than a century, although most of them are strongly prejudiced against it.

Listen! Ha! Now you have drawn near to hearken, O Brown Rock; you never lie about anything. Ha! Now I am about to seek for it. I have lost a hog and now tell me about where I shall find it. For is it not mine? My name is ------------.

This Is To Frighten A Storm

This formula is for driving away, or "frightening" a storm, which threatens to injure the growing corn. The first part is a meaningless song, which is sting in a low tone in the peculiar style of most of the sacred songs. The storm, which is not directly named, is then addressed and declared to be coming on in a fearful manner on the track of his wife, like an animal in the rutting season. The shaman points out her tracks directed toward the upper regions and begs the storm spirit to follow her along the waving tree tops of the lofty mountains, where he shall be undisturbed.

The shaman stands facing the approaching storm with one hand stretched out toward it. After repeating the song and prayer he gently blows in the direction toward which he wishes it to go, waving his hand in the same direction as though pushing away the storm. A part of the storm is usually sent into the upper regions of the atmosphere. If standing at the edge of the field, he holds a blade of corn in one hand while repeating the ceremony.

Listen! O now you are coming in rut. Ha! I am exceedingly afraid of you. But yet you are only tracking your wife. Her footprints can be seen there directed upward toward the heavens. I have pointed them out for you. Let your paths stretch out along the tree tops on the lofty mountains (and) you shall have them (the paths) lying down without being disturbed, Let (your path) as you go along be where the waving branches meet. Listen!

What Those Who Have Been To War Did To Help Themselves

This formula may be repeated by the doctor for as many as eight men at once when about to go to war. It is recited for four consecutive nights, immediately before setting out. There is no tabu enjoined and no beads are used, but the warriors "go to water" in the regular way, that is, they stand at the edge of the stream, facing the east and looking down upon the water, while the shaman, standing behind them, repeats the formula.

On the fourth night the shaman gives to each man a small charmed root which has the power to confer invulnerability. On the eve of battle the warrior after bathing in the running stream chews a portion of this and spits the juice upon his body in order that the bullets of the enemy may pass him by or slide off from his skin like drops of water.

Almost every man of the three hundred East Cherokees who served in the rebellion had this or a similar ceremony performed before setting out--many of them also consulting the oracular ulû'nsû'tï stone at the same time, and it is but fair to state that not more than two or three of the entire number were wounded in actual battle.

In the formula the shaman identifies himself with the warriors, asserting that "we" have lifted up the red war club, red being the color symbolic of success and having no reference to blood, as might be supposed from the connection. In the first paragraph he invokes curses upon the enemy, the future tense verb *It shall be*, etc., having throughout the force of *let it be*.

He puts the souls of the doomed enemy in the lower regions, where the black war clubs are constantly waving about, and envelops them in a black fog, which shall never be lifted and out of which they shall never reappear. From the expression in the second paragraph, "their souls shall never be knocked about," the reference to the black war clubs moving about like ball sticks in the game would seem to imply that they are continually buffeting the doomed souls under the earth. The spirit land of the Cherokees is in the west, but in these formulas of malediction or blessing the soul of the doomed man is generally consigned to the underground region, while that of the victor is raised by antithesis to the seventh heaven.

Having disposed of the enemy, the shaman in the second paragraph turns his attention to his friends and at once raises their souls to the seventh heaven, where they shall go about in peace, shielded by (literally, "covered with") the red war club of success, and never to be knocked about by the blows of the enemy. "Breaking the soul in two" is equivalent to snapping the thread of life, the soul being regarded as an intangible something having length, like a rod or a string.

The warriors are also made to shield themselves with the white war whoop, which should undoubtedly be the red war whoop, consistent with the red war club, white being the color emblematic of peace, which is evidently an incongruity. The war whoop is believed to have a positive magic power for the protection of the warrior, as well as for terrifying the foe.

The mythological significance of the different colors is well shown in this formula. Red, symbolic of success, is the color of the war club with which the warrior is to strike the enemy and also of the other one with which he is to shield or "cover" himself. There is no doubt that the war whoop also should be represented as red. In conjuring with the beads for long life, for recovery from sickness, or for success in love, the ball play, or any other undertaking, the red beads represent the party for whose benefit the magic spell is wrought, and he is figuratively clothed in red and made to stand upon a red cloth or placed upon a red seat. The red spirits invoked always live in the east and everything pertaining to them is of the same color.

Black is always typical of death, and in this formula the soul of the enemy is continually beaten about by black war clubs and enveloped in a black fog. In conjuring to destroy an enemy the shaman uses black beads and invokes the black spirits– which always live in the west–bidding them tear out the man's soul, carry it to the west, and put it into the black coffin deep in the black mud, with a black serpent coiled above it.

Blue is emblematic of failure, disappointment, or unsatisfied desire. "They shall never become blue" means that they shall never fail in anything they undertake. In love charms the lover figuratively covers himself with red and prays that his rival shall become entirely blue and walk in a blue path. The formulistic expression, "He is entirely blue," closely approximates in meaning the common English phrase, "He feels blue." The blue spirits live in the north.

White—which occurs in this formula only by an evident error—denotes peace and happiness. In ceremonial addresses, as at the green corn dance and ball play, the people figuratively partake of white food and after the dance or the game return along the white trail to their white houses. In love charms the man, in order to induce the woman to cast her lot with his, boasts "I am a white man," implying that all is happiness where he is. White beads have the same meaning in the bead conjuring and white was the color of the stone pipe anciently used in ratifying peace treaties. The white spirits live in the south (Wa'halä).

Two other colors, brown and yellow, are also mentioned in the formulas. Wâtige'ï, "brown," is the term used to include brown, bay, dun, and similar colors, especially as applied to animals. It seldom occurs in the formulas and its mythological significance is as yet undetermined. Yellow is of more frequent occurrence and is typical of trouble and all manner of vexation, the yellow spirits being generally invoked when the shaman wishes to bring down calamities upon the head of his victim, without actually destroying him. So far as present knowledge goes, neither brown nor yellow can be assigned to any particular point of the compass.

Usïnuli'yu, rendered "instantly," is the intensive form of usïnu'lï "quickly," both of which words recur constantly in the formulas, in some entering into almost every sentence. This frequently gives the translation an awkward appearance. Thus the final sentence, which means literally "they shall never become blue instantly," signifies "Grant that they shall never become blue, i.e., shall never fail in their purpose, and grant our petition instantly."

Hayï'! Yû! Listen! Now instantly we have lifted up the red war club. Quickly his soul shall be without motion. There under the earth, where the black war clubs shall be moving about like ball sticks in the game, there his soul shall be, never to reappear. We cause it to be so. He shall never go and lift up the war club. We cause it to be so. There under the earth the black war club (and) the black fog have come together as one for their covering. It shall never move about (i. e., the black fog shall never be lifted from them). We cause it to be so.

Instantly shall their souls be moving about there in the seventh heaven. Their souls shall never break in two. So shall it be. Quickly we have moved them (their souls) on high for them, where they shall be going about in peace. You have shielded yourselves with the red war club. Their souls shall never be knocked about. Cause it to be so. There on high their souls shall be going about. Let them shield themselves with the white war whoop. Instantly (grant that) they shall never become blue. Yû!

Figure 4
Native American Petroglyphs Of Supernatural Beings

Birth Totem

According to Native American tradition, everything in life is a circle. They saw that the Sun moves in a circle, from morning to night and then back again to another morning. They saw that, from the waxing and waning of the Moon from full moon to dark moon and back, the Moon too moves in a circle. And through observing the changing of the seasons, they knew that the Earth moves in a circle as well.

The Native people saw that it took twelve moons (i.e. moon cycles or months) to go through a complete cycle of the seasons (or a complete turn of the Wheel). And so the twelve moons, along with the four seasons, found their places on the Wheel. They believed that each of these moons had its own set of animal, mineral, and plant totems (as well as others), and that each of these totems possessed certain qualities that could be passed onto people depending upon the moon under which they were born. Additionally, they believed that, not only could one possess the traits and qualities of their own birth totems, but that one could also explore and experience the traits of any and all of the totems at various times in her or his life. As one walked one's way around the Wheel (i.e. went through life), she/he would experience many lessons and encounter many challenges, and the totems along the way would be there to guide them and to help them grow during these experiences.

It should be noted that the characteristics listed for each birth totem are not necessarily the traits that everyone born under that totem possesses. Every person is unique, and each has her or his own unique personality. Each person moves along the Wheel in their own way and at their own speed. Personalities are fluid, and over time they change and evolve. But those born under the same moon tend to share certain broad characteristics. Therefore, the qualities mentioned here are of a general nature, and describe traits that one may possess for a long or short period in their lives, or traits that one may lack and needs to develop at some point during their lifetime.

Birth Totem Dates

March 21 - April 19
Budding Trees Moon

April 20 - May 20
Frogs Return Moon

May 21 - June 20
Corn Planting Moon

June 21 - July 21
Strong Sun Moon

July 22 - August 21
Ripe Berries Moon

August 22 - September 21
Harvest Moon

September 22 - October 22
Ducks Fly Moon

October 23 - November 22
Freeze Up Moon

November 23 - December 21
Long Snows Moon

December 22 - January 19
Earth Renewal Moon

January 20 - February 18
Rest & Cleansing Moon

February 19 - March 20
Big Winds Moon

Budding Trees Moon: March 21 - April 19

Birth Moon: Budding Trees

Animal Totem: Falcon

Mineral Totem: Fire Opal

Plant Totem: Dandelion

Directional Totem: Golden Eagle

Elemental Clan Totem: Thunderbird

Affinity Color: Yellow

Personality Traits: energetic, independent, outspoken, enterprising, adventurous, frank, courageous, enthusiastic, imaginative

Like the falcon, people born during this moon are fearless hunters, always in search for something new. New places, new experiences, and new ideas are their prey.

These people, like their totem, have the ability to reach great heights, though sometimes, however, they can lack the patience, concentration, or persistence to be able to see things through to the end. Although they begin each new endeavor with great enthusiasm, they can easily get bored or distracted and, therefore, will quickly change directions and leap onto the next new thing that comes along, leaving the other endeavor behind never to be finished.

They may have a whole trail of unfinished projects behind them. To combat their tendency towards boredom, Falcon people may have several different projects going on all at once. Even so, they may still eventually lose interest in all of them and dive into something new that piques their interest. Falcon people, therefore, are often good at starting things, but not so good at finishing them.

Fire Opal: The mineral totem for the Budding Trees Moon is the Opal, or more specifically, the Fire Opal. Opals are formed under a lot of pressure, and therefore can be of assistance to those who find themselves under a lot of stress or emotional pressure.

Opals contain silica, which is also found in the human eye. Therefore, opals can aid in the quest to find clarity and to see the truth. Falcon people are inquisitive by nature, and Opal can enhance one's ability to see deeply into things.

Due to its reflective nature, opals amplify the traits of the one holding it, and so it can strengthen one's good traits (as well as their bad ones!). Falcon people tend to have a fiery nature and a fiery temper. Fire opal can disperse emotional negativity and help one to master their emotions.

Frogs Return Moon: April 20 - May 20

Birth Moon: Frogs Return

Animal Totem: Beaver

Mineral Totem: Chrysocolla

Plant Totem: Blue Camas

Directional Totem: Golden Eagle

Elemental Clan Totem: Turtle

Affinity Color: Blue

Personality Traits: resourceful, conservative, creative, methodical, practical, persevering, reliable, patient, productive

Beaver: People who have Beaver as a totem are hard workers. Just like a busy beaver, they keep themselves busy whether it is at work, or at home, or at play. They have no trouble keeping themselves occupied. Even when it seems that there is nothing that needs to be done, Beaver people are creative and will always find something to do, even if it is just changing, adjusting, tweaking, or rearranging things that they have already done.

Keeping busy helps to make Beaver people feel comfortable and content as well as giving them a sense of security. Beaver people are also persevering and patient and so, if they have their minds set on something, they usually end up getting what they want.

They are quick to learn and are readily adaptable to new things, though they also have a tendency to want to make things fit to themselves rather than the other way around. Sometimes so much so, that it may get to the point where they end up reorganizing the lives of those around them. But they usually don't do so selfishly, but rather with the intention of it benefiting all those around them as well as themselves.

Chrysocolla: Chrysocolla is an earth stone and is the mineral totem for the Frogs Return Moon. Take a sphere of chrysocolla and look at it from a distance. Most often, it will resemble the Earth as viewed from space, with its swirling greens resembling land, and its blues the ocean.

As an earth stone, chrysocolla can assist you in reaching into the highest realms of consciousness while keeping you grounded on the Earth. Therefore, chrysocolla can be used to balance the earth and sky elements within you.

Chrysocolla is a healing stone holding much strong and good medicine within it. It can purify on all levels, from the physical to the mental, emotional, and spiritual. It helps to ground and bring balance to the one using it, as well as bringing about a feeling of strength and well-being. It promotes stability and peacefulness within, thereby strengthening your sense of being connected with the Earth.

Corn Planting Moon: May 21 - June 20

Birth Moon: Corn Planting

Animal Totem: Deer

Mineral Totem: Moss Agate

Plant Totem: Yarrow

Directional Totem: Golden Eagle

Elemental Clan Totem: Butterfly

Affinity Color: Green

Personality Traits: quick, alert, expressive, charming, curious, friendly, versatile, intuitive, compassionate, witty, understanding

Deer: Deer people are fast-movers on every level. Not only do they move fast physically, but they also talk fast, think fast, and their emotions tend to change quickly. Due to all of their fast-moving, they are likely to often bound from one topic to another, from one idea to another, and from one project to another, many times failing to accomplish what they had set out to do.

They are resourceful, however, and have an eye for beauty, and so they are capable of making something beautiful out of something simple. Deer people often have a short attention span, as well as a tendency to interrupt conversations because their minds are always racing, a part of the conversation might set their thoughts off on a tangent, and then they will want to express those thoughts immediately, thereby not allowing the person who was speaking to finish what they were saying.

However, they are also intuitive and sensitive and are usually compassionate and understanding towards others. Deer people often have an uncontrollable wild side to them which can sometimes make it difficult for others to understand them and for them to even understand themselves. With all of their fast-moving and occasional wildness, Deer people are often unorganized and easily lose track of time.

Moss Agate: Agate, specifically moss agate, is the Corn-planting Moon's mineral totem. Agate, in general, is a very stabilizing stone on all levels. This is good for Deer people whose emotions tend to run wild.

Agate can also help Deer people with stabilizing their thoughts and actions, thus enabling them to take the time to see the truth of things. Moss agate, in addition to these properties, is also an overall healing stone and can help one in finding their inner truth and courage when facing difficult situations.

Moss agate is a grounding and energizing stone that is also helpful in alleviating depression and enhancing one's dreams.

Strong Sun Moon: June 21 - July 21

Birth Moon: Strong Sun

Animal Totem: Woodpecker

Mineral Totem: Rose Quartz

Plant Totem: Wild Rose

Directional Totem: Coyote

Elemental Clan Totem: Frog

Affinity Color: Pink

Personality Traits: emotional, sensitive, sympathetic, protective, vulnerable, imaginative, loving, thrifty, kind, considerate

Woodpecker: To Native Americans, the rhythmic pecking of the woodpecker reminded them of the sound of the shaman's drum. The people who have Woodpecker as a totem also tend to be musically inclined. The Natives saw that the woodpecker not only did its pecking out of necessity in the search for food, but that they also pecked for the sheer joy of it. Woodpecker, then, as a totem can teach people how to feel and express joy.

Woodpeckers take great care with building their nest and raising their young, and so too do those with this totem. Woodpecker people find their greatest joy in building a comfortable, harmonious, and happy home for themselves and their children. They are usually excellent parents, and sometimes have difficulty with letting go of their children when it is time for them to leave the nest.

Close relationships are important to Woodpecker people, and they can become very unhappy or even bitter if they do not have someone towards whom to direct their love, energy, and devotion.

Rose Quartz: The totem mineral for the Strong Sun Moon is Rose Quartz, also known as the Love Stone. As a love stone, rose quartz is excellent at promoting love in all its forms, not only the love that can be experienced between two people, but also the love between friends and especially among family.

It helps to strengthen family bonds, especially between parents and their children. Woodpecker people have very strong family relationships, and are usually willing to make sacrifices for the happiness of their children. Rose quartz works on the heart chakra, and therefore, is a strong emotional healer, helping to release the sorrows, fears, trauma, anger, and resentments that burden the heart.

Woodpecker people are naturally good at handling emergency situations, intuitively knowing what to do and what is needed in order to deal with such situations. Rose quartz is a helpful support in times of crisis, and so it is a good stone to carry with you.

Ripe Berries Moon: July 22 - August 21

Birth Moon: Ripe Berries

Animal Totem: Sturgeon

Mineral Totem: Garnet & Iron

Plant Totem: Raspberry

Directional Totem: Coyote

Elemental Clan Totem: Thunderbird

Affinity Color: Red

Personality Traits: confident, authoritative, energetic, self-assertive, dramatic, fastidious, generous, trusting, optimistic

Sturgeon: The sturgeon is a symbol of strength and longevity to Native Americans. Like salmon, sturgeons swim upstream to get to their spawning grounds. So sturgeon have the strength to swim against the current and the ability to survive despite hard times, and so too do those whose birth totem is Sturgeon.

Sturgeon (and Salmon) are very graceful swimmers, causing very little disturbance as they move through the water. Water is the element of the emotions, and so it is one of Sturgeon people's life tasks to learn to master their emotions and to swim gracefully through their lives causing little friction or disturbance.

Sturgeon people can be resistant to change which can cause them a great amount of emotional upset. Demands that are put on them by others can also be a source of emotional upset and a lot of stress for Sturgeon people.

Garnet & Iron: Garnet and Iron are the mineral totems for the Ripe Berries Moon. Both are good for the blood and the heart. The heart is the center of the emotions, and Garnet can enable one's emotions to flow freely.

It can also be of aid in getting to the heart of a matter. Iron can help you to temper your emotions as you go through life's experiences. It can also give you the strength and hardness to be able to say no when it is needed.

Harvest Moon: August 22 - September 21

Birth Moon: Harvest

Animal Totem: Brown Bear

Mineral Totem: Amethyst

Plant Totem: Violet

Directional Totem: Coyote

Elemental Clan Totem: Turtle

Affinity Color: Purple

Personality Traits: industrious, unassuming, reasonable, hardworking, modest, warm-hearted, good natured, helpful, dependable

Brown Bear: Brown Bears are independent and self-reliant, and so too are those whose birth totem is Brown Bear. These people are usually slow in acclimating themselves to change, and will often retreat to their dens for a time, where they can feel comfortable and secure within the familiar.

Brown bear people are constructive and have a knack for fixing just about anything, from repairing a broken down car to mending a torn relationship. These people are usually quite gentle, like their totem animal, and handle their relationships with much tenderness and understanding.

The Native peoples regarded the Brown Bear as a dreamer. People with this totem often love to daydream and have a vivid imagination. Sometimes they can get so wrapped up in their daydream that they become unable to distinguish it from their physical reality, which may cause others to think that they are liars.

Amethyst: Amethyst is the mineral associated with the Harvest Moon. It is a strong protector stone and is said to guard one against everything from black magic, to hailstorms, to alcohol intoxication. It is also a very spiritual stone and can help one to find spiritual attunement, as well as helping to find balance between the spiritual and the physical.

Amethyst is calming and soothing and can help one with finding the cause(s) of their anger and thereby enable them to release it. This stone is especially good for Brown Bear people as it helps to calm and clarify the dream state.

Ducks Fly Moon: September 22 - October 22

Birth Moon: Ducks Fly

Animal Totem: Raven

Mineral Totem: Jasper (Bloodstone)

Plant Totem: Mullein

Directional Totem: Grizzly Bear

Elemental Clan Totem: Butterfly

Affinity Color: Brown

Personality Traits: tolerant, talkative, pleasant, idealistic, diplomatic, cheerful, fun, artistic, tidy, efficient, easy-going, tactful

Raven: Ravens and crows like to be together in numbers. They travel together, eat together, and live together. Raven people have this trait as well, preferring the company of others to being alone and on their own. They feel the happiest and most secure when they are with others. They work best when they are in a group, and are extremely loyal to any group that they are a part of, and like the Raven, they are always ready to defend it when necessary.

Like the birds, these people are often cautious and wary which may make it difficult for them to make decisions. They are often indecisive and slow to make up their minds, preferring instead to remain neutral rather than to choose one side or one thing over another. However, once they have made a decision, they will act on it with conviction.

Since ancient times, the Raven and Crow have been associated with magick and mystery, and have been regarded as the guardian of secrets. Almost like magic, Raven people often have an uncanny ability to turn their wants and desires into realities. They are also usually very good at being discreet and keeping secrets.

Jasper (Bloodstone): The mineral totem for the Ducks Fly Moon is jasper, particularly bloodstone jasper. Among the many purported abilities of bloodstone includes stopping bleeding, making its wearer invisible, restoring lost eyesight, ensuring a long life, bringing rain, and drawing poison from a snake bite.

Bloodstone is a grounding stone that harmonizes one with the Earth's energies and helps one to find balance in their life.

Freeze Up Moon: October 23 - November 22

Birth Moon: Freeze Up

Animal Totem: Snake

Mineral Totem: Copper & Malachite

Plant Totem: Thistle

Directional Totem: Grizzly Bear

Elemental Clan Totem: Frog

Affinity Color: Orange

Personality Traits: purposeful, determined, imaginative, intense, impulsive, mysterious, discerning, ambitious, clear, decisive

Snake: Because of its ability to periodically shed its skin, the snake represents transformation, change, and renewal. And those born with Snake as their birth totem are inclined to shed their skins by way of making dramatic, and sometimes drastic, changes in their lives from time to time, letting go of their current ties and attachments, and starting again anew. They may make sudden decisions such as to quit their job, or change their occupation, or sell their house, or move to a new city, or totally reinvent themselves. Sometimes, however, they make these changes at inopportune times, thereby causing unnecessary upset and suffering to themselves as well as to others.

Change isn't necessarily always easy for Snake people, but they are adaptable to anything that is new to them. For Snake people, their lives are usually a lifelong transformation. They may start out making changes that are for purely selfish reasons.

However, as the Snake person goes through life, their selfish changes will usually eventually transform into more constructive changes which benefit not only themselves, but others as well. Snake people may also start out as insensitive and hurtful towards others, but then their ability to wound will usually turn into the ability to heal. Snake people can be especially helpful to those suffering from alcoholism or drug abuse.

Copper & Malachite: The mineral totems associated with the Freeze Up Moon are malachite and copper. Malachite is a spiritual stone which can help you to hear the voice of spirit and to cultivate your psychic powers.

As a metal, copper is a conductor of energies that will spread them out evenly over a surface or throughout a person. It can also help you to understand your own energy. Copper is a good purifier of the spirit, and it promotes strength, power, and balance.

Long Snows Moon: November 23 - December 21

Birth Moon: Long Snows

Animal Totem: Owl

Mineral Totem: Obsidian

Plant Totem: Black Spruce

Directional Totem: Grizzly Bear

Elemental Clan Totem: Thunderbird

Affinity Color: Black

Personality Traits: philosophical, independent, jovial, confident, dependable, fun loving, versatile, individualistic, bold, frank,

Owl: Owls have large eyes and keen eyesight which enables them to see and catch their prey in the darkness of night. Owl people are very observant as well with very little escaping their attention. They have a keen eye for detail as well as a deep insight into whatever they find of interest or importance. The owl is associated with hidden wisdom and the Moon, which is the light that shines through the darkness.

Owl people usually have very good intuition, and may often find that they become aware of certain things before it becomes obvious to others. Though they are drawn to the esoteric and mysterious, they are usually able to keep themselves grounded in practical reality. From time to time, Owl people may feel the urge to disappear into the darkness like their totem animal.

They may become quiet and withdrawn, and may even feel the need to be alone and will thus avoid being in the company of others. They may even suddenly break away from a situation or project in which they have been deeply involved. Because of their sudden withdrawal, Owl people may appear to others as antisocial. They might be and feel misunderstood by others and, during these times, may inadvertently hurt the feelings of those around them.

Obsidian: Volcanic lava that cools and solidifies very quickly forms into a type of natural glass called Obsidian, the totem mineral associated with the Long Snows Moon. Being a natural glass, Obsidian is highly reflective and can reflect a person's thoughts to the one wearing it, bestowing upon them a sort of clairvoyance.

Obsidian can be very sharp and can help one to cut straight to the heart of a matter. It can also sharpen one's outer and inner vision, thus enabling them to have foresight, the ability to see into the future.

Obsidian is a powerful grounding and centering stone which grounds its wearers to the Earth's energy, and teaches them how to use this energy within themselves to center their being with the Earth, thus bringing about stability.

Earth Renewal Moon: December 22 - January 19

Birth Moon: Earth Renewal

Animal Totem: Snow Goose

Mineral Totem: Clear Quartz

Plant Totem: White Birch

Directional Totem: Buffalo

Elemental Clan Totem: Turtle

Affinity Color: White

Personality Traits: self-demanding, reliable, prudent, ambitious, practical, resourceful, shrewd, patient, persevering

Snow Goose: The large white snow goose travels great lengths, some as far as 5,000 miles, during its yearly migrations to and from its nesting grounds in the North Arctic. As a totem, Snow Goose people will often go to great lengths to make their aspirations a reality.

They have clear ambitions, and their imaginative minds, strong determination, sheer energy, and bubbling enthusiasm can make the seemingly impossible become attainable for them. Their persistence and determination often makes them successful at attaining long-term goals that they have set out for themselves. Snow Geese will spend hours picking insects off of each other.

Snow Goose people will often do ordinary things extremely well, sometimes to the point of perfection. These perfectionists can also sometimes be nitpickers, letting small and insignificant matters bother and frustrate them. When they feel that they're not getting their goals accomplished quickly enough, or they perceive an obstacle, even a minor one, in their path, Snow Goose people often have a tendency to become despondent and depressed. Snow geese travel in large flocks, sometimes numbering in the thousands.

Like their totem, Snow Geese people are usually very social and enjoy being in the company of others.

Clear Quartz: Clear quartz, the totem for the Earth Renewal Moon, is a very powerful energy stone. It is an amplifier, transmitter, and receiver of any and all energies, including healing energies.

It is also a stone of clarity, enabling one to see the truth of things. Clear quartz can also strengthen one's psychic and prophetic energies.

Rest & Cleansing Moon: January 20 - February 18

Birth Moon: Rest & Cleansing

Animal Totem: Otter

Mineral Totem: Turquoise

Plant Totem: Quaking Aspen

Directional Totem: Buffalo

Elemental Clan Totem: Butterfly

Affinity Color: Turquoise

Personality Traits: broad-minded, lively, unconventional, perceptive, inventive, self-assured self-reliant, dynamic, friendly, artistic

Otter: Otters are known for their playfulness, and thus, Otter people are friendly, playful, and love to have fun.

Like their totem, Otter people are usually very helpful, considerate, and compassionate towards others and are often involved in charitable activities. They are very giving and throughout their lives they will spend a great deal of their energy working to benefit the Earth and its inhabitants.

Otters have a strong sense of family and are very passionate and devoted to their loved ones, and will mourn the loss of a mate for a long time. They love being parents, and are exceptionally good at it, and are very nurturing towards their cubs. Otter cubs stay with their parents for much longer than those of most other wild animals.

Just like their animal totem, Otter people are also usually very devoted and loving towards their families, and may have difficulty letting go of their children when they decide to move out into the world and be on their own.

Otters are great organizers and keep their living areas very neat and tidy. Otter people are just the same and will often feel ill at ease and uncomfortable if their living and working environments are not clean and orderly. Otters are intelligent, creative, and inventive. As they float in the water on their backs, they place a rock on their tummies to use as a tool to crack open their shellfish dinners. And you can bet that Otter people are just as intelligent, creative, and inventive as their totem animal.

Turquoise: Because of its bright sky-blue color, some Native Americans referred to turquoise as the "sky stone". As a stone of the sky, it was linked to the higher spiritual realms. Otter people are often attracted to mystical things, and turquoise can help them to find a balance between the physical and the spiritual.

Turquoise is a calming, peaceful, and energy balancing stone; therefore it is a good stone for meditation. It is also a good stone for Otter people to keep with them for they are usually quite vulnerable to deceit or trickery, and are susceptible to emotional disturbances.

Turquoise is a very strong protector stone, as well as a great healer, and is said to ward off physical danger and illness by absorbing harmful vibrations. Native Americans often wore turquoise to protect themselves from injury, especially from broken bones. They believed that the turquoise would fracture instead of their bones. They put turquoise on their shields to protect them from weapons, and they also tied turquoise onto their horses to protect them from injury or breaking a limb.

Big Winds Moon: February 19 - March 20

Birth Moon: Big Winds

Animal Totem: Wolf

Mineral Totem: Silver

Plant Totem: Plantain

Directional Totem: Buffalo

Elemental Clan Totem: Frog

Affinity Color: Silver

Personality Traits: sympathetic, adaptable, intuitive, impressionable, benevolent, trusting, sensitive, generous, gentle, warm

Wolf: The Native Americans regarded the wolf as an intellect in both mind and spirit, a keeper of knowledge, and a great teacher, as well as a guide to the sacred. Those born during the Big Winds Moon are most often intellectuals, like their totem, and are usually hunters of knowledge, especially with regards to philosophy, religion, and anything else that they feel might bring meaning and purpose into their lives.

Like the wolf, they are often very good with handling children and make excellent teachers. Wolf people are usually quite intuitive, and can often quickly discern the intentions and attitudes of others, even when they are hidden.

Both wolves and Wolf people have a need to have a well-defined territory. For Wolf people, this territory not only includes their home and work spaces, but also their relationships with others. Wolves are very social animals and companionship is important to them. Usually they partner for life. And so it is too for the people with this totem.

Wolf people are usually quite sensitive and, for them, a break-up can be devastating. These people often have difficulty handling their emotions. They feel vulnerable if they express them too freely, yet become depressed when their emotions are repressed. Their emotional imbalance may cause difficulties in their relationships.

Silver: Silver is the mineral totem for the Big Winds Moon. It can remove blockages in both emotional and spiritual energies and can help them to flow freely again, which is a quality that is especially beneficial for Wolf people.

Silver can help one to reach, awaken, and heal their High Self. It can also enhance intuition, telepathy, clairvoyance, and foresight.

Cherokee Legend Of Crystals

In ancient times, people lived in harmony with Nature. They spoke the same language as the animals and plants. They hunted for food only to satisfy their hunger and needs, always offering a prayer of thanks for what they had taken from Nature. As time went on, humans lost this innocence and harmony. They took more than they needed. They forgot their prayers of gratitude. They killed animals, and each other, for sport or pleasure.

The Bear Tribe, chief among the animals, called a meeting of all the animals. They decided that something had to be done. The Bears suggested that they shoot back when the humans shot at them, but the bow and arrow required too great a sacrifice, for one bear would have to give up his life so that his sinew could be used for the bowstring. The bear's claws were too long for shooting a bow anyway, and would become entangled on the string.

The Deer Tribe offered another method of dealing with the problem. One of their members said, "We will bring disease into the world. Each of us will be responsible for a different illness. When humans live out of balance with Nature, when they forget to give thanks for their food, they will get sick." And in fact the Deer did invoke rheumatism and arthritis; each animal then decided to invoke a different disease.

The Plant Tribe was more sympathetic and felt that this was too harsh a punishment, so they volunteered their help. They said that for every disease a human gets, one of them would be present to cure it. That way, if people used their intelligence, they would be able to cure their ailments and regain their balance.

All of Nature agreed to this strategy. One plant in particular spoke out. This was Tobacco, the chief of the plants. He said, "I will be the sacred herb. I will not cure any specific disease, but I will help people return to the sacred way of life, provided I am smoked or offered with prayers and ceremony. But if I am misused, if I am merely smoked for pleasure, I will cause cancer, the worst disease of all."

The close friends of the Plant Tribe, the Rock Tribe and the Mineral Tribe, agreed to help. Each mineral would have a spiritual power, a subtle vibration that could be used to regain perfect health. The Ruby, worn as an amulet, would heal the heart; the Emerald would heal the liver and eyes, and so on. The chief of the mineral tribe, Quartz Crystal, was clear, like the light of Creation itself. Quartz put his arms around his brother Tobacco and said, "I will be the sacred mineral. I will heal the mind. I will help human beings see the origin of disease. I will help to bring wisdom and clarity in dreams. And I will record their spiritual history, including our meeting today, so that in the future, if humans gaze into me, they may see their origin and the way of harmony." And so it is today.

This is a Cherokee legend, but it has been told in almost every tribe in the Americas. It tells of an ancient time of peace, a mythical homeland known to every culture on Earth. The Native Americans call it the "old way" or the "original way."

The Cherokee thought that crystal had " great power to give aid in hunting and also in divining." One Cherokee individual kept his magic stone wrapped up in buckskin and hid it in a sacred cave. At certain times he would take it out of its repository and 'feed' it by rubbing over it the blood of a deer. This goes to prove that the stone was considered to be a living entity and as such required nourishment.

Noted anthropologist James Mooney who studied the Cherokee in the late 19th century elaborates on the magical crystal of the Cherokee which, he noted, was called the Ulûñsûti – "Transparent":

"It is like a large transparent crystal, nearly the shape of a cartridge bullet, with a blood-red streak running through the center from top to bottom. The owner keeps it wrapped in a whole deerskin, inside an earthen jar hidden away in a secret cave in the mountains. Every seven days he feeds it with blood of small game, rubbing the blood all over the crystal as soon as the animal has been killed. Twice a year it must have the blood of a deer or some other large animal. Should he forget to feed it at the proper time it would come out from its cave at night in a shape of fire and fly through the air to slake its thirst with the lifeblood of the conjurer or some of his people."

This problem could be avoided if the owner told the crystal that it would not be needed for sometime, for then the stone simply sleeps until needed again. Mooney went on to say "no white man must ever see it and no person but the owner will venture near it for fear of sudden death."

Upon the owners death the stone is buried with him to protect the rest of the tribe. Why take such risks for this crystal? The owner is assured of success in hunting, rainmaking, business, prophecy and love.

Natives of the Mount Lassen area in California also valued quartz crystal as charm stones and kept them safely hidden in rattlesnake dens. The charms owner would secretly rub them on himself to gain good luck in gambling or other pursuits.

Sacred Herbs Of The Native Americans

Northern White Cedar:

It is called the "Tree of Life." It is a fragrant, soft, pliable, handsome tree. It attains heights of 70-80 feet. The leaves appear in flattened sprays. Life cannot be sustained without it. The fibers of it can be made into clothing. It is insect resistant. It prevents mosquitoes from bothering by putting some leaves in the fire. It will also hold a fire for days. The leaves can be used for tea...especially when starving. But one must not overdo it, if used over a long period of time, it could cause harm to the body. Pregnant women should not use it. The leaves and twigs are boiled with oil to make salves. Used for removal of warts and fungous growths. It is useful as a counterirritant in the relief of muscular aches and pains, chronic coughs, headaches, fevers, and sudden attacks of acute pain in the joints. It is also used to make offerings, because it stills the mind and gives back. Cedar keeps a place "clean."

White Sage Or Ghost Sage:

From the Artemisia Family. It is a highly variable aromatic perennial. It grows to about three-feet tall. The leaves are white-felty beneath. It is a very sacred plant, a ghost plant. It is very attractive in an herb garden. It is used for good energy, healing, and protection. It is vital to be healthy. The aroma relieves stress. It is used as an astringent, to induce sweating, curb pain and diarrhea. Used as a weak tea for stomachaches and menstrual disorders. Leaf snuff used for sinus ailments, headaches, and nosebleeds. Externally, wash used for itching, rashes, skin eruptions, swelling, boils, and sores. Compress used for fevers. Used in steam baths for rheumatism, fevers, colds, and flu.

Sweet Grass:

It is a vanilla scented grass. It grows 10-24 inches tall and is found throughout the U.S. on the borders of ponds and marshes where the soil is constantly moist and rich. It is unique among grasses. It is a female plant because it is soft, pliable, and fragrant. It represents feminine energy. You can bathe with Sweet Grass, wrap hides in it, and store things in it. It keeps things nice. It is also a defense (warrior) plant. American Indians widely used Sweet Grass as incense for healing ceremonies. It is usually burned after the first two sacred herbs. It acts like a barometer and brings balance to the ceremony. It is frequently used for heartburn. Tea used for coughs, sore throats, chafing, and venereal infections; to stop vaginal bleeding, expel afterbirth. It is a symbolism for welcoming good, positive energy. Sadly, it is growing increasingly rare because of over harvesting.

Traditional Native American Prayer To Start The Day With Good Luck

O Great Spirit,

whose voice I hear in the winds,
and whose breath gives life to all the world
-hear me-
I come before you, one of your children.
I am small and weak.
I need your strength and wisdom.
Let me walk in beauty and make my eyes ever behold
the red and purple sunset.
Make my hands respect the things you have made,
my ears sharp to hear your voice.
Make me wise, so that I may know the things
you have taught my People.
The lessons you have hidden in every leaf and rock.
I seek strength not to be superior to my brothers,
but to be able to fight my greatest enemy,
myself.
Make me ever ready to come to you,
with clean hands and straight eyes,
so when life fades as a fading sunset,
my spirit may come to you without shame.

Figure 5
Native American Magic Symbols

Figure 6
Apache Mother and Children on Horseback, Painting by Carl Moon

Lost Indian Magic: A Mystery Story Of The Red Man As He Lived Before The White Men Came.

By Grace Purdie Moon & Carl Moon

Illustrations and Decorations by Carl Moon

Figure 7
"He Raised His Arms In Salutation To The Great Light-Maker"

FOREWORD

Out in the region of the sage and the pine; in the far reaches of the ever-mysterious desert, the Indian campfires of the long ago heard many a tale well worth the telling. Some there were that have been handed down, through the channel of an unwrit tongue, from age to youth – told, retold, and told again until they come to the hearing of even you and me. Thus the ancient tale of Kay'-yah and the Lost Magic comes to be set down. It may be that the legend loses somewhat in parting with the strange tongue that gave it birth, but the thread on which the crude beads of its adventures are strung runs back even to the first account, and may be of the same spinning.

THE AUTHORS.

Pasadena, California, 1918.

Figure 8
Navajo Medicine Man, Pesothlanny (much money), Photo by Carl Moon

Figure 9
Indian Totem Pole – Picture by Timothy Green Beckley

PROLOGUE

PERHAPS the thing that, more than all else, governed the life and conduct of our American Indians, before the coming of the white man with his aggressive religious views, was superstition.

Like all primitive peoples they personified the hidden powers of Nature, most of which were feared, and they supposed that back of all disaster stood some evil intelligence that must be appeased, or fought, with the aid of some other power possessing greater virtue.

Naturally enough, the power that, in their opinion, brought the greatest protection against evil, and produced the greatest blessings in abundant crops, successful hunting, and strength in battle, was symbolized by some image or object which took to itself the mighty power and gave out its magical charm, or great medicine, to the fortunate tribe who possessed it.

All good fortune, great or small, was credited to its power. All evils were thought to be less vicious than they would have been had the great Magic not been on duty in the medicine lodge, or hidden away on some secluded altar. It was most jealously protected and regarded as the tribe's most priceless possession. Gradually such a tribal fetish would come to be looked upon as the vital link between the power of the gods and the humble earth people; their charm against all the wiles of the witches, and evil spirits that were ruled over by the chief of all trouble makers – the Shin-di.

Thus the people of Ah'-co, with whom our story deals, placed the highest earthly value upon a little carven bear of turquoise – their mighty Magic, handed down to them out of a mysterious past; an inheritance from generations of their forefathers who had received its constant protection, and the blessings of its power for good. Its fame spread abroad, and at last a powerful neighboring tribe began to covet it, and the unscrupulous young chief of the tribe laid careful plans to secure it by a subtle method of his own.

One eventful night, five years before our story opens, the great Magic disappeared from the sacred altar of the medicine lodge of Ah'-co, and with its loss came the looked-for train of want, woe, and disaster. One heavy shadow lay upon the hearts of the men – the loss of their Magic; one determination remained uppermost in their minds – its recovery.

Seasons passed, bringing their varying fortune, and then dawned the day of Kay'-yah who, with ever constant faith in Joho'-na-ai, the Great Spirit whose symbol was the sun, went forth to find the little blue bear and restore it to his people.

Figure 10
Indian Totem Pole – Picture by Timothy Green Beckley

Chapter I
The Theft

Over the desert and through the brush
The dawn-wind came with a cooling rush;
The dark night-shadows turned pink and gold,
And the buttes shone forth with an outline bold,
And over the farthest rim of the world
The sun great arrows of gold light hurled
That guilded the brush and sage and sand,
And day had come to Nag'-a-pah land.

WITH the first light of morning Kay'-yah pushed aside the swinging hide at the door of his hogan and stepped out. The air was clear and cold and he drew it into his nostrils with delight. He stretched his long arms and legs and threw back his head, keenly alive to the joy of being awake and strong and young and in such a glorious world.

All about him lay the desert in the purple and blue shadows of early morning, with the far-away buttes standing like sentinels on the horizon.

The village of Ah'-co, principal camp of the Nag'-a-pahs, was situated at the mouth of a canyon whose sandy floor was level with the desert, and whose rocky walls grew farther and farther apart as they reached out into the sandy spaces of the plain like the mouth of a great river entering the ocean, and ended in a few detached monuments of fantastic shape and brilliant coloring. Far back and beyond the camp, the sides of the canyon drew rapidly together in high, precipitous cliffs which kept the narrow passage between in an almost perpetual state of gloom. High up in the rocky walls could be seen the remains of cliff-dwellings, the homes of the "Na-ya-kaed'," the lost people, as the desert tribes called them, and here and there an eagle had built his nest.

From the sandy floor of the canyon, bubbling up from the underground, came a stream of water once rushing and plentiful: but now, a mere thread of silver, it wandered lazily down into the desert and disappeared in the sand.

Sage-brush, mezquite and cactus grew everywhere, with here and there a dwarfed pinyon tree or the big, red ball of a tumble-weed. The little fields that had been cultivated by the men of Ah'-co seemed almost swallowed up by the desert which came to the very edge of the camp and was separated from it only by the width of the narrow stream.

The camp consisted of about two hundred hogans or houses; round huts built of wattled poles and plastered with mud and clay and with a small shelter in front of each door made of poles and tree boughs. In the center of the camp was a much larger hogan, the Medicine Lodge, whose door or opening, as did all the others, faced the east.

The camp was still quiet with sleep, a few thin wisps of blue smoke rising from one or two of the hogans, giving the only evidence that some of the women were awake and about to prepare the morning meal.

Kay'-yah, with a glance at the growing light in the east, gave a tightening twist to the knot in the girdle about his waist and set off on a brisk run for the small shelf of rock, several hundred yards from camp, from which he loved to watch the sun rise. Every movement of his limbs was free and swinging, and the warm blood glowed through the bronze of his skin.

He was tall and straight and strong as the young pines that grew far up the canyon and his face as open and clear-featured as his own desert, with eyes set well apart and absolutely fearless in expression, a rather prominent nose and strong chin, and a mouth which, though straight and firm, could smile readily enough and soften into tender lines for those he loved.

He was about eighteen years of age but looked older, as do most young Indians of either sex, and his body had reached an almost perfect state of development. Bright bits of blue turquoise hung in his ears and a band of red-stained deerskin bound his hair; these gave color to his costume, if what he wore could be dignified by such a name, his only garments being a breech-clout or loin cloth and moccasins of soft doe-skin, leaving his limbs and body free in every movement and exposed to the bracing air. Old men say that such was the usual summer dress of the desert people before the coming of the white man.

The soft "pat-pat" of his moccasined feet in the sand raised little puffs of dust with every step and sent scurrying many tiny animals of the desert: a little white-tailed rabbit whisked across the trail in front of him and a horned toad, airing himself on a flat rock, watched him with bright, jeweled eyes as he passed. The east grew brighter and he quickened his steps, reaching the little cliff just as Joho'-na-ai, the sun-god, peeped over the edge of the desert. He raised his arms in salutation to the great light-maker and, as the gleaming disk swung clear of the horizon, let his eyes wander over the desert, now sharp and distinct in the clear atmosphere and glowing with color: bands of rose and lavender, the sandstone cliffs with out-croppings of shale; the warm yellow of the dry sands, and here and there the bright red of a butte worn by erosion and the gray of a rocky mesa. As he looked, his eye leaped suddenly to a tiny spot of color that rose straight into the air above an ancient pinyon-tree some hundred yards to the north; it rose and dropped to the tree and rose again and dropped a second time; a bit of brilliant red that shone in the sun like a large drop of blood.

"A bird," thought Kay'-yah, "but a strange looking bird, with strange actions," and he jumped from the shelf of rock and started for the tree with keenly aroused interest and curiosity.

He kept his eyes on the twisted branches as he approached, but could not see the bird; and when he was within an arm's length of the tree a To-to'-me warrior, deadly enemy to himself and tribe, leaped, without a moment's warning, from behind it and straight at him. Kay'-yah was instantly on the defensive, and quick as thought reached for his knife; but the other, with a hand as swift, and prepared for the action, struck the weapon from his fingers before he had it fairly in his grasp and it went spinning into the sage. He made to grip Kay'-yah about the waist but succeeded only in getting his arms half way, for Kay'-yah, though not so heavy, was quicker than the To-to'-me and slipped under his hold.

They fought fiercely for a moment, each trying to get the underhold, and Kay'-yah soon saw that the To-to'-me, oiled as he was and more slippery than an eel to the touch, was more than a match for him; but suddenly a trick he had learned in camp came to his mind. The To-to'-me was trying to force him back against the tree: Kay'-yah chose a moment when he felt the man's whole strength exerted against his resistance, then he suddenly stepped back, pulling the warrior toward him, and throwing out his right thigh. As the man stumbled forward Kay'-yah whipped his right arm over his neck and bearing down with all his strength, threw him over his thigh and he fell heavily on his back. Kay'-yah sprang instantly for the man's knife; but at that moment his arms were grasped from behind, his hands twisted together, and he was jerked up from the body of his enemy, who immediately jumped to his feet, drawing his knife from his girdle as he rose.

Kay'-yah tried to struggle free but was held as in a vise. The two men had him at their mercy and he believed it was only a question of moments until they should end his life. He stood motionless now, and did not so much as quiver an eyelid when the first of the two men threatened his throat with the point of his flint knife and said, with a sneer of triumph;

"*Now*, dog of a Nag'-a-pah — "

But he was cut short by the man who held Kay'-yah.

"Enough, Chot'-zu! Wau-ko'-ma waits. There is no time for words. The bag! The bag!"

He spoke as one in command, and Kay'-yah understood his words, as the To-to'-me language had been taught him as a child. But he made no sign of having understood and indeed he had not comprehended, for the words conveyed little meaning to him until the first man again approached his throat with the knife and with a swift movement severed the thong about his neck and possessed himself of the small skin bag that dangled at its end. Immediately Kay'-yah felt his feet tripped from under him and was thrown violently on his face in the sand.

When he arose the two men were dodging through the sage several yards away, running silently and evidently taking precautions not to be seen from the Nag'-a-pah camp. He could not have caught them had he tried and it would have been more than foolish to make the attempt; for the men were now well armed, as they had picked up, in their flight, bows and arrows that had been left near by and could have shot him where he stood had they so desired. Why they did not was part of a mystery surrounding the affair which seemed to Kay'-yah to grow more inexplicable as he stood watching them. The men had knives and could have used them when they sprang at him; and the To-to'-mes were deadly enemies not inclined to mercy in the past. Failing to kill him they could easily have taken him prisoner; but that they also had failed to do. They had simply taken the little bag from about his neck, placed there by his dying mother and containing, she had told him, good medicine to protect him from all evil. All the boys of his tribe wore them and he had never given his a second thought. Why should To-to'-mes, evidently at the command of their chief, for they had mentioned the name of Wau-ko'-ma, come a journey of a day and a night simply to obtain his fetish?

Kay'-yah could think of no explanation for such strange actions and, troubled by these puzzling thoughts, turned back toward camp, as the men had now disappeared from his sight. In turning, his eye again caught the bright spot of red that had attracted him to this place. In one of the branches of the tree hung a To-to'-me arrow, and tied to its shaft with a bit of thong, a warrior feather with a bright red tip and three black bars. That signified three lives – Nag'-a-pahs probably – men who had died at To-to'-me hands: and yet they had spared him.

Kay'-yah walked slowly back to camp, searching in his mind for some possible explanation of the morning's strange adventure: but none came and he was so occupied with his thoughts that he did not hear the greetings and jokes called to him by his friends as he made his way to his hogan.

The camp was now awake, with noise and motion everywhere. Women were attending several camp-fires and bending over baskets of tightly woven reeds whose contents bubbled and boiled as the red-hot stones were thrown in and sent forth appetizing odors. The men were sharpening spears and arrow-points, restringing hide bows, and dressing raw skins from the killing of yesterday. And children and dogs were everywhere, sniffing at the smell of food, nibbling at old bones, and rolling in the dust. It was the familiar, every-morning scene of camp life and Kay'-yah paid little attention to it as he passed. His thought was to snatch a hasty bite of food and go straight to the Medicine Lodge, where old Dee-nay', Medicine Chief of the Nag'-a-pahs, and his sole councilor and advisor since the death of his father and mother, might be able to throw some light on the morning's strange happening.

But there was a small group in front of his hogan, gathered around a steaming pot attended by an old woman with straggling gray locks, and they greeted him hilariously and made way for him in their circle as he approached.

Kay'-yah sat down and took the meat and bread offered him by the old woman, Diz'-pah, the one who knew him perhaps better than anyone else in Ah'-co, and who read his every mood. She watched him now keenly, with eyes sunken far down in the wrinkles of her face. That something troubled him she felt intuitively, but it was not her way to speak what was in her heart. Her lean jaws were well known in camp for their sharp clacking, and their garrulous tones had concealed many a heartache and a longing to sympathize with those she loved. She spoke lightly now but there was an undercurrent of questioning in her voice.

"Ah, Kay'-yah, my son, why so sad and silent? Was the huge rabbit you shot for your breakfast too large for you to carry home?"

The others laughed loudly at this, and Kay'-yah smiled as he answered her;

"Your cooking, Mother Diz'-pah, does not give me strength enough to hunt."

There was louder laughter at this: for, in all Ah'co there was no better hunter than Kay'-yah, and Mother Diz'-pah was equally famous for her cooking.

She shook her gray head in pretended anger.

"If it is my cooking that has made you sad, then it must have been *you* who took the seed cakes that I had made for the corn festival!"

There was a shout of merriment at this, and Kay'-yah rose hastily, in pretended guilt, and left the group. He walked directly to the Medicine Lodge and, drawing aside the hide at its entrance, peered in. The interior seemed dark in contrast to the outdoor sunshine, and for a moment Kay'-yah could see no one. But a quiet voice spoke.

"Enter, my son, if it is Dee-nay' you seek."

Kay'-yah entered, and his eyes soon grew accustomed to the light within. The hogan was the largest in camp and its circular wall more smoothly finished than were the others. Here and there hung feathered prayer sticks and ceremonial rattles, and little hide bags that Kay'-yah knew contained earth and pollen of many colors for the sacred sand paintings. Deerskin mats lay in a circle around the floor against the wall, and opposite the door could just be distinguished in the shadows the big medicine drum. The only light came from the smoke-hole in the center of the rude dome ceiling and from a small fire which burned feebly beneath it.

Bending over the fire, as if to gather all its warmth to himself, sat a very old man, seamed and wrinkled as a walnut. Kay'-yah could easily see why he was called, by many, the "Moon man"; for in the dim interior, as he sat with his back to the entrance, wrapped in dark hides, the bright patch of his silver head, seeming to float in the shadows, immediately caught and held the eye until the other objects became clear. And "Moon man" he was in another sense; for he rarely was seen in the daylight, preferring to spend his time in quiet thought in the Medicine Lodge during the sunlit hours and venturing out among his people when the fires were ablaze at night, when he would appear suddenly in one group and then another with a few words of greeting or a silent nod and then disappear. He was looked upon almost with awe by the Nag'-a-pahs, as his wisdom was great and it was thought that no act or word or happening in camp was unknown to him.

Kay'-yah entered in silence and sat down by the old man, who did not look up or make any motion of recognition, though the relation between them, through long years of close friendship, had become almost that of father and son.

"Father," said Kay'-yah, "my thoughts are puzzled by a happening of this morning – perhaps your wisdom may throw light upon it."

"My ears are open, Kay'-yah, my son," answered Dee-nay'.

As Kay'-yah told of the two To-to'-mes and the theft of the bag, the old man sat silent, the expression of his face did not change, though he turned toward Kay'-yah eyes that gleamed with an inner excitement he did not attempt to disguise. He did not speak until the narrative was finished and then his questions were short and to the point.

"What did the bag contain?"

"I know only from the words of my mother, that it contained a charm – good medicine to ward away evil," answered Kay'-yah.

"Umph! Then you could not have looked within without spoiling its charm," said the old man meditatively. "When did it come into your possession?"

"The night my father came home: that last night when he fell in front of our hogan shot through with To-to'-me arrows, my mother took this fetish from him, from his hand or from about his neck, and kept it for me until the day she died."

Dee-nay' leaned forward and his eyes flashed.

"The To-to'-me wolves have a good scent for an old trail! But this is strange news, Kay'-yah, my son – strange news. I should have known of this before. You knew not what was in the bag, and yet *they*, the To-to'-mes, knew. Yes – that is strange. Wau-ko'-ma sent for it – a two-days' journey. He would have done that for no ordinary fetish – can it be — " His voice trailed off into silence as he sat with knitted brows deep in thought over this strange problem.

A tingling sense of excitement began to grow in Kay'-yah as a half-formed thought took shape in his mind. He watched Dee-nay' with a tense expectancy, awaiting his next words.

The moments grew into what seemed a long time to Kay'-yah and still the old man sat thinking; he nodded his head slowly several times, and his lips moved noiselessly. It was evident that he was deeply stirred, and when he finally looked up and began to speak his eyes burned with a fire that Kay'-yah had never before seen in them.

"Kay'-yah, my son, if this bag contained, what I greatly fear it did, and others knew of it, even I could not keep our tribe from war with the To-to'-mes – a war for which we are not prepared. But there is a doubt; this matter is not yet perfectly clear to my mind; it will take thought. For that I must be alone. Go now, and when the sun is four fingers above the desert's rim return to me; I will then have words for you. But first answer for me one question. Have you spoken to anyone of this?"

"You are the first, Father."

"It is well; see that I am the last. Go, and return as I have said."

Kay'-yah walked out of the Lodge with many strange thoughts troubling his mind; he was in no mood to talk with his usual companions and, after walking some distance toward the canyon, found a spot under a large rock by the narrow stream where he hoped to be alone.

When, in a little while, he heard the soft shuffle of approaching moccasins, he made a movement to leave the place, but decided to wait and see who came. A slender girl came around the corner of the rock, carrying a jar on her shoulders. His first thought at sight of her was of relief. Here was one who never disturbed his thinking and who never urged him to talk. He could not remember the day when he had not seen Sah'-ne pass with her water-jar, and he liked the little smile that came to her lips and the droop of her eyes as he nodded to her, though they seldom spoke to each other. She knelt now without a word by the stream, which widened and deepened into a small pool just here and made it possible to dip the jar into its cool depths.

Figure 11
"He Could Not Remember The Day When He Had Not Seen Sah'-Ne Pass With Her Water-Jar"

She seemed to feel Kay'-yah's eyes on her as she worked, and stooped low to hide the deep red that dyed her cheeks. A look of admiration shone in his eyes, for she made a pretty picture in her buckskin dress, outlined against the silvery gray of the sage. He spoke to her.

"Why are you different from the other girls of the camp, Sah'-ne?"

She gave a half-frightened little look up at him and down into the pool again and the red burned more deeply in her cheeks, but she did not answer.

"Why are you always alone, Sah'-ne?" he asked again. "Why are you never with the others?"

She rose to her feet, and there was more than embarrassment in her manner now.

"You do not know?" she asked, looking away from him.

"No, I do not know – why?"

She hesitated for a moment, and then lifted her head proudly, but did not look at him.

"I am To-to'-me," she said; and Kay'-yah, through his astonishment, felt his heart grow heavy within him. A gulf had opened up between them; a gulf fixed by all the laws and traditions of his people and hers. He stood looking at her in silence as his thoughts tried to adjust themselves to this new condition. She slowly turned her head to meet his eyes.

"You do not like that?" she asked quietly.

"No, I do not like that – but I like *you*, Sah'-ne."

The smile came back to her eyes but could not quite hide the pitiful little droop of her mouth as she drew the water-jar to her shoulder and waited a moment as if for him to speak again, but as he did not she gave a shy nod and walked back the way she had come.

He stood looking after her – Sah'ne, of an enemy tribe. Why should such a thought cause his heart to throb with a dull pain? He could not understand the sense of depression that had come to him, nor did he like it, and forced his thoughts back to Dee-nay' and the morning's adventure; but at thought of the little medicine bag his heart again began to beat fast – what if it *did* contain what Dee-nay' had hinted – and he waited with impatience for the afternoon hours to slip away until he could get back to the old man. Finally the sun drew near to the horizon and he found himself again seated in the Medicine Lodge with Dee-nay', who did not speak immediately on his entrance but still sat with head bowed in thought, as though he had not moved since morning. At last he spoke:

"It has not been in vain that I have made prayers to the Great Spirit, Kay'-yah, and our path is now more clear. It would take more than a rat to draw the To-to'-me wild-cats from their den. We may be sure they came seeking big game – none other, so it seems to me, than our great Magic."

Kay'-yah gave a sharp exclamation, though the words but affirmed what had been in his mind since morning.

Dee-nay' nodded slowly.

"The honey draws the bees, and a rotting carcass the vultures, but the To-to'-mes have ever been keen on the trail of our Magic, and it may be that they have now hunted it down. How it came in the little bag, we know not; but our work is now clear before us. This is what has been made plain to me – you must go to the To-to'-me camp and, if our gods are good to you, find the way to recover this bag. We know that the Great Spirit protects those who seek their own. If the bag did not contain the Magic, we must know what it did contain. What has value for the To-to-'mes may have value for the Nag'-a-pahs also. Do you know the country of these people, Kay'-yah?"

"Only as a hunter, from a distance," answered Kay'-yah.

"You do not know Qua'-ma, the mountain which rises to the north of their camp?" continued the old man.

"I have seen it many times from the plain below but have never explored its trails."

Dee-nay' nodded slowly.

"Beware of the To-to'-me trails! They are as rabbit-tracks in the desert. Make your way only where the mountain goat has led – for I know you to be sure of foot. It is to the foothills of this mountain you must go, for they overlook the To-to'-me camp, and from there you can watch their actions. Remember, Kay'-yah, it is by their actions that men and beasts betray their secrets – the wild-cat skulks when the prey is in his mouth, but the eagle flies to his nest and the eaglets cry – the To-to'-mes will make gay with feasting and dancing if they have succeeded, after these many seasons, in capturing our Strong Medicine. It is in that way that you will learn their secret; and once sure that they have the Magic it will be for you to discover where it is kept. This you may not do from the hills. In this, all I have taught you of caution will be necessary. Remember that the dark is a faithful aid to those who would not be seen, but the dark also has dangers for those who have not ears trained, as have our brothers of the night – and a dog's nose is as keen at night as in the sunlight, my son. The To-to'-me camp is so situated that you may not easily enter it without being seen, nor can you overlook it near at hand; it will be difficult to learn the information you seek.

"I have not given you an easy task, Kay'-yah, my son, but one which holds much in its accomplishment – for, if it is learned by our enemies that the power of the Magic is gained only when it is placed on the altar of the Medicine Lodge and sprinkled with the sacred meal, and if they so place it, then it will take all of the medicine of our wisest men and the strength of our warriors to bring it back to its rightful place, and it may well be that even then we would fail. And if we fail – the abundant crops, the clear springs, the prosperity and success in hunt and battle, and the protection from all enemies – all these, that should belong to the Nag'-a-pahs will be with the To-to'-mes. Does your heart fail, Kay'-yah, or is it strong to do this task?"

Kay'-yah reddened at the direct question, and his voice was husky with embarrassment, but he looked Dee-nay' squarely in the eyes as he answered;

"My heart is strong to do it."

"It is well. I have not said how you will find where the Magic is kept – that is not for me to say. But we know that when our cause is right, the Great Spirit opens the way, and so it will be for you. Make no attempt to get the Magic unaided, for it will be well guarded, and in such an attempt you might give your life without return. It is well that I have taught my children the tongues of the tribes about us, for it may be of service to you to know the language of these To-to'-mes; you may hear their talk from the trails. If you find they have captured the Magic, return quickly to me, for I have further plans; do not linger on the way; five suns should see you here again. Have my words been plain?"

"Yes, Father."

"It is well. You must go tonight. There is no moon and the trail of the To-to'-mes is still clear in the canyon sands. Go, before the earth has swallowed it. Is there aught you would ask, my son – the words of Dee-nay' are for your counsel."

"You have made the way plain for me, Father. There is nothing that I would ask, but I would like to tell of what had been in my mind these many days past."

"Speak, Kay'-yah."

The boy hesitated, with some slight show of embarrassment, but an earnest tone came to his voice that had not been there before.

"When I have been alone – before the Great Spirit – at sunrise, I have made a vow – within my heart, and it is – this that I would give my life to this one purpose – to bring back to my people the Magic which is their own. When my mother placed the bag about my neck, my own heart tells me that she did not know what it contained; but if it did contain the Magic, and if it was by her action that it was lost, then it shall be mine, Father, with the help of the Great Spirit, to bring it back."

"It is well, Kay'-yah." A warm light came into the old man's eyes as they rested on Kay'-yah and he looked well pleased.

There was silence for a short while, and then Kay'-yah looked up suddenly.

"Father, how is it that we have a To-to'-me girl among our women?"

"That is to go far back, Kay'-yah – you speak of Sah'-ne?"

"Yes, the girl who is as unlike our women as the pine-tree that lifts itself above the sage."

Dee-nay' smiled to himself but looked up keenly.

"The laws of our tribe are strict, my son. See that you keep them in mind. A Nag'-a-pah must not take to wife a woman of another tribe."

"I do not forget." There was a tinge of bitterness in the boy's tone. "But of this girl – you have never told me how it happens that she is of an enemy tribe."

"It was many summers ago," began the old man, "perhaps fourteen – when a hunting party of our people went out toward the north. They were gone long and when they returned they had with them a man – Gō'-me (you must remember him), and a baby girl of about two summers, his daughter. The man claimed to be of a small tribe friendly to us, who had all been killed by To-to'-mes; even he himself was left for dead beside the body of his wife. This was his story, and it was borne out by his many apparent injuries, and you will remember he was a hunchback."

Kay'-yah nodded in silence, and Dee-nay' continued;

"The baby had been overlooked or spared, he said. A quiet man, was Gō'-me, and of good behavior and with a wonderful skill in taming animals and birds. That was why, in time, he was made keeper of the sacred eagle in the Medicine Lodge, where he remained until the night he was killed. His baby was much loved by the women. It was not until after the night he was killed that it became known that he was To-to'-me; that his story had been false, and that he had been sent to our camp as a spy. Since this was known, our women have looked away from Sah'-ne."

A strangely bitter look came into Kay'-yah's face as the old man ceased speaking.

"And yet," he said, "I have been told the To-to'-mes were once a great and good people."

Dee-nay did not answer, and again there was silence for a few moments. Presently Kay'-yah looked up.

"Was not this Gō'-me killed the night my father was also killed?"

"The same, my son."

"Was he in the Lodge when it was discovered that the Magic was missing?"

"He was in the Lodge and alone when I entered and found our Great Medicine gone. But he could not have taken the Magic; he was searched then and later, and if he had been able to give it, in some way, to the To-to'-mes it is certain that they would not have continued their efforts to obtain it, which they have done from that day to this."

"Could he not have buried it?" asked Kay'-yah.

The old man shook his head.

"You, yourself, have helped to search the plain and canyon."

Kay'-yah felt his face grow hot with the thought that was in his mind, and he forced it away from him as a vision of Sah'-ne, sweet and girlish, came before his mental vision – what could *she* know of the Magic – and if she *had* known of it, the fact that it had not reached the To-to'-mes was surely proof of her loyalty to her adopted people.

"Then it must have been in the little bag that my father brought back, the bag that my mother placed about my neck when she died. And now I will go, to recover it at your word."

"It is well – prepare here for your journey. You will find food and weapons also," and Dee-nay' indicated the articles with a gesture.

Kay'-yah arose and soon found the things he needed. Dried meat and piki bread he stuffed into the girdle at his waist, and also a knife in the same place. A deerskin bow-case, containing a stout bow and quiver of arrows, he drew over his shoulder; he tested the thongs of his moccasins and girdle, and was ready for his journey. Dee-nay' looked up when Kay'-yah again stood before him.

"I send you alone for two reasons, my son. One man can go where two might be discovered. And a secret ceases to be a secret when shared by too many – and my words have told you why this mission must remain secret for a while, at least. So now the wisdom of your way lies in caution and silence – it is well to remember what you have learned of the ways of the fox and the snake – they make few mistakes. The trail is there – go – and return as I have said in five suns from now – and the Great Spirit of all be with you."

Kay'-yah stepped out into the twilight. He avoided the groups about the supper fires and walked quickly out of camp toward the canyon, where, shrouded already in the shadows of early night, lay his trail.

Figure 12
Indian Chief, Painting by Carl Moon

Chapter 2
The Wrong Bag

A stretch of rocky mesa, and a sweep of desert sand;
A narrow ledge along a cliff; a strip of stony land;
The sharp horizon of the hills; an eagle's startled cry;
The mountain trail leads on and on and over it, the sky.

THE two To-to'-mes, leaving Kay'-yah standing in the early morning sunlight, ran freely and easily, making a wide detour about the Nag'-a-pah camp and arriving in the shadows of the canyon before the sun was more than two hands above the horizon. Chot'-zu, the larger and heavier of the two, ran always a few feet behind his lighter companion and kept closely in his track. Their pace was in the nature of a dog-trot and could be kept up for many hours without weariness, even when the trail began gradually to rise and grow more difficult with sliding sand and rocks and rolling gravel.

It has been said that Chot'-zu was the larger of the two: his features carried out the general lines of his figure and were also large and coarse, with a heavy forehead which overhung eyes set a trifle too closely together in his head and a nose with bulbous nostrils. His lips were thick and loosely hung together and not over-inclined to silence. He was altogether in striking contrast to his companion, Ha-wal'-li; for where Chot'-zu was thick Ha-wal'-li was slim, in neck and thigh and nostril: and where Chot'-zu gave the impression of brute-force, Ha-wal'-li showed the alertness of skill and training, and the refinement of thought. As they ran Chot'-zu still held the little bag in his hand and glanced at it from time to time.

"What do you think is in this bag, Ha-wal'-li? One little look would show."

Ha-wal'-li stopped abruptly and reached forth his hand.

"Give me the bag, Chot'-zu. You know well that Wau-ko'-ma said to bring it safe to him unopened."

"Wau-ko'-ma!" sneered Chot'-zu, as he handed over the bag with reluctance. "Wau-ko'-ma – and are you then so faithful to Wau-ko'-ma?"

Ha-wal'-li did not answer, but with head held high, turned and again broke into his easy run, the little bag tucked safely into his girdle. But Chot'-zu was not to be so easily silenced.

"Did not Tag-a'-mo have a word to say about this bag, friend Ha-wal'-li?" His eyes glittered as he spoke and he leaned toward his companion as if to dare him to answer.

Ha-wal'-li answered shortly.

"Tag-a'-mo, as you know, is in the council of Wau-ko'-ma."

"Ah, do you say so! It may be there are those who say differently. Tag-a'-mo has been Medicine Chief these many moons, but he had better have a care! I, Chot'-zu, say it – he, and his followers" – He paused and looked significantly at Ha-wal'-li. "His followers are not unknown to Wau-ko'-ma, who is *still* chief of the To-to'-mes."

Ha-wal'-li shrugged his shoulders contemptuously.

"Thy tongue is over loose – it may well loosen thy head also, friend, some day."

Chot'-zu lapsed into surly silence, and the two began to go more slowly as the trail now led steeply up the side of the canyon. Once they dropped cautiously behind a large boulder as a hunting-party of Nag'-a-pahs passed below them, and at another time they were tempted to take a shot at a mountain sheep which ran swiftly up the trail ahead of them; but they did not let the arrow fly, as the sheep might plunge into the canyon below and betray their presence to possible foes.

By noon they had gained the level of the upper country and left the canyon behind. The heat of the sun set them both to looking for water signs and it was not long before a little pile of rocks with its pointing stone on top led them to a sheltered pool, where they drank their fill and plunged their faces into the refreshing depths. They also ate a little from their small supply of dried meat and hard maize cake, and after a very few moments continued their journey. Their way now lay across country, much like the desert below save that it was more rolling and broken by many gullies and canyons, some of which were of almost as much importance as the one they had left behind. The food seemed to loosen Chot'-zu's tongue again, and an inner excitement brought a strange gleam to his eyes. He spoke to Ha-wal'-li in a tone very different from the one he had used before, and the words came slowly from his tongue.

"Have you thought, Ha-wal'-li" – he hesitated – "what this bag may contain?"

Ha-wal'-li gave a slight shrug to his shoulders, that may have meant affirmation or negation, but did not speak.

"Have you thought — " and Chot'-zu leaned forward that his words might, the more surely, be caught – "that it might contain the Magic of the Nag'-a-pahs?"

Ha-wal'-li answered impatiently.

"You have the chatter of a squirrel, Chot'-zu, and with less reason. Would a Nag'-a-pah boy wear their treasured Magic about his neck?"

"Then why such caution and secrecy about a bag? What think you does it hold?"

"Would Wau-ko'-ma talk to me – Tag-a'-mohow should I know?"

Chot'-zu gave a grunt of disgust, and they ran in silence after this.

Through Ha-wal'-li's mind ran thoughts of those who awaited them in the medicine lodge of the To-to'-me camp – Wau-ko'-ma, who for fifteen harvests had been chief of the To-to'-mes, though not much more than twice that many years old: a man brutal in instinct and action and with a following like himself. Though the whole tribe openly acknowledged him as their chief, yet the greater part of them were not with him in heart, and the camp was thus divided into two factions – Wau-ko'-ma's followers and those who morally supported Tag-a'-mo, the medicine chief – Tag-a'-mo, the wise and fearless, who though with the heart of a child, knew no mercy in the cause of justice. His white head was loved by friends and feared and respected by his enemies; for in addition to great physical strength, which at sixty years had weakened not one bit, he had at his command all the magic and superstition of a long line of medicine men and knew the history and family of every member of the tribe from the smallest papoose to the oldest grayhead who had long forgotten the number of his years. The followers of Tag-a'-mo were those who loved justice and peace, while the other faction, the wilder of the young men, gloried in the brutal and lawless rule of Wau-ko'-ma. There had been no open break between the two factions, and might never be, for an Indian, though he may in his heart hate his chief, yet will he remain loyal to the end, for old tradition and superstition hold him in their grip. So Ha-wal'-li, though hating Wau-ko'-ma and despising Chot'-zu as his follower, gave open expression to neither feeling. He realized that Wau-ko'-ma himself had no faith in his own following; for had he not, in sending for the bag, chosen one he knew to be of the opposing faction as more worthy of trust than his own men?

With the first pink light of morning the two men drew near to the To-to'-me village of Ta-pau'-wee. With the exception of the few stops they had made for water, they had kept up the same swinging trot for a day and a night, and yet they appeared as fresh as at the start and approached the camp with heads thrown back and a quickened pace. They did not slacken their speed until they reached the door of the medicine lodge, pushed aside the curtain, and stepped within.

Seated in a circle on the floor of the lodge were five men, smoking; the haze from their pipes hung in the air like a fog and gave a weird, uncertain aspect to their faces. Wau-ko'-ma faced the entrance: a man with a heavy, square face, high cheekbones and a thin, cruel mouth. Tag-a'-mo sat next to him, or rather towered, for he was a giant of a man, with the face of a lion and the voice of one. It was a common joke in camp to say, when it thundered, "Tag-a'-mo speaks!" The other three were elders of the tribe without whom no ceremony was complete.

Ha-wal'-li stepped forward, laid the little bag at the feet of Wau-ko'-ma, and stood upright, waiting.

Wau-ko'-ma made a gesture toward the door.

"It is well! Go – you and your companion."

And they passed out, dropping the hide at the door behind them.

There was silence in the medicine lodge. The little bag lay where Ha-wal'-li had placed it, on the beaten floor, and the clouds of smoke curled upward. No man had moved; each, seemingly intent on his own thoughts, gazed into vacancy.

Presently Wau-ko'-ma, with deliberate motions, drew a flint knife from his girdle and, picking up the little bag, severed the thong that bound its throat. Then, drawing out the only article it contained, he placed it on his palm for all to see – a heavy ring, curiously carved and of evident antiquity.

The silence seemed greater than before. Wau-ko'-ma's eyes were fastened on the ring, but the others, after one long look at it, had shifted their gaze to Wau-ko'-ma himself, who, seeming to feel the intensity of their regard, looked up with something like defiance in his eyes, mingled with growing anger.

"Call back the messengers!" he commanded; and when Ha-wal'-li and Chot'-zu again appeared at the door, he spoke harshly to Ha-wal'-li.

"I sent for the bag about the neck of Kay'-yah, the Nag'-a-pah, and you bring me this! The meaning – what is the meaning of this? Speak quickly!"

Ha-wal'-li stood motionless.

"This is from the neck of the Nag'-a-pah. There is no mistake," he said, and his quiet tones were in striking contrast to those of Wau-ko'-ma, who now turned to Chot'-zu with a puzzled frown on his face.

"Chot'-zu, what say you of this?"

"Ha-wal'-li speaks what is so, Wau-ko'-ma. I, Chot'-zu, and no other, cut it from about the neck of the Nag'-a-pah dog. Three suns we watched for him, and when he came — "

"Enough! Go – both of you; but wait outside."

Again there was silence in the lodge, but not for long. Tag-a'-mo's eyes had not left Wau-ko'-ma's face since the opening of the bag: he seemed thinking deeply and now his voice boomed suddenly forth from the smoky haze:

"Wau-ko'-ma, what means this?" and his finger indicated the ring. "How comes it that a Nag'-a-pah wears that which you have claimed to have?"

There was a sneer in Wau-ko'-ma's voice as he answered, and his eyes flashed.

"How comes it that the fox has the fur of a hare in his den? Are thieves unknown to you, Tag-a'-mo? This Nag'-a-pah, like all his tribe, is a thief, and – " his fury rising – "his life shall pay for this!"

Tag-a'-mo and the elders smoked quietly for a moment, and then he reached for the little bag, which still lay at Wau-ko'-ma's feet, and looked at it thoughtfully. The sinews were old and stiff, and the thong which had bound it nearly worn through on the side that had lain next the flesh of its wearer. He fingered the two small silver beads that dangled from the bag, and looking within, noted the worn hollow left by the ring. Then he spoke:

"This fox went hunting young, Wau-ko'-ma. The ring has lain within its nest for many seasons."

Wau-ko'-ma rose to his feet and his voice was harsh with anger.

"I care not – the time has now come for his thieving to end, and I – Wau-ko'-ma – shall end it. By the sacred symbol of Joho'-na-ai, I swear it!" And taking the ring and bag he strode out of the medicine lodge without one backward glance.

The old men smoked in silence until Tag-a'-mo again spoke. He addressed the man on his right.

"Speak, Dis'-din! What know *you* of the bag worn by this Nag'-a-pah?"

Dis'-din drew deliberately at his pipe for several moments before answering; his thin, silver hair fell over the brow of a patriarch and his features gave evidence of a refinement of thought unusual among his people. He was the father of Ha-wal'-li, and the likeness was marked. Presently he let his long pipe rest on the beaten floor and watched its smoke curl upward as he talked.

"When our spy, Gō'-me, was sent to the Nag'-a-pah camp, these many summers past – for reasons well known to you, brothers – " the others nodded over their pipes – "he found the Magic of the Nag'-a-pahs guarded by two men: Dee-nay', the medicine chief, and Qua-hi'-da, the father of this boy, Kay'-yah." He drew again at his pipe. "This Qua-hi'-da was chosen, that night we know of, to bury their treasure – this we learned from the man we afterward captured. And with Qua-hi'-da went another. We received the word from Gō'-me – the way is known to you also."

Again the others nodded in silence.

"The two were at the mouth of the canyon when our scouting party found them, returning to their camp. They were both mortally wounded by our warriors, but Qua-hi'-da, with the speed of a dying deer, escaped to die at his own door. One of our party followed him and saw him hand to his woman a little bag from which the firelight caught the gleam of silver beads; he made an effort to speak but no words came and he fell back dead. The other man was conscious for some time before he also died and he was made to speak about his people. He said it was useless for the To-to'-mes to capture Ah'-co, the Nag'-a-pah camp, as the treasure was no longer there. When tortured, to tell the whereabouts of the Magic, he said only that it was in the keeping of Qua-hi'-da, and it was then that the runner returned with his tale of what had happened at camp and of the bag handed by Qua-hi'-da to his wife, who thrust it into the bosom of her dress. The captured man smiled when he heard this and died in peace."

Dis'-din picked up his pipe as the others listened expectantly for his next words';

"One other incident there was that night," he continued. "As the men stood considering, a sound of hurrying feet came to their ears – someone who came running in fear or excitement and, before he could be stayed, one of the To-to'-mes had put an arrow to the string and let fly straight at the approaching figure, who leaped high into the air and fell on his face. As they turned him over the features of Gō'-me could be plainly seen in the starlight. Only four words could he gasp out before he also was gone. 'The Magic – the bag' was all he said. And since then, brothers, we have had spies constantly watching for the reappearance of the little bag with silver beads, the bag which Wau-ko'-ma now carries."

He ceased speaking abruptly and Tag-a'-mo made a guttural sound which seemed to express many things.

"We trailed a wolf and caught a fox. But what of this Kay'-yah – think you he still holds the Magic and knows it not?"

The others did not answer, and Tag-a'-mo continued;

"Brothers, there is much here that calls for explanation and to me it seems there would be interest in speaking to this Kay'-yah, interest for us as well as for Wau-ko'-ma. I shall send men to follow his runners and see that the Nag'-a-pah is not killed, and if he is captured he shall be brought here. We shall talk to him and it may be that we shall learn much that is now wrapped in mystery." And Tag-a'-mo also passed out of the lodge, leaving the three elders pondering what had just occurred.

The next day toward evening Tag-a'-mo was conscious of an undertone of excitement in the village: men and women hurried toward the rock which was Ta-pau'-wee's one gathering place, and from the words they spoke he soon discovered that the cause of interest was a captured Nag'-a-pah who had been caught in the act of spying from the foothills. He walked slowly in the wake of the others, half-consciously following where they led, until presently looking up he found himself on the edge of a crowd and over many heads he looked into the face of a young Indian whose eyes, though looking straight into his, seemed to look through and beyond him with an indifference and pride that gave little indication of the rebellion that was surging within him; for it was Kay'-yah – filled with fury at himself for the carelessness that had placed him in the hands of his enemies.

Figure 13
Daily Chores, Painting by Carl Moon

Chapter 3
Kay'-Yah At Ta-Pau'-Wee

Perched like an eagle on its nest
Ta-pau'-wee lies.
Set high upon a rocky crest
Against the skies.

LOOKING downward upon it from the precipitous slope of the first rocky foothill that towers above it on the northern side, the To-to'-me mesa rises sheer out of the desert like an island in a becalmed sea. Even a casual glance at it and the immediate country about it would suffice to tell why the To-to'-mes had chosen its top as a site for their permanent camp – the village of Ta-pau'-wee.

The great perpendicular walls of this rock-ribbed base drop down on all sides of the camp except one, but at a point on the side nearest the mountain nature has provided an approach that not only gave the To-to'-mes a direct level path to the foothills, but the narrowness of the passage made it possible for a very few men to protect the camp from an invading party of almost any size. This long narrow approach ran along the top of a rocky ridge that seemed to project itself from the foothills to the mesa as though the thin arm of stone were loath to permit this island of rock to be separated from the parent mountain of which it had, at one time, doubtless been a part. Beyond bow-shot from the hills on one side, and protected from the open desert that lay below it on the other, the place seemed impregnable. The area of the mesa was not large, yet there was ample room on its level surface for the two or three hundred hogans that housed the tribe. The main portion of the houses were erected in the shape of a crescent whose outward curve fronted the narrow approach to the mesa. Small bushes, tumble-weed, and a few stunted pinyon trees dotted the outer margin of the mesa, giving a still more secluded appearance to the houses that clustered within. Over and beyond the mesa to the southward, the great level desert stretched monotonously out to the faint purple buttes on the horizon line.

On the eastern side ran an energetic little stream that coursed downward in a curve from the mountain-side a mile or more away, and then flowed in an almost straight line to the foot of the mesa. Reaching its base, it skirted around it on the desert side, and, turning back toward the mountain for a little way, wandered off again westwardly across the plain, where, after several miles of snake-like twists and turns, it emptied itself into a shallow lake that sparkled in the sun like a small disk of burnished copper.

On the west side of the camp, at a point where the narrow approach joined the mesa, a steep little trail that led zig-zagging downward to the stream below, had been cut into the sides of the cliff. Over this trail the women brought the daily supply of fresh water for the camp's use. If the supply was cut off by an enemy, a little pool, deep in the rocks on the western side of the mesa, where the seepage from winter snows and rains kept it filled, could be drawn upon and be made to last longer than the enemy would care to remain below.

At late evening the low golden light of the setting sun flooded the desert and gilded the western walls of the mesa that cast its great purple shadow streaming out to the east. It sharply outlined the cliffs at the base of the foothills and turned the stream into a thread of gold. Such was the scene that spread out beneath the wondering eyes of Kay'-yah as he looked down from the sheltering pile of rocks high up on the nearest foothill. His uneventful journey of a day and a night was at an end, and he was thankful that the sun was yet high enough for him to inspect the enemy camp before darkness fell. As he looked downward, his trained eyes took in the unusual surroundings and he carefully noted each detail that would be of use to him in the task that lay before him. As his eyes wandered along the little stream on the eastern side of the mesa he noticed that the bank nearest the foothills was very steep and contained no trail, while the opposite bank was piled high with great boulders and thick underbrush. Small trees and bushes grew about the stream as it neared the cliffs, and dotted the little slopes that ran upward in drifts at the base of the mesa.

It seemed plain enough that if he was to enter the village he must find some point at which he could scale the walls from the desert side, as an entrance by way of either of the two trails was out of the question. He must get to the plain below, and under cover of darkness follow the little stream around the foot of the mesa to the eastern side, which seemed to be the most promising place to find a break in the wall up which he might ascend.

Down in the village he could see men and women, looking no larger than ants, as they moved about among the hogans. On the southern side of the camp, not far from the mesa's edge, stood a hogan that was much larger than the rest. "The medicine lodge," thought Kay'-yah, as he carefully noted its location. Within its walls, and perhaps upon its altar, the little bag might even now be lying. His heart beat fast with the thought and his hopes, almost shattered at finding the enemy camp so wonderfully protected from an intruder, now began to return.

As his eyes searched for the best way down to the plain, a way that must be traveled after darkness came, he saw several tiny figures, of men or boys, running in the desert at the foot of the mesa. As they came nearer he saw they were having some kind of game or race, as they were kicking a small object with their feet as they ran. He suddenly remembered that he had been told of a To-to'-me game in which the contestants, usually three on a side, tossed a smooth round stick with their toes as they ran over a given distance. The side that brought their stick to the goal first won the game. Now, as the nude runners came on around the mesa he became so intent in watching them that he forgot, for the moment, all else, and, rising from his shelter in the rocks, moved a little nearer the edge of the slope to get a better view. Suddenly he heard the sound of steps at his back; and as he turned he felt the quick clutch of strong arms, and before he could make effectual resistance found himself at the mercy of three To-to'-me men. The oldest of the three, a man of great strength, and one who seemed to be accustomed to leading men, was the first to speak.

"A nice place for a Nag'-a-pah rabbit to choose when spying upon the den of wolves. Are your young eyes satisfied with what they have seen?"

Kay'-yah's blood ran hot within him and he inwardly cursed the carelessness that had made him such an easy prey to his To-to'-me captors, but his face instantly became a mask that effectually hid his thoughts; a mask of cold dignity that could give little satisfaction to his enemies.

"For one who walks alone, you are far from your campfire," said another, who now produced a stout thong which he handed to the two men who held Kay'-yah.

Pretending not to understand their language, Kay'-yah made no reply. They now tied his arms securely behind his back and pushed him forward, indicating that he was to go with them. He knew enough to make no struggle, as escape was now out of the question. He also knew that his captors would take him to the camp below, as it was the custom of all desert tribes to bring their captives into the presence of the people before they were put to death. Evidently he had fallen into the hands of a hunting party that had been returning to camp, as one of the men now picked up some rabbits and birds that had been deposited in the rocks just before they had attacked him. What a fool he had been to be caught like a rabbit, just as one of the men had said! The To-to'-mes, seemingly satisfied that he did not understand their language, talked together as they walked. One of them strode ahead of him to lead the way, and the remaining two followed in the rear.

"Wau-ko'-ma has said we would have much fun with the next Nag'-a-pah brought in," said one, and after a short time he continued: "He has said that we can try the flying knife, and this is a fair mark at which to throw the knife."

"It is because Wau-ko'-ma cannot shoot an arrow straight that he always talks of the flying knife," said another man. "Perhaps Tag-a'-mo will have words to say," he continued, "and my ears are better pleased with what he says than with the talk of Wau-ko'-ma."

"Wau-ko'-ma is chief," reminded the third man; and after that the party fell silent.

Soon Kay'-yah saw that they were on a zig-zagging trail that led directly downward to the narrow approach to the mesa, and after a very short time he found himself marching along the narrow ridge.

As the four men advanced, dogs, naked children, and a few old women ran out to meet them, as they had seen from a distance that the hunters brought a captive with them. The news that a captured enemy was being brought into camp quickly spread over the village and in a few moments a crowd gathered about the approaching party as they passed between the row of houses. In the clamor of voices that arose, questions, jibes, and insults were all hurled at Kay'-yah at once: but pretending not to understand, he held his head high and walked more like a conqueror than a captive. Soon several of the people who knew the Nag'-a-pah language began to taunt him in his own tongue: but he paid no more attention to these than to the former remarks. Something in his quiet dignity began to make the childish clamor sound foolish to the crowd, and they now followed the party in silence to the public gathering place in the center of the camp. As soon as he was halted in the level opening in front of the circling hogans, he looked into the antagonistic faces of those about him with an indifference that was not forced. If death was to come – and he did not doubt that it would come – he knew how to die like a man and a warrior; even the torture would not move him to any show of pain, as that would bring pleasure to his captors.

His thoughts turned to Dee-nay' and, as he fully realized how unworthy he had proven himself of the trust the old man had placed in him, his heart grew hitter with self-condemnation. But it was useless to lament the past, and as he thought of the peril that confronted him his mind turned to an oft-repeated admonition given him by his aged counselor: "A warrior may lose his spear, his arrows, and his knife, but his thoughts may still remain with him and prove to be his most powerful weapons." Realizing that he must keep his thoughts acting to some purpose, he stood upright and motionless, his height enabling him to see over the heads of most of the men about him.

A heavily built To-to'-me now pushed his way through the crowd, and, coming close to Kay'-yah, called out with triumphant voice:

"Aha! It is soon that I get even with the Nag'-a-pah dog who tried to throw me – me, Chot'-zu, who could throw two like him and use but one arm!" And then with mock kindness he asked: "Do you come to Ta-pau'-wee for the little bag I took from your neck?"

At the sound of Chot'-zu's remark a second figure came up and the crowd made way for him as he approached. He also was heavily built and near Kay'-yah's height. His face, like that of Chot'-zu, was coarse and brutal, but he made a great effort to carry himself with a dignified bearing that was plainly unnatural.

"Wau-ko'-ma comes," said a low voice in the crowd near Kay'-yah.

As he strode up into the circle he stopped to speak in a low tone to Chot'-zu. At that moment Kay'-yah noticed a gray-haired old man approaching the outer edge of the crowd. His great shoulders towered above those about him and his large black eyes seemed to blaze out of a face that revealed unusual power and dignity. Then the man with the brutal face, whom Kay'-yah now knew to be Wau-ko'-ma, the To-to'-me chief, walked up to him and in a voice that was meant to be awe-inspiring said:

"So here is the thieving Nag'-a-pah who stole the little bag, and now sneaks back like a skulking dog to steal again. Your life was spared when my men took the bag from your neck two suns ago," then raising his right hand as if to make his words more impressive, "but tonight you pay the price."

Kay'-yah seemed to look straight through and beyond the man as he spoke, and his perfect mask of cool indifference angered the less-gifted young chief, who inwardly realized the mental superiority of the captive who stood before him. Stung by the thought, he grasped Kay'-yah by the hair, and wagging his head back and forth he shouted: "Tonight, young whelp of a slink-dog, you die!" The humiliating and cowardly act of Wau-ko'-ma brought the hot blood leaping to Kay'-yah's face as he tugged vainly at the thongs about his wrists; then he looked up and his eyes met those of the white-haired old giant who now stood before him. Something in the wonderful face, more kindly than the other faces of the crowd, quieted him and he again stood erect and motionless. Then the old man's expression suddenly changed, as though some important thought had flashed into his mind, a thought that demanded definite action. "Be'-ta-atsin, be'-ta-atsin!" (Eagle-wings, eagle-wings) he exclaimed under his breath, but loud enough for the words to reach Kay'-yah's ears; and, turning with more of the movement of a young wrestler than that of an old man, he faced Wau-ko'-ma. The last red glow of the setting sun shone full upon the bronzed old face that now held an expression of almost unnatural calm, and Kay'-yah felt as though he looked upon the face of a god. In a deep voice that rumbled as if from a cave, he addressed Wau-ko'-ma.

"Let not your word go forth to the people that the Nag'-a-pah spy shall die this night. It is my wish, for a reason that I will give before the council, that he be made a prisoner and given trial before he is put to the death."

Anger blazed up anew in Wau-ko'-ma's voice as he shouted:

"No Nag'-a-pah is given trial in a To-to'-me camp! My word is given! It shall be as I have said – if I have to kill him with my own hand!"

Turning to the crowd, the old man raised his arms, and in a voice that thundered out in the evening stillness like the booming of a mighty drum, he cried:

"Listen, then, my people! You have heard the word of Wau-ko'-ma; hearken unto me. All of you, from the child to the hoary-headed, know that I raise not my voice except it be for good purpose. This Nag'-a-pah shall *not* die this night! If any attempt his life he shall answer to me with his own. I, Tag-a'-mo, have said it, and by the gods of our fathers it shall stand."

At this unprecedented action of the old medicine man, in publicly opposing the word of the tribal chief, a death-like silence fell upon the crowd that stood a moment as if dazed. Then repeated exclamations and low murmurs of approval came from a group of the older men who stood about Tag-a'-mo; but several of the younger men moved nearer the young chief who had stepped aside at the sudden and unlooked-for action of the old man. Recovering from his momentary surprise, and gaining courage from his followers, Wau-ko'-ma said:

"We will see whose word shall stand – and I shall know how to deal with all who oppose me!"

With a look of defiance and hatred that swept both Tag-a'-mo and Kay'-yah, he strode away to his hogan, followed by the men who had shown their loyalty.

Turning again to the crowd, the old medicine-man quietly gave orders to release the captive's hands, and to place him in a guarded hogan for the night. Then announcing that he would call the council for a trial at sunrise, he turned and with head bowed in thought walked away into the gathering gloom.

Two men stepped forward and after cutting the thong about Kay'-yah's wrists, led him away toward a hogan that stood on the farther side of the village. His guards made no attempt to mistreat him; in fact, they seemed to regard him with a puzzled questioning in their eyes that plainly told that they had been as mystified as he by the strange action of Tag-a'-mo. He was not to be given the usual treatment of a spy, at least not until after trial, and the strange turn of affairs that had prevented his being immediately put to death, now occupied his mind more than all else.

Groping around in the dim light within the hogan that was to serve as his prison, he found food and water as well as a very poor bed of old skins. Seating himself on the latter, he tried to bring his confused thoughts together in an effort to find some reason for the strange actions of both Tag-a'-mo and the young To-to'-me chief. Many questions that could not be answered crowded into his mind. Why had Wau-ko'-ma accused him of stealing the little bag that they, the To-to'-mes, had stolen from him? Why had the manner of Tag-a'-mo changed so suddenly while looking at him, and why had he asked that he be given trial as a law-breaker when it was the custom of all tribes to show no mercy to an enemy, especially one who had been caught while spying upon the tribe? Did the old To-to'-me hope to force him to give some information about the Nag'-a-pahs? And what had he meant by exclaiming, "Be'-ta-atsin"? Some charm word possibly, as medicine men used many such words, though seldom outside of the medicine lodge.

And what about the little bag with its precious contents? There was nothing about the To-to'-me camp to indicate that Dee-nay's suspicions were correct, for there were neither signs of feasting nor merry-making of any kind. If the priceless Magic were in the bag, would not Wau-ko'-ma have boasted of it?

A slight stir outside the hogan attracted his attention, and he caught the words of a low conversation between his guard and someone who had just arrived. "I come, at the word of Tag-a'-mo, to guard in your place, as you have been all day in the hunt."

The first guard, evidently willing to make the change, moved away. A few moments later he heard the cautious approach of another and the voice of Chot'-zu speaking in a low tone to the new guard. "The trick did its work well; he believed that you *did* come from Tag-a'-mo."

"What is Wau-ko'-ma's plan?" asked the guard.

"This," said Chot'-zu, "and it must be carried out as he directs. This dog is not to be treated like a great chief; he is an enemy and a spy. This is the plan – No, there is no need for caution, the men who brought him in say he knows no word of our tongue. The way is to be left open for him to escape: the door unguarded. He will want to get away; he will look and see no one; then when he tries to run an arrow will do the work and no one will know the bow that sent it. Who then can say a word?"

"But if the Nag'-a-pah should suspect something, and not try to escape?" questioned the guard.

"That also is provided for. Wau-ko'-ma has said that he dies tonight, and so it will be. Tag-a'-mo is not chief, and the people will laugh at him and the old men who follow him when we show them this night that the word of Wau-ko'-ma is law and that the Nag'-a-pah has been put to death as he said."

"When is this to be done?" asked the guard.

"Soon, for Tag-a'-mo may decide to come and make a change in the guard himself, and so our plan be made to no purpose."

Kay'-yah remained very quiet. The words of Chot'-zu, though spoken in a very low tone, had been heard by him, and he doubted not that the plan spoken of would be carried out immediately. If he was to defend himself, or if there was any possible chance for an escape, he must act quickly. Then his eyes searched about the hogan for anything that could be used as a weapon, or for any way, other than the door, by which he could get out of his prison.

His search seemed fruitless. The lodge was an unusually large and well-built one, and its smooth-surfaced walls offered no possibility of making a passage through them. With the exception of the skins on which he sat, and the large flat firestone in the center of the room, there were no furnishings. The night was rapidly growing dark, and he welcomed the darkness. Black clouds that had begun to drift upward from the east, swept across the sky and obscured most of the starlight. Only occasionally did the round smoke-hole overhead become clearly visible in the uncertain light. He turned his face toward it, watching the passing clouds, and wondering what course of action he would follow if one of his guards should enter the hogan to make an end of him.

Suddenly he jumped to his feet as he realized that the smoke-hole might offer a possible means of escape. He leapt upward with all his strength in an effort to grasp its rim, but found, as he might have known, that the hole was too high to be within his reach. But there was another way that it might be reached, and as the plan formed in his mind, he stepped to the doorway and listened. All was silent, and he realized that the To-to'-mes had probably withdrawn to give him his false opportunity to escape. He knew they could not be far away, but just how far he could not guess.

Cautiously drawing aside the hide at the doorway he looked out. He could see no one in the dim light; the camp seemed deserted, and save for the sound of the rising wind that whistled among the rocks and bushes, all was silent. He wondered how many steps he could take out of the doorway before an arrow or knife would strike him down. Feeling for the top of the door curtain, he found, as he suspected, that it was firmly bound to a pole of about the thickness of his arm, and as he felt for the ends of this he found that they rested on other large poles at the sides of the door, and were kept in place by thongs that had once bound them closely but were now dry and loose.

Cautiously, and as silently as possible, he worked the pole back and forth a few times, and was soon able to slide it through the dried fastenings and lift it from its resting-place. The noise he had made was slight, but he stood for a moment, hardly breathing, as he waited for an expected movement on the part of the guards: but they were evidently giving him every opportunity to come out, and made no sign that would indicate that they had heard him. Returning to the center of the hogan, he felt among the skins of the crude bed, and selecting two of the smallest and thinnest among them wrapped them as tightly as he could about the ends of the pole. Then stepping to the firestone directly beneath the smoke-hole, and standing with the pole poised for action, he waited for the light again to shine brightly enough to aid him.

After what seemed a long time the sky above the hole brightened a little, but it was enough for his purpose. Tossing the pole high through the opening and leaping at the same time with the hide, he jerked it to one side as the pole fell squarely across the hole. He heard a low exclamation from some one outside, but there was still no movement toward the door, and his heart beat high with hope as he drew himself up through the blackened aperture to the top of the hogan and cautiously crouched down on its curved roof. The darkness was so great that he could distinguish nothing, and he could hear no sound save the rising wind. Determined that only immediate action could save him, he slid cautiously down on the side of the hut that he knew to be opposite the entrance, and waited a moment for some sound to guide him. He could now see the dim dark mass of another hogan not far from the one he had just left, and as he moved swiftly into its deeper shadow, a hand came out of the darkness and laid itself on his shoulder.

"Is that you, Chot'-zu?" The voice sounded familiar somehow, but he did not stop to identify it and jerking himself free he started to run, but it seemed as if a dozen forms separated themselves from the shadow, and he was helpless among so many.

"It is the Nag'-a-pah," said another voice. "But how did he escape? He came by the back way."

Exasperated by the realization that his one chance of escape had come and gone, Kay'-yah made a mighty effort to free himself from his captors, and as he struggled in their grasp the voice he had first heard spoke again, and this time in very poor Nag'-a-pah.

"We do not mean you harm, Nag'-a-pah, but if you struggle you bring punishment upon yourself and you fight to no purpose. Come quietly and I give you promise that no harm will come to you this night."

Kay'-yah became quiet as the hopelessness of his situation became apparent to him, and all but two of the men let go of him and conferred among themselves.

"Tag-a'-mo is in the medicine lodge and will not call the council before the dawn," said one. "What think you, Ha-wal'-li, is his interest in this man, and why should Wau-ko'-ma wish him put to death now, since it is Tag-a'-mo's wish that trial be given?"

"You have heard as much as I, and the answer I know not," came the reply.

At the mention of the name of Ha-wal'-li, Kay'-yah remembered the last speaker to be the companion of Chot'-zu when the two had taken the bag from him, and knew it was his voice that he had recognized in the darkness.

"But we must see that he is kept safe, or answer to Tag-a'-mo as you have heard, and you all know what that means," said Ha-wal'-li.

"We can keep him safe enough," said another, "for Wau-ko'-ma will not dare to defy Tag-a'-mo openly and bring a fight among us, as he knows that Tag-a'-mo has the greatest number of the tribe for his followers."

"As to that I know not," said Ha-wal'-li, "but the guards must be men we can trust. Kee'-to, you will guard the door, and give place to no one unless I bring another guard from Tag-a'-mo to stand in your stead."

"And I," spoke another voice, "will go on guard with Kee'-to."

There was a slight hesitation in Ha-wal'-li's voice as the last offer was made, but he replied:

"You, Tal-lak'-kin? Are you ready to answer with your life for the Nag'-a-pah's safety?"

"I am ready," came the reply.

"It is well then; let us go," said Ha-wal'-li.

They walked swiftly for some little distance, and finally Kay'-yah was pushed through the entrance of another hogan and the hide curtain dropped behind him. He looked about his new prison, giving attention to every detail. A small fire burned in the center of the room, and by its light he saw that soft skins lay about the floor; large woven reed mats, the beds of the more ease-loving To-to'-mes, lay near the walls, and an abundance of food in finely woven baskets was placed about the cheerful blaze on the firestone. Here were luxuries of almost every kind; but why had he been given them? One possible reason came vaguely into his thoughts. At some time he had heard tales of a people who often gave their captured enemies many luxuries just by way of contrast to the torture that always followed. Ha-wal'-li had said that he should not be ill treated – during the night: and Tag-a'-mo, the chief medicine man of the tribe, had sworn that anyone who attempted his life should answer to him with his own – but he was only to be protected until after trial. Was he simply being used as an excuse for a fight between the strong will of Tag-a'-mo and that of the young To-to'-me chief, or was it all some strange trick to humiliate him and his people through him? The latter seemed the most reasonable explanation.

As he looked down at the little fire, he derided at once that it must be extinguished, as he knew that out in the darkness a guard was stationed at his door, and he did not like the thought of eyes peering in at him. The little blaze seemed friendly; but darkness was a needed ally, so after looking about him he found a reed water-bottle and poured its contents on the flames, stamping out the few remaining sparks with his feet. Then he pulled back the hide at the door and threw it over its pole, and now felt more on an equality with those who watched from without. Escape seemed impossible, yet he did not permit discouragement to occupy his thoughts. No fear was in his heart; on the contrary, a strange exultation seemed to grow within him, and a great desire to triumph over the young To-to'-me chief whom he now hated.

The storm that had been growling in the distance was drawing nearer, and heavy clouds now shut out the light of the stars. The low rumble of distant thunder was welcome to Kay'-yah, as he knew it would be an aid if a second opportunity to elude his enemies came. The man Kee'-to kept careful watch in front of the lodge, as his form could dimly be seen at intervals passing the paler patch of light framed by the doorway. The guard at the back was also on duty, as he could sometimes be heard as he moved about near the wall of the hogan.

Was this man at the rear of the hut of Wau-ko'-ma's faction? From the conversation he had overheard he decided that he might be, and this would be the man he would have to reckon with in case he made a second attempt to escape. As matters stood, he was for the present in no danger, and would have to wait, with what patience he could, until events took some new turn.

The heavy darkness around him, the sighing of the wind, accompanied by the distant rumble of the approaching storm, seemed to lull his senses into a drowsiness that was hard to overcome. He pondered more and more hazily over his situation, while loss of sleep the night before, his long journey, and the hard exertions of the evening now arrayed themselves against his constant efforts to remain awake.

Just when he lapsed into slumber he did not know, but he was suddenly conscious of a disturbance from without. Instantly, he threw off the haze of sleep, and his brain was clear and active. He sprang noiselessly to his feet, every faculty alert; his ears straining to catch any sound. A loud peal of thunder hoomed out and its many echoes rolled away into the distant canyons. Could it have been thunder that had awakened him? His instinct told him no. Storms seldom disturbed his night's rest. Then his ears caught the murmur of voices from the rear of the lodge, and though the voices were low he recognized one of them to be that of the young chief whom he now felt to be his greatest enemy. "Go!" commanded the voice. "I will take your place. Go without noise, and keep a still tongue in your jaws." The sound of the soft steps of the guard as he moved away told that the first part of the command at least was being obeyed.

"Ah," thought Kay'-yah, "the young chief fears that his men may not guard me well, and comes to do the work himself."

As he followed the line of thought this led him into, he heard the sound of men scuffling near the front of the lodge. Then the roaring of a passing gust of wind drowned the sound; but a moment later came a low groan, and one of the men fell heavily and evidently lay still. Then came the sound of heavy breathing from the victor, who seemed to be approaching the door of the hogan. Instantly the whole situation straightened itself out in Kay'-yah's mind. Wau-ko'-ma had come to carry out his threat to kill him with his own hand, and after dismissing the guard at the rear of the lodge, who, it was now evident was one of his followers, had killed the man who guarded the entrance so that there could be no alarm given, and no witness. He had waited until the late hour to make certain he would not be disturbed, and the noise of the storm would drown the possible sounds of conflict. It was well planned, and the very treachery and cleverness of it sharpened Kay'-yah's wits, for he knew that here he had an adversary who would call forth all that was in him of strength and skill if he was to escape death.

By the dim light that filtered momentarily from between the storm clouds, Kay'-yah could barely see beyond the square opening of the doorway, and stepping quickly to the left side of it, he crouched for the spring that must be made at his antagonist the moment he entered, as he evidently intended doing. Armed with the killing-knife, and knowing Kay'-yah to be unarmed, the odds were all with Wau-ko'-ma, and the result of the impending fight seemed certain.

In the dead silence that now reigned, in which Wau-ko'-ma seemed to be listening, Kay'-yah decided on his one possible course of action. Being on the right side of his antagonist, he could only hope for light enough to see the arm that held the knife if the young chief entered the doorway. The darkness was his greatest aid, and he felt thankful that no spark of the fire remained to light up the interior of the lodge. Wau-ko'-ma was evidently waiting to fully recover his breath after his fight with the guard. He also probably hoped for some sound from within the hogan, as the interior loomed black, and offered no suggestion as to where Kay'-yah might be. The pause became so long that Kay'-yah began to think that his enemy would not come inside until some movement of his own betrayed his position.

Then very slowly a dim light came from a rift in the clouds and the dark bulk of the crouching chief was revealed some four feet from the entrance. Instantly Kay'-yah sprang like a mountain cat at its prey. The impact of the young Indian's body against his antagonist was a powerful one, and would have resulted disastrously for the To-to'-me had he not been somewhat prepared for such a move on Kay'-yah's part: and as it was, his heavier weight was all that saved him from losing his balance.

Half twisting in a short backward step, Wau-ko'-ma instantly drew his right arm for the knife thrust; but Kay'-yah's left hand had the wrist before the blow could fall, and his right arm had gone about the neck of his enemy. Both men knew that it was now a test of strength and skill. No sound passed their lips as each, for very different reasons, wanted silence. Wau-ko'-ma because he wished to kill Kay'-yah secretly, and Kay'-yah because he wished to make way with his antagonist and escape. Backward and forward the two figures struggled, Wau-ko'-ma depending upon his superior weight, and Kay'-yah upon his skill and agility. With a roar the passing storm broke overhead, and as the wind swept over the mesa it drove great sheets of rain upon the struggling men, drenching their bodies and making their hold upon each other more difficult to retain. Kay'-yah was thankful for the rough rock footing beneath, as a slip or fall made by the unarmed man in such a fight could mean only one thing. Twice did Kay'-yah try the wrestler's leg-hold to trip his enemy, and each time Wau-ko'-ma evaded him with a skill that showed that he too knew the tricks of the wrestler. Again and again Wau-ko'-ma exerted every ounce of his strength to bring the knife down or wrench his arm from his enemy's grip. Twice its point pricked Kay'-yah's wrist, but each time he again forced the arm of his enemy upward. The strain was now growing terrible and Kay'-yah realized, with grim satisfaction, that Wau-ko'-ma was breathing more heavily than he.

Suddenly, with a mighty effort, the young chief pulled in savagely on the left arm that was about Kay'-yah's waist, and bent him backward with all the strength that could be brought to bear. The move took Kay'-yah off his guard, and he felt himself bending to a point where he would fall beneath his foe. But one possible course of action now stood between him and certain death, and he put it to instant test. With a quick movement, for which he was famous among the wrestlers of his own camp, he threw his left leg out as far as possible to one side; then suddenly letting go of Wau-ko'-ma's wrist, he twisted his whole body downward to the left, breaking the hold that bound his waist, and instantly brought his left forearm beneath his antagonist's chin. The knife descended but struck only a glancing blow that ripped into the shoulder. Before it could be raised again, Kay'-yah had forced the head of his enemy backward, and had at the same instant turned his own body until his back was almost against the back of his foe, his right hand gripping Wau-ko'-ma's left arm from the rear. With back arched as a powerful brace, he now slowly pulled downward.

Figure 14
"Stepping Quickly Backward, His Foot Went Into Empty Space, And He Felt Himself Falling Through The Air"

Kay'-yah's unlooked-for action had been executed so quickly that Wau-ko'-ma, intent only upon the use of his knife, did not realize until too late that he had been caught in the strangle hold of "Thal-kin," the choke-neck throw. Savagely, though ineffectually now, he struck downward with the knife, but could only reach his antagonist where no telling blow could be dealt.

Then for the first time Kay'-yah spoke. In perfectly good To-to'-me he said;

"The Nag'-a-pah dog shakes the To-to'-me rat in his teeth."

Wau-ko'-ma dropped the knife, and with both hands he now clutched frantically at the arm that was slowly but surely crushing the breath from him. A moment later the To-to'-me's body relaxed, and Kay'-yah threw him to the ground, where he lay still.

In the starlight that broke through the last ragged clouds of the passing storm, Kay'-yah knelt over his senseless foe, and picking up the knife thought, for a moment, to make sure of the death of his enemy: but as he raised the weapon, now red with his own blood, his eye suddenly caught sight of a little bag about Wau-ko'-ma's neck. Its familiar shape and color needed no close scrutiny. Quickly severing the thong that secured it, Kay'-yah stuffed it into his belt.

Again he bent over Wau-ko'-ma with the knife raised; but he could not strike, for the words of Dee-nay' rang clearly in his mind, "Never strike an enemy if the last sleep is upon him; the gods alone deal with the dead." His teaching proving more powerful than instinct, he rose to his feet. Then he realized, for the first time, that the cut in his shoulder was bleeding profusely. Again the clouds shut out the dim light and darkness settled down, blotting out the view of all things except the shadowy outline of large bushes that grew close at hand. But suddenly a flare of light cut the darkness a short distance away, and he heard the voices of men who were carrying a torch and coming around the lodge in which he had been held a prisoner.

Stepping quickly backward, to place one of the bushes between himself and the men, his foot went into empty space, and clutching out frantically to regain his balance, he felt himself falling through the air.

Figure 15
Indian Totem Pole – Picture by Timothy Green Beckley

Chapter 4
The Hidden Passage

They built in ages long ago, the Na-ya-kaed'
In stony cliff and wall and rocky height.
But they have gone the long trail of the dead
And left no tale, no record of their flight.

WHEN Kay'-yah stepped backward over the cliff he believed that he went to his death. In the flash of a second all of the events of his past life seemed to pass before his mind with astonishing clearness, ending with the triumphant battle with his enemy above.

Then came a crash as though his body were hurtled through a cloud of wet brush and crackling twigs. From this moving mass he rolled with terrific speed, fell a little way, and clutching out desperately, caught and held what seemed to be a mass of stout twigs. His body whipped downward as his grip held firm, and with a jarring blow it struck heavily the unresisting limb of a tree.

A sharp pain in his side, like the stab of a blunt knife, caused a groan to escape his lips. Quickly lowering himself from the scratching branches of the thick-topped juniper into which he had fallen, he felt the rocks of the steep slope below him and crouched down beneath the tree, still holding to the twisted trunk.

The light from a torch now flickered from above, and he heard the voices of the To-to'-mes, who were running to and fro on the cliff edge above him. He waited in silence for a moment, trying to recover the breath that had almost left his body, and realized that he had narrowly escaped death. A lighted torch was hurled from above and came spinning in great circles through the air, throwing showers of sparks in its descent. It struck a projection in the canyon wall some feet from him, bounded out and down into the space below. Evidently it was thrown with the hope that its light would reveal his position, but in this it failed, as the dense top of the tree above him protected him from the sight of his enemies, and he was safe for the moment at least. The flare of the torch had revealed two important things to him: in one he saw the real reason for his escape from worse injury and possible death, and in the other a possible way to get safely to the level country below.

All about the tree, in great black piles, were masses of tumble-weed balls that had loosened from the mesa above during the storm, and had blown over the cliff to lodge among the tree tops and bushes below. Into one of these drifts of wet tumble-weed he had fallen, breaking the force of his descent before he had crashed into the top of the juniper-tree.

His side now throbbed with dull pain and the smarting wound in his shoulder reminded him that the blood must be staunched. Quickly tearing a strip from the soft buckskin about his loins he bandaged the cut as best he could, drew the knot tight with his teeth, and started downward as silently and as rapidly as the darkness and steep slope would permit.

He had made considerable progress when a large stone, loosened by his feet, went crashing down into the brush below. Its loud noise indicated his position to the watchers above and almost instantly a shower of rocks fell about him. Then loud voices, as if the men were quarreling, came to his ears, and no more stones were thrown. Evidently some of each faction were among the men, and the followers of Tag-a'-mo had probably persuaded the stone-throwers to cease. But the noise of the falling rock had told them what they were waiting to know, that he was alive, and he knew they would immediately dispatch a party of men for every trail that led downward, to head him off.

From a little way below him now came the sound of the stream, swollen into a torrent by the heavy rain, and as he reached its low bank he plunged his face into the cooling water. He remembered from what he had seen that morning from his position on the mountain, that the northern bank of the stream, on which he now found himself, was comparatively smooth, and took comfort in the fact that as no trail led directly down the cliff, which was much too steep for climbing, his pursuers would be compelled to go out around the base of the mesa, and could not get to him from his side of the stream, as the great crags and boulders would make their passage too slow and dangerous in the darkness. But he could not remain here, as the very obstacles that prevented his enemies from reaching him barred his own escape.

He took the only possible trail, which followed the stream and led directly to the mountain, and he could only hope that with the darkness as an ally he could gain the foothills before the To-to'-mes could intercept his path. As he ran he thought carefully of all the methods his enemies would probably use to recapture him. The swiftest runners would doubtless take the trail that followed the foot of the mountain, from which they could cut across his path a mile or so farther along, where the stream curved downward from the foothills. Then perhaps a second party would be sent out into the desert from the other side of the camp and would attempt to head him off if he turned away from the mountain and sought to escape across the plain. The fact that the path he was now traveling was a far shorter cut to the foothills than any his pursuers could take was almost discounted by the certainty that his wound and desperate struggle with Wau-ko'-ma had taken half of his usual strength.

He ran steadily, with no attempt to attain the speed that he could make if he exerted all his strength. He knew that the testing-time would come as soon as he commenced to climb into higher ground that lay ahead. Again and again did he have to stoop low as he ran, to ease the pain in his side, but he kept his mind fixed on the one thought – the bag was his again, and he must not be caught.

Presently he heard the sound of waterfalls that told of higher ground ahead, and soon he found himself on a narrow trail that ran sharply upward, zig-zagging across the side of a steep foothill. Immediately ahead loomed the great dark mass of the mountain and he realized that he had reached comparatively safe ground ahead of his pursuers.

He was now forced to walk and climb as fast as his strength would permit, and after a few moments came out onto level ground. Quickly lying down, he put his ear to the earth and listened. He could distinctly hear the *pad-pad* of moccasined feet some distance away, and arose, staring about him in the dim starlight to get his bearings.

A cliff loomed ahead and he saw that he stood on a wide trail that led around it and doubtless rose to a higher level. There was no other path visible, so he ran on and when he had rounded the cliff he found himself on a second ledge of rock well up on the highest foothill very near the base of the mountain. Here the trail ran into another that seemed to cross it at a sharp angle. Again there was no time to stop to make a choice and, turning to the right, he ran for some distance along a smooth level shelf of rock, that skirted the first great rock wall of the mountain. Soon it began to widen out gradually, and then ended abruptly in a mass of huge rocks that had fallen from above. Arriving at the end he peered out over the rocks and could see that the wall dropped sheer down in a great precipice just beyond them. Turning about he saw the even stones of a whitened wall in the deep shadow at the base of the cliff, its center cut by the sharp, black opening of a doorway.

"The home of the Na-ya-kaed'," he said to himself; and, turning, swiftly ran back to see if the trail he was on did not branch off and lead to a still higher level. But he had not taken many steps before he heard the sound of his pursuers running along the trail a little lower down. There was no time now to search for a back trail, and he turned about and retraced his steps to the ancient cliff dwelling. Above him loomed the overhanging wall of rock, the first mighty cliff of the great mountain: below was a drop in the darkness to depths he could not see. He knew it would be useless to hide in the fallen rocks. The To-to'-mes would separate when they came to any branch of the trail, and he knew there would be at least four men sent to explore each new trail that opened along the way. Each party would have a torch that would be lighted when search for his tracks began, and his every footprint would be plainly visible in the moist sand of the rock ledge.

He knew that neither his own people nor the To-to'-mes ever entered the ancient abodes of the Na-ya-kaed', the vanished people of the cliffs: but putting all superstition and fear from his thoughts he entered the doorway of the dwelling, deciding that he could here sell his life more dearly than he could in a fight on the open shelf of rock; and he had a vague hope that the To-to'-mes, who were the most superstitious people of all the desert dwellers, would not attempt to enter the witch-ridden old building to take him. Then too he must find a weapon of some kind, as the loss of the knife, when he had fallen over the cliff, had left him again without means of defending himself. Now that he had probably killed Wau-ko'-ma, and again had the coveted bag in his possession, he believed the To-to'-mes would give no thought to sparing his life.

As he sought his way blindly into the low-roofed room he felt for some object, stone or wood, that could be used as a weapon. He would fight to the last, but before he gave up he would throw the little bag over the cliff; for if he could not take it back to Dee-nay' he would do all that was possible to keep it out of the hands of the To-to'-mes.

As he groped hastily about, his hands came in contact with a pile of crumbled rock and dirt three or four feet high. He knew enough about the construction of these ancient dwellings to know that the ceiling above was always of short poles, usually a little smaller than a man's arm, laid close together and held firmly by small stripped branches or wattles, woven in and out among them. He climbed up on the pile of fallen rock and reached upward, hoping to find a loose ceiling-pole that could be used as an effective weapon while his strength lasted. As he caught hold of the small ceiling timbers he found, to his surprise, that not only one pole but a whole section of them was movable, and although it could not be forced downward it could be pushed upward with apparent ease.

As he pushed upward a cool draught of air poured over him, and a quantity of fine dust sifted down over his head and shoulders. Evidently there was an opening above, and probably the back of the structure had a second story. Perhaps the pile of crumbled rock and earth on which he stood had been some kind of a stairway, long ago tumbled into ruins. Again he pushed upward and outward on the poles and found that they could slide to one side far enough to admit his body through the opening thus made.

Weakened as he was, and almost unnerved by the pain in his side, he knew that it would require every ounce of his strength to draw himself up and through the hole. Clenching his teeth as if to shut out the pain that would be caused by the exertion, and drawing a deep breath, he clasped the poles at the sides of the opening and drew himself up until he could sit on the edge of the hole. As he drew his feet up he heard the noise of a party of his pursuers who had just arrived on the ledge outside. Cautiously, and as silently as possible, he moved to one side far enough to slide the section of poles back into place, and finding it secure sat down upon it, leaning wearily against the cliff wall that continued up the back of the room or opening in which he now found himself.

The darkness around him was intense. He could see nothing, but could distinctly hear the conversation of the men who now had gathered near the door of the dwelling. He could hear the *whirr-whirr* of fire sticks as one of the men made a fire to light the torch. The men spoke in low guttural tones, for they had not yet seen his tracks and did not wish their remarks to be heard in case he was hiding in the rocks beyond them. Presently the snapping of the burning bark came to Kay'-yah's ears as the torch was lighted, and almost instantly a shout went up as his tracks were discovered.

"The dog has run to the end of his trail this time, and now hides in the house of the dead to save himself!" said a voice.

"Those are his tracks and he'll not make many more," said another.

Then a voice that he knew to be that of the man Chot'-zu spoke.

"The Nag'-a-pah dog has a witch in him. Here is another proof: for he enters the house of the dead, and no one who is not a witch would do that. No man who is not of the Shin-di (devil) people can kill an armed guard, take a knife from Wau-ko'-ma and strangle him."

"Wau-ko'-ma was not strangled to the death," replied another voice. "When I left Ta-pau'-wee he was alive and, although he could not speak, Ta-ga'-mo says he will live."

"But I say again that he is a witch!" spoke Chot'-zu. "For he can wrestle like the Shin-di. He almost threw *me* two suns ago."

This last remark was followed by the sound of other men joining the first party, and a voice that Kay'-yah recognized to be that of Ha-wal'-li called out:

"You should be the last to speak of the Nag'-a-pah's skill in wrestling, Chot'-zu. He threw you as easily as a man throws a child, and would have made an end of you had I not come to your assistance."

"You think I fear the dog of a Nag'-a-pah?" sneered Chot'-zu.

"If you do not fear him, go in there and bring him out," challenged Ha-wal'-li.

"You say that to save your Nag'-a-pah friend," replied Chot'-zu; "for you know that it is the ghosts of the dead that I fear and not the skulking Nag'-a-pah."

"*Ah-ee eee!*" exclaimed a fear-stricken voice. "Look you here – the tracks of Doh, the man-bear!"

Evidently the crowd gathered about the discoverer of the tracks, for there were many exclamations of awe and wonder.

"See!" continued the first to call. "There is the claw-foot, and there the twisted moccasin."

"The tracks are not fresh," said another voice; "but the rain did not wash them away as they were sheltered by the overhanging cliff."

Again came the murmur of many voices as the men looked for other tracks, evidently to see if the bear-witch had gone into the cliff dwelling.

Kay'-yah could not avoid a sudden feeling of fear that gripped him at the mention of Doh, the dreaded bear-witch. He had heard many tales from men of his own tribe who had crossed the tracks of this strange witch, who wore a twisted moccasin on one foot and made the mark of a great bear with the other. It was said that he had killed many men and that he always left the mark of his great claws upon them. Men who possessed more than usual bravery had followed the trail of the creature, but those who had lived to tell of their experience said that they tracked the witch until they heard the many growls and sounds that it made and then they dared not go further, for the sounds were fearful like that of the growls of many different animals.

"The bear-witch is not here; the Nag'-a-pah is here, and we must take him back to Tag-a'-mo," said the voice of Ha-wal'-li.

"The dog dies here," replied Chot'-zu; but his voice lacked strength and the remark sounded like an idle boast.

"Give me the torch," commanded Ha-wal'-li; and a moment later Kay'-yah heard his footsteps at the door.

"Come out to us, and you have fair trial before Tag-a'-mo," he called in Nag'-a-pah. Then, receiving no reply, he walked into the room, and Kay'-yah could see the flickering points of light through the poles beneath him, and the pungent odor of the burning juniper bark came to his nostrils. Other foot-falls about the doorway, and the sound of bodies crowding together, told him that several faces must be peering in, doubtless expecting to see the brave Ha-wal'-li in a death struggle with him, or being torn to pieces by the witch.

In a voice so husky with a nameless dread as to be scarcely more than a loud whisper, Ha-wal'-li said: "He is not here!"

Then, as if the terror of the situation struck them all at once, the crowd fled down the trail.

The fear of the To-to'-mes was for the moment shared by Kay'-yah, but he drove the fear from his heart and rose slowly to his feet, feeling about him in the darkness as he did so. He could not go down again into the room below, as he knew that the dawn was near, and that the To-to'-mes, in spite of their temporary fear, would not leave any trail unguarded from below. As he felt about him in the darkness he found to his surprise that he could touch four walls of solid rock. He must be in a sort of chimney cut out of the cliff itself. He felt carefully over the walls with his hands and presently his fingers slipped into a small slot or hole which he instantly knew to be a crude step or foothold to be used in climbing. The little hollow was filled with fine dust but he pushed his fingers through this and found that the depression slanted downward at the back for a good finger length, thus forming a hand as well as foothold. Above, as far as he could reach, were similar depressions cut at regular intervals into the solid rock.

As he looked upward he could see nothing, but the means of climbing, which he had found, made it certain that there was some opening or passage above. Feeling somewhat revived after his rest, and encouraged by the discovery of the holes in the rock, he tightened his belt and started slowly upward. Up and up he went, and was soon thankful that the Na-ya-kaed' were little people and had therefore been compelled to make the hand and footholds close together: otherwise he felt he could never reach the top, as his muscles almost refused to work and his strength was nearly gone.

After what seemed an endless climb, he could feel the sides of the passage narrowing, and the back wall of the great crack or opening was now so close that he could lean back against it, and with feet securely braced in the holes, he could thus rest his right arm, now stiffened by the wounded shoulder. A little farther up the steps ended, and feeling to the left with his foot he found that it rested on a level ledge of rock. He stepped out and cautiously moved along the ledge. He knew that he must be in a great crack or crevice in the mountain-side, for there was little more than room for his body to move sidewise between the walls.

He had noticed that the air was growing fresher and it now blew down on his face and fevered body in cool refreshing gusts that told he was nearing the opening. He was still in complete darkness and each movement told him that his strength was fast leaving him. He must reach some place where he could rest, and reach it as soon as possible. His hand came in contact with more of the depressions in the rock, and he wearily drew himself together again for what he hoped was the last stretch of his climb.

He had gone only a few yards when he again found himself able to stand on level ground and this time the passage was wider and illuminated by a great patch of gray light that shone at its other end. He walked slowly toward the light, which grew brighter with every step, and in a moment more he again stood in the open air. Even in his exhausted state he noticed how cleverly and securely Nature had hidden this upper outlet of the passage through which he had climbed. The cleft through which the passage ran could not have been visible a few feet away, so perfectly did the grain and coloring of the rock run together. He had arrived on a long level shelf of rock that topped the great cliff rising up from below, while above him rose another bulging wall that frowned darkly in the uncertain light.

He gave one look at the pale sky that was slowly taking on the faint rose of dawn, then sank down to the rock and lay back with a weary sigh of relief. Through half-open eyes he looked about him and felt more as though he were in a land of dreams than in a land of reality. In one direction he could look out into empty space whose farthest outlines were lost in the early morning mists, while in another he could look along the wide ledge on which stood three large cliff dwellings more elaborately built than the one he had left below. He wondered hazily what their builders could have been like: then the ancient dwellings seemed to fade from his sight; the mountain seemed to move and slowly to turn around and around. He closed his eyes and extended his arms on the ground in an effort to steady his reeling senses. His thoughts went whirling through a jumble of events in which the pain in his side seemed to be a kind of animal witch that was trying to lower him into a bottomless pit. Then, into his confused thoughts came the sound of a voice singing. It came nearer and nearer. The voice was that of a To-to'-me man, and now the words crowded out all of the weird impressions that had thronged his mind and rang clear and distinct in his brain.

"The sun-god comes: the sun-god comes:
He draws his bow and the shadows fly.
The night is fleeing across the sky.
He lifts his head, and the day is nigh.

O Mother Earth, the light is come.
O Brother Stars, the night is gone.
The sun-god comes: the sun-god comes."

At the sound of the To-to'-me language, alarm seemed to battle for advantage in Kay'-yah's fevered brain, and in a moment he had raised himself upon his elbow, turning his face toward a bend in the shelf of rock from whence the voice of the approaching To-to'-me seemed to come. He made a great effort to rise, then all turned black about him and he fell back into unconsciousness.

Chief Pow Wow at Enchantment

Figure 16
Publisher of Lost Indian Magic. Timothy Beckley. is photographed in the Land of Enchantment by Charla Gene'

Chapter 5
Dee-Nay's Narrative

To-night the council sits, within the glow
Of firelight in the shelter of the hogan walls,
And wise men talk in guarded voices low;
While from the plain the gaunt coyote calls.

MANY days Dee-nay' waited for word from Kay'-yah, and as time passed and no message came, his heart grew heavy within him. Kay'-yah was as a son to him and dearly loved, and the successful outcome of this mission would have meant the recognition of Kay'-yah as one of the chief young men of the tribe. But now he feared the worst – that Kay'-yah had been captured while spying on the To-to'-me camp and had, in all probability, been shot with arrows – the usual fate of a spy – and his thoughts grew dark with foreboding.

Toward evening of the seventh day he summoned the chief medicine-men of the tribe to council in the lodge, and they were now gathered about the little fire while the daylight waned outside. They were silent and expectant, these wise men, and sat watching Dee-nay' as he gravely touched the lighted end of a stick to the filled bowls of their ceremonial pipes. The remains of a sand-painting were on the smooth floor of the lodge, which gave evidence of a ceremony of importance completed before their entrance; the altar still remained and in it were stuck twenty bahos, or prayer sticks, one for each man present, and the sacred grain and pollen were scattered over its surface. The deerskin mats on which they sat had been carefully arranged in a circle with an open side which faced the east and also the door of the lodge. Dee-nay' sat directly opposite this opening, facing the entrance, with ten men on either side of him. After having lighted their pipes he drew from his belt a small bag containing a fine powder, a little of which he sprinkled on the fire, and a pungent aromatic odor filled the room. He picked up his pipe and drew on it, sending a puff of smoke first to the east, then to the west, the north and south, up and down; the others gravely followed his example and while the smoke still hung in the air he began to speak:

"Brothers, I have called you here
To the circle of our council:
To the quiet of our hogan:
To the smoking of Na-tōt'-se;
For a reason I have called you;
For a reason that lies heavy
On my heart, and I would tell you
Of the reason, that your thinking
And the wisdom you have gathered
From your many quiet camp-fires,
And the silence of your hogans –

That your wisdom, if it may be,
May reveal the way that's hidden."

Dee-nay' paused and drew thoughtfully at his pipe for a few moments.

"That I may be clear, my brothers,
I will tell again the story
Of our tribe from the beginning,
Though you know it well, my brothers."

The wise men nodded in silence and the smoke from their pipes curled upward in a piling cloud toward the smoke-hole overhead.

"Long before our fathers,
Or the fathers of our fathers,
Had beheld the light of morning;
Long before the deer and bison
Had been frightened from this valley:
From the north a Great Chief journeyed;
Journeyed south and brought his people;
Searching for a better hunting:
For a land more rich and fertile:
Searching for a sheltered valley
That was from his foes protected.
Up a hill the Great Chief journeyed;
Up a mountain that was higher
Than the world that lay below him.
All around him spread the desert
And beyond, the mountains rising;
And the many sheltered canyons.
Long and careful was his searching –
Then his eyes crept to a valley –
Green it lay before him, smiling;
Rich in many-varied verdure;
Watered by a stream that sparkled:
Sheltered by a mighty canyon.
Long he looked and then he whispered;
'Thou, Great Spirit, hath directed:
There below me lies our homing.' –
And 'twas thus our camp was founded."

Again Dee-nay' paused, and the others gave guttural sounds of approval and affirmation.

"In those days of the beginning,
Peaceful was the tribe, and happy;
But the Chief was of a nature
That for long could not stay quiet:
In his heart the roving spirit
Ever grew more strong and urgent:
But his people were contented

And desired to roam no longer.
It is known to you, my brothers.
How the time grew long, and longer
When the roving Chief was absent:
Absent from the tribe and council.
But at last there came a morning
When he came back to his people.
Strange in look and strange of manner,
And called all the tribe to council;
Young and old he called to council."

Dee-nay' paused and looked thoughtfully at the fire.

"These the words he gave in council:
'Brothers, it has been my ruling
That all men should live as pleased them –
If they but obey the council.
They who choose the quiet living
Of the field and camp and council.
They have chosen well, my brothers;
They who do protect our camp-fires
In the fighting of our foemen,
They have chosen well, my brothers.
They who bring us food and clothing,
Hide for bows and flint for arrows,
From the canyon and the forest,
They have chosen well, my brothers.
But *my* way is not as your way;
It is not the field or camp-fire,
Not the hunt or fight or council,
Not the ways of men that draw me:
But the quiet of the forest
And the simple ways of beast folk;
It is there my path lies, brothers.
But I would not leave you helpless.
I have brought for your protection
Medicine of might and power:
Medicine that will protect you
From all foes, or dire disaster;
That will bring you peace and plenty.
Many crops and rushing waters.
It is here, the Mighty Magic!'
And he placed upon our altar,
Sprinkled with the sacred pollen,
The small bear of carven turquoise;
The Great Magic of our people
That you know so well, my brothers."

The others nodded without speaking.

"Then again the Chief spoke further:
'I shall not be far, my people,
From the circle of your camp-fires.
I shall still be Chief and ruler
Though my name and form be different,
And all men shall call me "Bear Chief."
I shall still give words of counsel
To the wise men of my people
When they seek me in the forest.
Now, my brothers, I have spoken,
And my way is not as your way,
Peace be with you, peace and plenty.'
And he left his people gazing,
As he walked into the forest:
Walked no longer as a man would
But as bear upon his four feet.
And 'twas so it happened, brothers,
That we first received our Magic."

Dee-nay' drew the little bag again from his belt and scattered a pinch of the fragrant powder on the flames. His listeners waited expectantly for him to continue.

"From that day our people prospered:
In the battle always victors;
In the hunt they were successful;
In the field the many green things
Grew abundantly and ripened.
From the canyon came our river,
Giving to the valley water.
And the mountains gave us turquoise;
Gave us wealth in many turquoise.
From that day our people prospered;
From the day our Mighty Magic
Lay upon the sacred altar
In the sacred meal and pollen."

Dee-nay' looked about him at the circle of faces: each head drooped and the pipes lay before them on the floor held in inert hands. He nodded slowly.

"Now our fields are dry and yellow:
Strong our foes seem to our weakness.
Gone our treasure, gone our turquoise:
And the bow-arms of our hunters
Often idle hang beside them
For the lack of any hunting.
And the river that flowed, singing,
From the canyon to our valley,
Barely creeps across the pebbles,
Barely saves our lips from parching.

And our altar – Brothers, look you!
See – the altar top is vacant!
Only scattered meal and pollen
Lie upon its empty surface.
Where! Oh, where! has gone our Magic?"

He stopped abruptly and every head was raised. An old man opened his mouth as if to speak, but Dee-nay' raised his hand, commanding silence.

"No – I would not have you answer.
For I yet have much to tell you:
I, who saw and knew, can tell you
Of that night when strange things happened.
But five summer suns have passed us,
But five winter snows have melted
Since the night our people hurried
To prepare our camp for leaving.
For the season was the springtime
When we fare into the desert
For our yearly springtime hunting,
As you know so well, my brothers.
When we leave our sun-baked hogans
For the hide tents of the desert
And become again a people
Of the open plain and mesa,
Roving hunters for a season:
When our treasured stores are hidden
In the rock caves of the canyon
And our Magic always guarded
By the one who is appointed.
(And 'twas always guarded safely
'Til the night, the night we know of.)
Two were sent to hide the treasure,
Two were sent far up the canyon:
One to guard and one to hide it,
Where the night and dark were thickest.
When the patter of their footsteps
Had been swallowed by the canyon
I returned then to the hogan;
To the lodge where was our altar.
I, Dee-nay', who was to guard it,
Was to guard our Mighty Magic.
As I entered at the doorway
One came out whose name was Gō'-me,
Keeper of the Sacred Eagle,
And his face was gray as ashes.
'Gone!' he cried, 'look to your altar!'
And I looked and saw it empty.

Then I seized this man and shook him,
'Til his jaw-teeth clicked and rattled;
And I tore away his girdle:
Drew his hair from out its binding,
Thinking thus to find the Magic.
But he had it not, my brothers.
'They have hid it with the treasure!
I will bring it back!' he shouted.
And was gone from out the doorway
While I stood and watched him running;
Stood and waited, only thinking
Of the altar that was empty.
And you know the rest, my brothers,
How we found this Gō'-me later
With an arrow through his body.
How Qua-hi'-da, who had hidden
Our great treasure in the canyon,
Dying, dropped before his hogan,
And could speak no word or whisper.
With a body full of arrows.
How the other, sent to guard him,
Fell into the hands of foemen,
Of a party of To-to'-mes
Who were scouting in our canyon,
And whose fate we never heard of.
This is known to you, my brothers.
So our Magic and our treasure
Both were lost beyond the finding.
We have searched the rocky canyon,
Searched the camp and every hogan.
Every man and child and woman,
All have aided in the searching.
But to no avail, my brothers.
But to no avail, my brothers."

Dee-nay' stopped and bowed his head. The ashes in his pipe lay cold and gray and he emptied them into the little fire and laid aside the pipe; the others followed his example.

"All here know the boy named Kay'-yah,
Son of him they called Qua-hi'-da
Who fell dead before his hogan
On the night of our disaster.
Kay'-yah, who has proved the bravest
Of our young men in the hunting,
Who is fearless as the eagle,
And as skillful as the beaver;
Kay'-yah, who has led the searching

For our Magic and our treasure:
Who has been my willing pupil
For these many, many harvests.
Is there one among you, brothers,
Who has doubt of Kay'-yah's valor?"

Every old head was shaken vehemently, and a gleam of pride came into Dee-nay's eyes as he continued;

"Early then one morning, brothers,
While you slept within your hogans,
Kay'-yah, as his daily wont was,
Went to view the sun-god's rising.
As he stood, all unsuspecting,
Two sprang at him from the bushes.
Spies they were, of the To-to'-mes.
And they sprang and held him helpless
'Til one of the two had taken
From his neck a bag that hung there,
Then they ran back to their people.

* * *

Brothers, we have all suspected
That our Magic lay, well hidden
With the treasure that was buried.
How we knew not – how Qua-hi'-da
Could have taken it we know not,
Nor his reason for so doing.
But a stranger thing has happened,
And the answer still is hidden.
For the bag from Kay'-yah taken
Was held by this same Qua-hi'-da
When he fell before his hogan
Pierced by many foeman arrows.
This was told to me by Kay'-yah,
Who knew only that his mother
Placed it on his neck when dying.
Saying that it held a fetish,
Medicine he must not part with.
Brothers – did it hold our Magic?"

Dee-nay's pause was dramatic, and it was as if an electric shock had passed through the men about the circle. They sat rigidly erect, but the fire in their eyes and their half-open mouths spoke of an eagerness and excitement their silence and immobility did not conceal.

"If our tribe thought that our Magic
Had been captured by our foemen

They would loudly cry for battle:
But we cannot fight, my brothers,
We are weak and the To-to'-mes
Are a tribe of mighty people.
Thus on every side I pondered,
And I sought the Mighty Spirit
For an answer to this problem,
And the answer – ? This, my brothers –
Kay'-yah, who is brave and fearless,
I have sent to the To-to'-mes,
To discover, if it may be,
Where they keep our Mighty Magic.
(If, indeed, it was the Magic
Which was in the bag of doe-skin.)
And I come now to the reason
Why I summoned you to council,
For no word has come from Kay'-yah,
Though for many suns the echo
Of his footsteps has been silent."

There was a slight sound at the door of the Lodge and Dee-nay' stopped abruptly, his keen eyes on the hide curtain which swayed uncertainly for a moment as if blown by the wind, but there was no wind. Every eye followed his, and there was a tense silence in the Lodge. Slowly the curtain was drawn aside and in the doorway, with bowed head, stood Sah'-ne. But not for long was her head bowed. With what seemed a gathering together of all her strength she drew it up and held it high, and before Dee-nay' could open his lips, stepped swiftly into the circle and began to speak.

"I have done that which no Indian has ever done and lived – I have listened at the door of your council."

The men half rose to their feet; but there was a look in the girl's face that held them silent and they fell back gazing with wonder – all but Dee-nay', whose brow was dark with anger.

She spoke again.

"For what I have done I may die, but before I die I would speak."

"Sah'-ne!" It was Dee-nay' who spoke and his voice was cold with disapproval. "Do you forget the laws of our tribe and of your maidenhood?" He spoke as a father would speak to a wayward child who has displeased him.

"I do not forget, but the matter is of life and death – hear me before I am condemned."

"It cannot be – a woman may not speak before the council."

"A woman! Then do not call me longer woman – I am an Indian and an outcast. And I would speak of that which calls you here – of Kay'-yah and of the Magic."

Dee-nay's eyes softened at mention of Kay'-yah's name, and the frown grew less apparent.

"What know you of Kay'-yah and of the Magic?" His cold tone had changed to one tinged with interest, though the mention of the Magic had caused a slight suspicion to enter his heart.

"Then I may speak?" Sah'-ne's hands were tight-clasped at her sides and spoke of nervous tension.

"Speak!" said Dee-nay'.

She looked at the circle of faces turned toward her and every eye was cold. The rigid attention of the men gave no suggestion of sympathy, and a wave of faintness swept over her. She closed her eyes for a second and sent a swift prayer for aid to the Great Spirit of all.

"You men of the Nag'-a-pah – already I see my condemnation in your eyes. You judge me before you hear me. It was so with the women. Because my father was a spy, an enemy, you think me the same. It is not true. I was born To-to'-me, but I am Nag'-a-pah now. If you do not believe, I shall give you proof. Listen – I cannot live here longer – so. The women turn away from me, the men make light talk as I pass. I have pride; I have honor – I cannot live so. I am of your people. Before the truth was known of my father you, Dee-nay', taught me of the sacred things. I made seed-cakes for our ceremonies, and danced in the Virgin dance of the Corn Festival. Heart and soul I am Nag'-a-pah, and the gods you worship at your altars I also worship. But words are not enough. I give myself to prove what I say. I was born To-to'-me and my father, Gō'-me, keeper of the Sacred Eagle, gave me a clan word to prove my birth. This word I cannot speak aloud or to any but Dis'-din of the To-to'-mes, or his eldest living son – but it will prove my birth and give me position in the tribe."

There was a movement among the men and an angry look passed over their faces, but before they could speak Sah'-ne continued.

"Wait! I have not spoken! I can enter the To-to'-me camp without suspicion — "

Dee-nay' leaned forward and his eyes narrowed in sudden comprehension.

"They will receive me there as I am not received here." She spoke with bitterness. "My father was a spy in your camp. I will be a spy among the To-to'-mes."

The men leaned forward and a murmur passed among them.

"If it is true, as you believe, that they have the Magic, I shall find where it is, and – " she spoke slowly now and her head drooped, "I shall find what has been the fate of Kay'-yah."

An old man spoke harshly;

"How do we know that you, of To-to'-me blood, will not take what you have learned tonight in council to the Lodge of your people. To me it is good reason for your going." There was an open sneer in his voice and the words stung Sah'-ne as if he had lashed her with a thong. The blood flew to her face and she held her head high as she answered:

"Your words lack wisdom. Why should I enter here if such had been my purpose? Could I not have gone to my people without your knowledge? My presence here is proof of my intention. I have offered you service. If you do not trust me, I can die, my heart is not afraid. I say no more." And there was a look of pride and exaltation in her raised face.

The men still shook uncertain heads, but Dee-nay' had not once taken his eyes from Sah'-ne's face as she spoke and he now raised his voice.

"The girl's words are true," he said quietly. "And it shall be as she says. We have much to gain and little, brothers, that is not already lost. She has done that which, under the laws of our tribe, demands her life in payment; but she offers what is more valuable to our people in exchange, and, brothers, it would seem wise to accept her offer. And, more, I believe the Great Spirit Himself has sent the answer to our problem. Daughter, I, Dee-nay', believe your words."

Sah'-ne still stood erect, but her hands crept to her face and she shook suddenly with sobs. The nervous tension that had aided her thus far left her, at Dee-nay's words, and she was again the modest, sensitive girl, and cried as if her heart would break.

The men of the council sat stolidly silent, but Dee-nay' again spoke and there was kindness in his voice.

"It is well, Sah'-ne. Return now to your hogan, and with the sun tomorrow come to me and I shall have words for you of this journey on which you shall start before the coming of another night. Go now, and see that you speak to no one."

And Sah'-ne passed silently out of the Lodge.

Figure 17
Indian on Horseback, Painting by Carl Moon

Chapter 6
The Cave Man

The Shin-di roams among the hills!
Mix strong magic — medicine-man.
With mighty tooth and claw he kills,
Till all be gone — but the Bear-witch clan.

WITH the first return of consciousness, after his collapse on the ledge of rock, Kay'-yah awoke to find himself staring up at the roof of a cave whose great rock walls arched outward into a low dome above him. He turned his head toward the light that flooded the room and saw a wide entrance through which a man of average height could pass without stooping. Then his eyes wandered about the cavern, his thoughts searching an answer to the first question that naturally entered his mind. Where was he? He tried to think of the immediate past; some great trial or disaster had befallen him, he was vaguely sure of that, but what was it? Of only two things was he certain. He was too weak to rise, or even care to rise from too the comfortable bed of skins on which he lay, and he was very hungry.

As he looked about his strange surroundings he saw the remains of a small fire in the center of the cave floor and near it two earthen vessels that doubtless contained food of some kind. Then, as though it were the memory of a dream, he had the dim recollection of having frequently tasted meat soup from the smaller of the two vessels held by a hand that pressed it to his lips. The owner of the cave must be away on some errand, for he was alone.

With an effort that brought a pain to his shoulder and side he rose on one elbow and stretched a hand toward the vessel. It was too far away. Then his eye caught a reed water-bottle that stood near his head against the cave wall. After a deep draught from the water it contained he leaned back and closed his eyes. Now he must collect his thoughts: try to remember what had happened to him. Searching back for the last thing he could remember he recalled the fight with Wau-ko'-ma. Then the fall over the cliff. Yes, that was when he had injured his side. Then slowly his mind unfolded the flight to the mountains, the ruin and the slow climb up and up and up through a great dark crack in the cliff. No, that must have been a dream, for there could be no such place in all the mountain. He smiled to himself at the foolishness of it. Yet how had he come to be in this cave?

Again he opened his eyes and looked about him. From wooden pegs, driven into cracks in the rock walls, hung many things. Here was a bunch of dried grass, there a rattle made of a tortoise shell and a worn moccasin: farther along, a bow and arrow case made from the skin of a mountain lion; and beneath it a stout bow was leaning against the wall. Kay'-yah's trained eye and skill as a marksman told him that the beautiful bow had been made by one who well knew how to select good material and how to fashion it in a manner that would balance its weight and preserve its strength. Then his eye caught the coils of a long stout rope made of many strands of twisted thongs. One end was worn and frayed as though it had rubbed back and forth on the rocks. He wondered for what purpose it could be used.

On the opposite wall hung a bunch of soft skins, some of fox, others of deer and mountain cat; and standing out near them at about the height of a man's head, hung the heavy skull of a bull buffalo, the eye sockets and cavity of the nostrils looming black against the pure white of the bleached bone. "My captor is a member of the buffalo clan," thought Kay'-yah, "as none but the clan have the death-head in their homes."

Near the skull hung a cluster of small bags of smooth doe-skin that doubtless contained colored sands and magic medicine. The cave-dweller must also be a medicine-man.

As he contemplated the little bags, Kay'-yah's thoughts suddenly jumped to the bag he had recovered from Wau-ko'-ma, and his hand stole to his belt. The little bag was gone. He felt among the skins on which he lay, but his search proved fruitless. Then his mind recalled the rock ledge to which he had somehow climbed, and the voice of the To-to'-me who came toward him singing the Sun God song. Then this was the cave of a To-to'-me, and the To-to'-me had taken the bag from him and now held him prisoner!

He had no desire to rise or make any effort to escape, and this fact seemed strange to him. In his weakness he felt like a child and was very content to lie still and rest. Then he noticed that the light of the sun on the left wall of the entrance struck the rocks with a pale rosy glow. The sun must be low and near the horizon. He now remembered that when he had reached the cliff outside it was before the dawn, and now the low sun told him that the day had almost gone. Then his thoughts wandered back to his home in Ah'-co and it seemed a long, long time since he had left Dee-nay' standing in the half gloom of the big medicine lodge as he bravely started on his mission over the canyon trail. His last meeting with Sah'-ne came vividly into his mind, and a little pain came into his heart as he recalled her blush and the joyless smile that was about her lips when she told him that she was To-to'-me. Why could she not have been Nag'-a-pah; and then he asked himself why was it that he cared so much.

As he stared out of the entrance into the gathering twilight, he heard the sound of footsteps coming along the sandy trail. As he listened he noticed something strange about the shuffling noise made by the approaching feet. One foot not only made more noise than the other, but it also ground into the sand as if the owner at each step twisted his foot before lifting it again. "A cripple," thought Kay'-yah. Then he heard a voice, a strange deep voice, that sounded like the low wind sighing in the canyon. As the singer came nearer Kay'-yah caught faintly the words of the song and knew the man to be To-to'-me. Then more clearly came the words;

"The chin-dog howls, he howls in the wind." A long-drawn-out whine followed the words – the whine of a dog in fear of a bear or mountain cat; the imitation was perfect.

"The bush-tail keeps to his hole," sang the voice.

"The bear sits back in his cave in fear." Then followed a sound so like the growling of a bear that Kay'-yah involuntarily arose on his elbow, with the feeling that a bear must be just outside the cave door. Then he sank back, realizing that it must have been the singer, for the voice went on with the song:

"The wolf sits back in his cave afraid." The low, half-growl, half-whine of the wolf followed.

"The Shin-di comes, the Shin-di comes."

The song ended abruptly as the singer neared the cave entrance. A moment later a white-haired old man entered, and Kay'-yah saw that he limped and his body twisted a little with each step. In one hand he carried a large pitch-covered water-bottle of woven reeds bound about by a thong that ran up over his shoulder to support part of the weight. In his other hand was a stout spear used for both climbing and defense. After setting down the water-bottle the man turned and looked at Kay'-yah, peering under his hand as if to see more clearly in the darkening cave. The two stared at each other for a moment in silence. Then, realizing that Kay'-yah had regained his senses, the old To-to'-me spoke.

"For three suns, young Earth brother, you have seen with the eyes only. Now you see with the head. It is well. Why did you not fall in front of the door, then I would not have had to drag you so far to my cave?" The old man's voice was kind, and his face held the expression of simple and friendly interest. The question he asked was a strange one and would have sounded foolish from even a child, but in the mouth of a patriarch it was without reason, and Kay'-yah could see that it was not intended as a joke. He therefore avoided an answer and simply asked:

"Who are you that treat me with kindness when I am hurt?"

"I am Tso – the eldest son of the Earth mother – own brother to the bear. But how did you fall from the great wall? You are an Earth brother that goes to the mountain's top above – where even I cannot go, yet you fall and I must drag you here."

"I did not fall," replied Kay'-yah; "I climbed."

At this the old man shook his head several times but said nothing. In the silence that followed Kay'-yah had ample time to study his strange benefactor and captor. In appearance he seemed a contradiction, a mixture of unusual strength and weakness. The face showed great refinement but seemed somehow to be lacking in strength, while the long arms and wide shoulders revealed power and great endurance in spite of age. Evidently the man's mind was not altogether right, yet it was plain from the surroundings that a certain saneness, and even cleverness, controlled most of his actions. Kay'-yah had known old men in his own tribe whose minds seemed to wander, yet at times they thought with perfect clearness.

The old To-to'-me now squatted down by the fire and began to rake some live coals from the ashes. Soon a blaze was crackling the dry sticks, and one of the earthen vessels was set upon them.

"I am very hungry," said Kay'-yah.

In reply the old man reached for the small vessel that remained beside the fire and handed it to him without a word. It seemed to Kay'-yah that he had never tasted anything so good as the meat stew that the bowl contained, and he ate with a relish. When the last of it was eaten he put down the bowl and, raising himself slowly into a sitting posture, made an effort to move back to the wall, where he could rest in a new position and see his strange companion and the surroundings more easily. Seeing his movement, the old man stepped over and lifted him to a comfortable position against the wall as easily as if he had been a child. Kay'-yah wondered at the man's strength, and then at his own feeling of weakness. He must get his strength back as soon as possible; then he must get the little bag from the old man, who doubtless had it, and return to the Nag'-a-pah camp with the first opportunity presented. Just now he could use his thoughts only, as his body was too weak to be of service.

Soon Tso, as he had called himself, had cooked the contents of the larger bowl and the firelight flickered over his wrinkled face as he removed the vessel to the floor. Seating himself on some skins near the opposite wall he leaned back and waited for his evening meal to cool.

"Why do you, who are To-to'-me, live up here in the mountain?" asked Kay'-yah.

"To-to'-me! To-to'-me!" ejaculated the old man. "There is but one To-to'-me: he is Tap-a-wan' and he is dead. The others are slink dogs that bark and run. To-to'-me! Umph! I was To-to'-me long ago, long ago, before the crow turned black or the mountain cat had fur."

In the now dim light the crouching figure of the old man recalled to Kay'-yah's mind the fleeting impression of some event of long ago. Some early meeting with Dee-nay' no doubt. Tso's remarks now filled Kay'-yah's thoughts and he began to wonder if the old man were an outcast or hermit who lived up here alone.

"Do not the To-to'-mes come here to see you?" he ventured.

A low laugh came from Tso, and then he replied; "The dogs cannot find Tso, and the oldest son of the Earth mother has medicine too strong for the To-to'-me children. None can come here but we of the Earth people. You know the way down from the top. I know the way up from below."

It was plain that Tso believed that he, Kay'-yah, had climbed down or fallen from the top of the ledge above, and he saw that it was useless to correct him again, but he now remembered distinctly having climbed up through some kind of crack in the cliff wall and recalled the hidden opening out of which he had crawled.

By the time the old man had eaten his meal, darkness had settled down in the cave and only the soft twilight suggested rather than revealed its interior.

"If all this strange man says is true, then I can leave here as soon as I am strong enough to travel," thought Kay'-yah. Then his mind returned to the little bag. Why had the old man taken it? After all, perhaps he had not. He would wait and find out later. Then he fell to wondering why neither the Nag'-a-pahs nor the To-to'-mes had found this cave long ago. Did they know of the old man? Perhaps he had some secret way up to the great ledge onto which the cave opened. All of these questions puzzled him. He was growing weary again and must lie down.

Just as this thought came to him the old man arose in the gloom and hobbled to the fast-graying ashes of the fire. The darkness had brought the chill of the high mountain air into the cave and both the light and warmth of the fire would be welcome before time to sleep. The little flames leaped up through the dry twigs and their light cast dancing shadows about the cave walls.

As Kay'-yah moved forward from the wall so that he could lie back on the skins, the old man again hobbled to his assistance. The firelight now shone out brightly and as the figure of the old To-to'-me bent over to assist him, Kay'-yah noticed that his right leg was badly bent and was wrapped about with a strip of skin covered with thick fur. Then as his eyes fell on the foot he gave a start of surprise, for it was the foot of a bear. As Tso eased him down on the skins and moved away, Kay'-yah's eyes followed the foot and in the brighter light he saw that it was indeed the great paw of a bear, but that it formed a strange moccasin within which the man's crippled foot was held by bands of bearskin attached to the sides of the paw. Instantly he realized that here was Doh, the man bear, the witch who was feared by both Nag'-a-pahs and To-to'-mes. This revelation explained why the Doh witch had a twisted moccasin on the left foot, as it was this foot that the old To-to'-me twisted as he walked. It also explained the terrifying sound of the growling bear that men had heard when they found fresh tracks of the man bear, for the old man had already revealed his weird powers in imitating not only the bear but the wolf and the dog. Kay'-yah laughed to himself as the full significance of the revelation came to him. The bear foot was strong medicine indeed, for neither a Nag'-a-pah nor a To-to'-me would care to follow a bear witch.

With a sigh, the old man sat down, and after humming for a few moments under his breath, began to speak.

"The Earth mother gives a name to all her sons, from Sug, the rat, to me, the eldest of them all. What name has she given to you?"

"I am called Kay'-yah," came the reply.

The old man repeated the name over and over. "The name has no meaning for Tso. I shall call you the 'Rain-boy' because you fell down from the clouds."

Kay'-yah thought best to let his aged host have his own way and made no objection to the new name. He had two reasons for deciding not to anger the old man in any way. His natural respect for old age was one; and the other lay in the hope that he would gain the confidence of the old To-to'-me, learn if he had the little bag, and perhaps even gain his assistance in finding the best way to return to the Nag'-a-pah camp. Intent on thoughts of the little bag, he forgot for the moment that he was with a To-to'-me and remarked in his own tongue:

"When I was on the rocks outside of your cave I lost something. When you brought me here did you find it and keep it for me?"

"Why do you talk Nag'-a-pah?" asked the old man roughly, as he arose and came toward Kay'-yah. Then without waiting for a reply he continued as if to himself:

"Yes, your hair and your moccasins are as the Nag'-a-pahs wear them. But the Earth mother chooses her sons from all people."

Then as he returned to his place by the wall he spoke still lower and as though to himself alone:

"Dee-nay' is Nag'-a-pah – yes, yes, he is Nag'-a-pah."

Forgetting his question about the lost bag, in his astonishment at hearing the name of Dee-nay' in the mouth of this To-to'-me, Kay'-yah asked;

"Do you know my father, Dee-nay'?"

The old man either did not hear or was too wrapped in thought to notice the question, for he made no reply. Again Kay'-yah asked the question, and this time Tso looked up, and after gazing at Kay'-yah for some time in silence, he said:

"Long ago, before the owl hunted by night, before the flat-bill ran on top of the water, when in the darkness of sleep the gray wolf messenger for the Great Spirit came in the night to Tap-a-wan' and brought his eyes to the long sleep, a mountain lion fought and fell over the cliff – down, down. But the Earth mother said, 'The lion shall not die,' so a man of strong medicine came to the lion and the lion lived. Yes, Tso knows Dee-nay' – and Tso knows more and more — " and now his deep voice trailed off so low that Kay'-yah could scarcely hear the words, yet he knew instinctively that he must not interrupt the old man's strange recitation.

"Yes," continued the low voice, "Tso knows where the sky paint grows. The earth sand-painting is good but it is not good medicine without the sky painting. Tso makes both and Dee-nay' makes both."

Kay'-yah waited as patiently as he could, his mind teeming with a hundred thoughts and conjectures. That this queer old To-to'-me was a friend of Dee-nay' seemed all but impossible to him, yet the To-to'-me spoke of Dee-nay' as of a friend. Surely then the old man would not wish to keep the little bag after he explained that it was Dee-nay's greatest wish that he, Kay'-yah, should return it to him. With this thought in mind he said:

"It is from Dee-nay' that I come for a little bag that I have lost. Do you have it?"

At the question the old man arose with a growl in his throat that was more like that of a beast than man.

"Yes, I have the bag, and I shall keep it – keep it!" he shouted angrily.

Then almost leaping over to where Kay'-yah lay, he shook his great arms above him and called out hoarsely;

"The lie is in your mouth when you say you come from Dee-nay' for the bag. The strong medicine is mine! Is mine! And you shall never have it!"

Then, stooping suddenly, he caught Kay'-yah up in his arms as though he were a child, and hobbling with all the speed of which he was capable, made for the narrow ledge the outlines of whose dangerous edge were lost in the blackness of the night.

Chapter 7
A Secret Council

The sands of the desert are free for all
And shelter many a clan,
Who have felt the lure of their mystic call
And flown from the haunts of man.

WAU-KO'-MA'S recovery from his fight with Kay'-yah was rapid, but it would have been difficult to recognize the true story of that night from the account he gave to Tag-a'-mo and others. The events, as they had happened, were far too belittling to his pride and self-importance to repeat to others and so the account he gave was a strange distortion of the facts, carefully rehearsed in his thoughts to give an impression of truth and accuracy. It was, therefore, with a feeling of fury that he saw, at the very outset of his carefully planned account, a look of unmistakable doubt in Tag-a'-mo's shrewd eyes; a doubt which grew into certainty as the young chief talked.

It was the day after the happening that he told what had occurred, as until then his throat had been closed to sound, and his voice was yet husky from the treatment it had received at the hands of Kay'-yah. He lay in his own lodge on a couch of soft skins, surrounded by Tag-a'-mo, Dis'-din, and some of his own following, and a restless impatience shone in his eyes and sounded in his voice as he spoke.

"The dog of a Nag'-a-pah has the strength of a devil-cat; but he never could have held me had I not been taken unawares," he said.

Tag-a'-mo did not attempt to disguise the note of skepticism in his voice as he replied:

"Is it so? Our ears are open wide to hear the account of this strange fight."

Wau-ko'-ma cast a venomous glance at the old man and his voice was harsh with anger as he continued;

"The night was thick with storm, as you know, but above the sound of the wind I thought I heard a cry from the hogan where the Nag'-a-pah spy was kept — " he broke off and raised himself on one elbow. "It had been well if my word had been heeded and this dog put to death at sunset. I do not forget, Tag-a'-mo, that you and others have put my word at nought – have defied me. Your age alone protects you but it does not protect all."

Tag-a'-mo answered only with a deprecating movement of the hand; and the other, after a moment of silence which seemed to vibrate with the intensity of his anger and hatred, went on:

"I went out into the night and approached the prison hogan: as I neared the door my foot touched something – I stooped to see and it was the body of the guard. As I bent over him – this dog of a thieving Nag'-a-pah sprang from the shadows and threw himself upon my back. I could not draw my knife or free myself before he had strangled me well-nigh into the long sleep — " He stopped, for Tag-a'-mo's eyes were looking into his and they spoke of unbelief. "Why do you stare like an owl in the sunlight?" he asked angrily, and looked down ashamed in spite of himself at having so spoken to an elder.

"This guard still held his knife, they tell me," said Tag-a'-mo; and his quiet voice was in strong contrast to the other. "The Nag'-a-pah was unarmed. Who killed the guard?"

"Who could have killed him – who but the Nag'-a-pah?" snarled Wau-ko'-ma. "I tell you he has the strength of a devil-cat!"

"This would take more than strength – and what of the man who guarded with him?" asked Tag-a'-mo.

"I saw no other – this Kee'-to was alone and dead." And there was a note of defiance now in Wau-ko'-ma's voice.

Tag-a'-mo did not speak for a moment. Then: "The mirage in the desert seems real to the man whose thoughts are fevered with thirst, but to those who observe it is upside down." And he rose with dignity and walked out of the lodge.

Wau-ko'-ma frowned more blackly than before, and he harshly commanded the remaining men to follow Tag-a'-mo and leave him in peace. When he was alone he lay for a long time looking up through the smoke-hole at the bit of blue sky that shone there. For several days he lay on the couch of hides as his strength came gradually back to him, but he was not idle in those days; party after party of searchers he sent into the canyons and foothills and mountain to find trace of Kay'-yah, but they all returned with the same report: "The Nag'-a-pah must be dead, as no living thing was to be found in the rocks or on any of the trails." But it was strange that they had not found his body nor was there trace of struggle on any trail. Wau-ko'-ma at length decided that his enemy had met his death in the cave of some wild beast, or lay shattered at the foot of some precipice whose dark depths were beyond exploration by the eyes of man, and it was with a feeling of great relief that he gave his thoughts to other things.

More and more marked had become the division between his followers and those of Tag-a'-mo, and mingled with the anger which this aroused in the chief had come a secret fear as to the possible outcome. He called together the men on whom he could most surely depend and made many plans. On this day, before the sun had shone above the desert's rim, a runner, leaving the door of Wau-ko'-ma's lodge, had sped down the mesa trail and disappeared into the great stretches of the plain. Tonight a secret council was to meet in his own hogan and he awaited the coming of the men with impatience.

They came in silently, one by one, and took their places in the circle on the floor. Guards were stationed at the door and watched outside. All felt that matters of importance were to be discussed and a sense of impending danger or ill was in the air.

The night was dark and the camp quiet, but other figures besides themselves were abroad and they glanced at one another significantly as several of Tag-a'-mo's followers passed at some distance from the lodge, barely recognizable in the gloom.

"There are other councils tonight," spoke a voice.

Wau-ko'-ma looked up quickly.

"My place is at the head of all councils in this camp!" he said. "None dare call the men together save at my word."

"Yet they meet," said the voice again. "For as I passed the medicine lodge but a moment ago, Dis'-din and others entered."

Anger darkened the face of Wau-ko'-ma, but he sat silent in thought before he spoke.

"I will let it pass this one time – important matters keep me here – but such things shall not continue long. Chot'-zu, move to the left – three places in the circle are to be left vacant – others will be here tonight."

The men looked at one another and a scarcely audible murmur of surprise passed among them. Wau-ko'-ma looked about at the circle of faces and a grim smile lifted the corner of his mouth. Their uncertainty pleased him; but he stooped to the fire that burned in the middle of the floor, and taking an ember with one blackened end touched it to the filled bowl of his pipe and passed it about the circle. He spoke no word and they smoked in silence until low voices were heard at the door. The guard who was posted outside spoke to another who arrived; almost immediately he came within the door.

"The runner, Tong-pah, has arrived with the Ta-pee-chi messengers," he said.

There was a startled movement in the group of men, and all eyes turned in amazement to Wau-ko'-ma. His face was inscrutable and he met no eye.

"Bid them enter," he said to the guard; and before protest could be made or word spoken three men entered the lodge followed by the runner.

The men who entered were giants in size, with large, fierce features and bushy heads of hair. They looked about at the walls of the lodge as if uncomfortable at the confinement they suggested. Wild men of the desert, these, who lived on the spoils of others more industrious than themselves. Pirates of the plains who owed allegiance to power only and whose only law was that of might. Their greatest weakness lay in greed, and this Wau-ko'-ma had learned long ago when he had bartered with them in the plains below. He now drew toward him a bundle of buffalo skin that had lain near and smiled as his fingers felt the outlines of flint knives, carved armlets and other articles that it contained.

The desert men stood close together and looked at Wau-ko'-ma, their glance passing over the heads of the others, and an expression of fierce inquiry was in their eyes.

"The desert wolves have come at the call of the mountain wolf," spoke the one who seemed their leader. "What word have you for them?"

"Brothers," answered Wau-ko'-ma, and his eyes still did not meet the eyes of any of his own men, "we have kept places for you in the circle of our council to signify that you are indeed our brothers. Be seated and smoke with us while we talk of many things."

There were dark looks on the faces of many about the circle as the strangers awkwardly and with an ill grace took the seats indicated to them. The desert men understood To-to'-me but spoke in a language that seemed a strange conglomeration of all desert tongues, and yet it was intelligible to the men present.

Wau-ko'-ma spoke long and in the end his gifts passed into the hands of the Ta-pee-chis. As he spoke, many and uneasy glances passed among his followers and they looked at him with uncertainty in their eyes, but such was his authority over them that they spoke no word though the feeling among them was strong.

At last one of the strangers glanced up at the smoke-hole where the glimpse of night sky was growing pale.

"The night is old," he said. "We must be far from here before the sun has come."

"It is well," said Wau-ko'-ma. "The trail lies well-guarded by my men as when you came. Will the desert wolves come again at the call of the mountain wolf?"

"I and my tribe will listen for your voice," said the man. "We shall come when you call."

"With claws prepared for fight?" asked Wau-ko'-ma.

The man's eyes gleamed.

"Yes, and with bared teeth!"

Again the grim smile twitched at the corner of Wau-ko'-ma' s mouth and he nodded toward the door.

"Go – and may the Sun God smite your enemies!"

The men passed out and there was silence in the lodge for the space of a few moments. Wau-ko'-ma was still smiling into the fire but his smile was not pleasant to see.

"The desert comes to our aid," he said. "Wau-ko'-ma is still chief of the To-to'-mes."

One, more brave than the rest, spoke up.

"I like this not – it is not plain to me – the desert thieves are not our brothers, and I like it not."

Wau-ko'-ma's expression did not change as he looked at the man, and he did not immediately answer. At this moment the hide at the door was pulled aside and a man walked in. He blinked blindly at the fire for a moment, as a man whose eyes had grown accustomed to darkness, then peered at Wau-ko'-ma and the circle of faces about him.

"I have seen the Nag'-a-pah!" he said.

The words were like an exploding bomb in the room and nearly every man gave a sharp exclamation of surprise.

Wau-ko'-ma spoke harshly in incredulous amazement.

"You have seen the Nag'-a-pah – *alive*?"

"Alive and in hiding," answered the man.

"Where did you see him? Have not our men searched every trail?" And there was a note in Wau-ko'-ma's voice that boded ill for those who had taken this duty lightly.

"You will remember that first night that we traced him to the ruin of the Na-ya-kaed'?" again spoke the man. "It was where the trail ends beyond there that I saw him."

Wau-ko'-ma sneered:

"You have seen a vision. The ruin and rocks were searched, and he could have found no food in that place."

"But it is not in the ruin or the rocks that he is hiding," spoke the man slowly and significantly.

"*Speak!* man, speak!" said Wau-ko'-ma. "Do not keep us waiting with your riddles. If you have seen no vision, tell us quickly."

The man spoke hurriedly now.

"I and four others were hunting in the canyon. As we rounded a corner of rock on the trail I looked upward, and standing far above was the Nag'-a-pah. He saw me and ran like a mountain-goat. There could have been no mistake – no man of our people wears a band of red on his hair, and I saw the band plainly. I called to my companions and ran up the trail, they following. We saw nothing of the Nag'-a-pah as we came near to where he had been. There was nothing but some strange tracks in the trail, and when the men saw these tracks they would go no further. 'It is the bear-witch that you follow,' they said and waited below. I put the fear out of my heart and went on alone. But there was nothing to be seen. The ruin was empty, for I looked within the doorway, and no living thing was in the rocks about it."

Wau-ko'-ma frowned again.

"Said I not that you had seen a vision? A goat perhaps, with a smear of blood on his head."

The man did not heed the interruption.

"When I had searched the rocks, I went backward down the trail, scanning the ruin and the wall of rock above. There was no trail up the face of the cliff, no foothold, and yet – I swear that I saw a face look at me from the ledge above; for the space of a breath it was there and then gone – but plain to see was the red band on the hair. It is there – on the shelf of rock that the Nag'-a-pah is hiding."

"Is he a spider that he can crawl up a sheer wall of rock?" Wau-ko'-ma's voice was still incredulous.

"It may be that he is a witch," said the man; "I know not, but he is there, on a shelf of rock that begins and ends plainly before the eyes, with no way up or down."

"Not even from above? What is the approach from above?" Wau-ko'-ma spoke with impatience.

"There is none," answered the man. "The wall that rises beyond the shelf overhangs by many hands and there is no way up."

"Of that you are certain?" asked Wau-ko'-ma.

"I am certain." And the man's tone left no doubt as to his conviction. "Until the sun went down I searched every trail and examined every cliff and rock from above and below and none climb better than I. There is no way up to the higher level above the shelf; it seems to be a part of the top of Qua'-ma itself, whose heights, as you know, no living man has scaled. And there is no way to the ledge itself."

"Why did you not shoot the dog?" Wau-ko'-ma spoke now with bitterness; he was at last convinced that his enemy still lived.

"The word has gone forth that your arrow alone was to reach his heart," said the man.

"I have not said so," Wau-ko'-ma replied quickly. "He is to die, but I care not how. Are men watching the trails?"

"I left two in front of the ruin and two further down the trail," and a note of sullenness crept into the man's voice. He had looked for and expected praise for his actions, but had met only criticism and sharp words.

"Good! See that more are sent to share their guard. The dog shall not escape this time. I would have him trapped like a bear in a pit." And Wau-ko'-ma's voice was not pleasant to hear.

"What of this bear-witch?" said another. "I myself have seen his tracks; they lead to a wall of rock and go no further. Are the Nag'-a-pah and the bear-witch the same?"

A shiver seemed to pass among the men.

"A witch he may be," spoke Wau-ko'-ma. "He fights as one. But man or beast or spirit, my arrow shall find its way to his black heart."

"There are those who say you fear the Nag'-a-pah," spoke a voice from the circle.

Wau-ko'-ma snarled his answer.

"My knife shall force his words down his lying throat who speaks so! Who was the man?"

"I but heard – I but heard," said the other hastily.

"You had better save your ears for better things, my friend, or lose them altogether," said Wau-ko'-ma.

"Shall we hunt the Nag'-a-pah with tomorrow's sun?" It was Chot'-zu who spoke.

"Not tomorrow, for my bow-arm has not yet received its full strength – but the day after – and no power shall then save him from my vengeance." There was a weakness in the words of the chief that seemed to be felt by all: even Chot'-zu looked down at the beaten floor of the lodge and moved uneasily.

The strong *tum-tum-tum* of a drum came to their ears. There was no mistaking the sound – it was the drum of the medicine lodge.

Wau-ko'-ma lifted his head and sprang to his feet, amazement, incredulity and anger in his face. Never, since he had been chief, had that drum been sounded except when he was present. It was beaten only on important occasions, occasions when he, as chief of the tribe, had presided. He strode out of the council circle.

"Come!" he said to those about him, and walked direct to the medicine lodge, where, with a sweep of his arm, he pushed aside the hide at the doorway and stepped within. A few followed him into the lodge, but the greater number stood without and waited for what would happen.

The drum still sent forth its pounding notes, and an old man chanted monotonously. All the elders of the tribe sat in a great circle against the wall, and the altar was piled high with sacred meal and pollen and ears of purple and yellow corn. Clouds of incense smoke arose from the fire that burned under the smoke-hole and the men had laid aside their pipes, but the tobacco smoke still hung in the air like a curtain of fog.

Wau-ko'-ma stood for a moment surveying the scene. He looked at the faces in the circle lit by the flickering flames and realized that here were all the head men of his tribe, the elders and wise men. While about *him* stood the hot-heads: the men who had done nothing but shout and flourish their knives at the suggestion of a battle or sporting hunt; who thrived on constant excitement and whose heads contained no wisdom. His anger flamed more hotly at the thought. His place was here at the head of his tribe: here, where they held ceremony without him.

Tag-a'-mo sat opposite the entrance, and he now raised his head and looked straight into Wau-ko'-ma's eyes. He was the first to speak.

"Enter, Wau-ko'-ma! Your place awaits you in the circle."

Wau-ko'-ma stood stiffly erect and folded his arms; he restrained himself with difficulty; his inclination was to take these old men by the hair of their heads and throw them into the night, but not so read the unwritten law: to dishonor age is a crime even a chief of the To-to'-mes would think long before committing.

"My place has awaited me thus far – it can wait longer. What is the meaning of this?" and he waved his arm indicating the circle of men. "I have called no council to this lodge." And his voice was harsh with pent-up rage.

Tag-a'-mo's face was calm, but there was a cold light in his eye. He spoke deliberately and quietly:

"And yet, the council has been called."

The veins in Wau-ko'-ma's neck seemed swollen to the bursting-point; his head grew hot.

"To your hogans – all of you!" he said in a thick voice. "I am chief of the To-to'-mes, and, by the gods, no council shall be held here that comes not at my word."

Some of the old men half rose and looked at Tag-a'-mo with uncertainty in their eyes. He raised a hand and they slowly sank back into their places. He spoke almost gently:

"Has it gone from your mind, Wau-ko'-ma, that you did call a council for this night?"

Wau-ko'-ma frowned and cast an uneasy glance over his shoulder at the men who stood behind him.

"Is there a law which says that I, chief of the To-to'-mes, cannot call a council when I so desire?" There was a deep sneer in the words; but the expression on Tag-a'-mo's face did not change, though his voice grew stern and boomed like distant thunder.

"A council of the To-to'-mes must include the chief men of the To-to'-mes – the men who sat in council before you, Wau-ko'-ma, were born. No council is complete without them."

"And yet I, Wau-ko'-ma, did hold council – a council of the To-to'-mes – a complete council: and the *wise* men" – a deeper sneer lay on the words – "were not called."

Like a thunderbolt from the blue came the quick reply:

"When was the law made that includes in a council of the To-to'-mes the thieving hounds of the desert? Those vultures who live on dead men's bones and who, until now, have never soiled a To-to'-me trail!"

The blood fled from Wau-ko'-ma's face and his fingers clenched deep into his hands. He stared at Tag-a'-mo, but no words came to his lips. The men of the council looked away from his face, for it was not pleasant to see, and the men at the doorway, who had followed him here, drew back, one by one, into the darkness.

Tag-a'-mo spoke again:

"The night is dark, but it has ears and eyes for Tag-a'-mo. And the dawn is near, when all may see."

He looked Wau-ko'-ma straight in the eyes, and Wau-ko'-ma's gaze wavered before his and fell.

"Go now. This matter will be clear to you at another time and before many suns have passed."

Wau-ko'-ma turned in the doorway; he was alone with the old men – the others had gone. He hesitated for a moment, then lifted the hide curtain and walked out into the paling night.

Chapter 8
The Mark Of The Bear-Witch

The law of the gods is the law of the hills:
Who saves a life is saved in turn,
And death awaits the one who kills: –
Justice for justice – the law is stern.

KAY'-YAH'S first impulse, as he was caught up in the ape-like arms of the angry old To-to'-me, whose apparent intention was to throw him over the cliff outside, was to fight for his life with such strength as he had; but he instantly realized that, in his weakened condition, he was as a babe in the hands of the old man.

As they passed through the entrance into the night the old To-to'-me hobbled straight across the level shelf of rock toward the edge of the precipice. Deciding that if he were thrown over the cliff he would make the old man pay for his madness by having to go with him, he threw his arms about his neck. Then as the thought came to him he called out:

"Does the eldest son of the Earth mother kill a child to whom he has given a name?"

The effect of the question was almost instantaneous. Reminded that he had renamed Kay'-yah, as a member of the Earth clan, the old man stopped and stood uncertainly on the edge of the cliff.

For a moment, that seemed an age to Kay'-yah, the grim old figure held his burden poised above the precipice; his partially unbalanced mind slowly taking in all that the question had implied; and then realizing, as Kay'-yah had hoped he would, that no Indian, least of all a medicine-man, could kill one to whom he had given a clan name without receiving the instant curse of the Great Spirit, he slowly turned toward the cave, and to Kay'-yah's surprise he laughed a deep-throated laugh that ended in a growl like that of a cornered animal. At the entrance he set Kay'-yah down on his feet, saying as he did so:

"Go back into the lion's den – Rain-boy. The star-brothers guard the sky, and no clouds are above for you to fall from."

Kay'-yah walked unsteadily to the bed of skins at the back of the cave and lay down. Tso did not enter, and a few moments later the sound of his queer twisted steps told that he was walking away into the night. Then came the sound of the deep voice as he sang:

"The chin-dog howls: he howls in the wind:
The bush-tail keeps to his hole,
And back in his cave sits the bear in fear,
And back in his den sits the wolf afraid:

'Tis the Shin-di comes on the roaring wind:
On the roaring wind in the bending trees,
And the mountain quakes as the pine-tree shakes.
The Shin-di comes, and the chin-dog howls;
The chin-dog runs with the wind."

As the voice died away in the distance, Kay'-yah thought of the strange turn of affairs that had so nearly cost him his life. It was now plain that the old To-to'-me not only had the little bag, but that he prized it above life itself and intended to keep it. But why should he want it, since he lived apart from the To-to'-me tribe, and the Magic had no virtue when separated from the tribal altar and the sacred meal that must be upon it?

He must learn where Tso had hidden it, whether about his person or in the cave, and then recover it: but not until he was able to escape with it, as it would not do to have the old man miss the bag and attack him again while in his weakened condition. He needed strength; his lack of it was a new experience to him, and impatient with the feeling of weakness that was upon him, he slowly arose and walked feebly about the cave.

As he neared the entrance he stopped. The cool night air blew in upon him, and from out in the silent desert that lay far below came the faint *ky-yi-yi-eee* of a lone chin-dog (coyote) calling to his mate. His surroundings seemed very strange, and Ah'-co, with its intimate shelter and many friends, seemed far away, yet he rather liked the feeling of loneliness that was upon him.

He had walked about the cave but a very short time when he grew too weary for further effort, and knowing that sleep would be his greatest aid in the recovery of his strength, he lay down and was soon lost in slumber.

Several uneventful days passed, and they were long wearisome days to Kay'-yah, as his weakness prevented him from wandering beyond the cave's entrance. Neither he nor Tso had mentioned the little bag since the night when both had so nearly gone over the great cliff outside. For a day and a night the old man had been absent, but at sunrise of the second day he entered the cave just as Kay'-yah awoke from his night's rest.

"The coming day bring good to you!" he said by way of salutation.

"The Sun-God smile upon you!" replied Tso, as he threw down some small game he had killed. "Weakness is not a good bow for so straight an arrow as the Rain-boy. Strength should come to your bones after the long rest."

"The feeling of strength is returning to me," replied Kay'-yah, "and soon I will be as I was before the great weakness came upon me."

"The stream that is filled with water has the strength to carry a tree upon its back," remarked Tso: "and strength is for the man with much blood about his bones. Your blood had run low like the little stream of water that goes feebly among the rocks."

After the morning meal was finished, the old man lay down and was soon sleeping heavily. Walking over to where he lay, Kay'-yah looked down upon him, wondering what circumstances could have made him the hermit and outcast he seemed to be. This was Doh, the bear-witch of the twisted moccasin; the creature most feared by both Nag'-a-pahs and To-to'-mes.

As he stood above the now helpless figure, lying like a twisted old juniper-tree that had fallen before the wind, he thought how easy it would be, if he had his usual strength, suddenly to bind the old To-to'-me's hands behind his back, and he could then search him and the cave with every hope of finding the bag. A flush of shame swept over him on second thought, for he knew that he could not mistreat an old man, and especially one who had saved his life and was now giving him food and shelter. He must bide his time until he could recover the bag without violence or shame.

As he walked out of the cave and stood on the ledge of rock, drinking in the cool morning air, new life seemed to rise within him as he realized that his accustomed feeling of strength had about returned, and that he would soon be able to go on with the task that lay before him. Far below, and stretching away beneath the blue haze of early morning, lay the desert. He walked nearer the edge and looked down to see if the To-to'-me mesa were visible from where he stood, but it could not be seen, as a projecting shoulder of the mountain obscured the view toward the west.

Deciding to learn more of his strange surroundings than his strength, up to this time, had permitted, he walked along the shelf of rock to the right, and after a short distance came to the end of the ledge. The downward continuation of the cliff above cut squarely across the shelf, making further passage impossible. Looking upward, he saw that at no point could an ascent be made to higher ground, as the overhanging cliff rose some thirty feet to the next possible level, and he smiled as he thought of old Tso's belief that he had fallen from above. From directly above his head came the shrill song of a catbird singing with delight in the morning sunshine. The little singer was perched on the limb of a gnarled pinyon-tree that leaned out over the cliff's edge.

At this sight of timber, the first he had seen since leaving the foothills below, Kay'-yah decided that the rock cliff above him must be the last of the great bare surface of perpendicular walls that could be seen from far out in the desert below, and that the long flat top of the mountain could not be very far above him. Before him, as if crouching in fear beneath the overhanging rock, stood the three ancient dwellings of the Na-ya-kaed', the buildings he had seen in the faint morning light when he had climbed out of the passage in the rocks. There were no signs of other cliff dwellings at this end of the ledge, but the thought suddenly came to him that the cave of old Tso had probably been the remains of such a dwelling, and that the old man had simply cleared it out for his own use. The outlet of the passage, up which he had climbed, must be near at hand, and he looked for it among the great flat rocks near the edge of the cliff.

Remembering that the tilted strata of rock ran parallel with the slight incline up which he had crawled, he looked for this tilt, and was soon standing in the narrow little entrance. Then he realized why Tso had never discovered the passage, and why no one attempting to find a way down from the ledge at this point, would believe that a way to lower ground existed, for even from the opening in which he stood, no trace of the little footholds could be seen in the great crack that shot downward into the darkness. Here, then, was one possible way of escape, if the To-to'-me trails about the ruin below could be passed, and no one but himself knew of its existence.

Stepping out of the passage, he walked thoughtfully back to the cave, and though he could not see the other end of the long ledge because of a curve that rounded a projection in the cliff a little way beyond the cave's entrance, he believed that the secret passage he had discovered made it practically certain that the ledge was everywhere cut off from those above and below, as the little cliff people had doubtless used it as a secret retreat when hard pressed by an enemy. Yet there was another exit somewhere along the other end of the shelf, as Tso had approached the cave from that side, and had always departed in the same direction. His also must be a secret way, as he had said, "You know the way down from above, and Tso knows the way up from below."

He would explore the end of the ledge that he had not yet seen, and would then find the old man's secret passage; but not now, as Tso might awaken any moment, and such investigating must be done at some time during the absence of his aged host.

Reaching the cave and finding the old To-to'-me still wrapped in slumber, he moved quietly to his bed and sat down. He decided to rest a while, and if Tso awakened and left the cave he would follow him and learn how he got down to the country below. Then stretching himself out luxuriously, he closed his eyes and thought over the many strange adventures that had befallen him since he had departed from the lodge of old Dee-nay'. Many suns had risen and set since he had left the Nag'-a-pah camp, and he wondered what his old friend and counselor would think of his long absence. Had Sah'-ne missed him, and would she care? No doubt the entire Nag'-a-pah camp now knew of his mission, and believed he had been killed by the To-to'-mes.

As he lay thinking, he heard the old man move, then yawn as though awakening from his nap. Something within him, something contrary to his usual frank way of acting toward his host, decided him to keep his eyes closed and pretend to be asleep. He even began to breathe more deeply and regularly, that the deception might be the more complete. And now through narrowly opened eyelids he watched the old To-to'-me as the latter rose to a sitting posture, and after stretching his great arms in an effort to overcome the relaxation of sleep, got to his feet. Then after taking a deep draught from the water-jar, he walked to the back of the cave and looked down at his sleeping companion.

For a long time he thus stood, and Kay'-yah became so uncomfortable under the gaze that he had about decided to open his eyes and act as though he had just awakened when Tso began to talk to himself in a low voice no louder than a whisper.

"The eagle doesn't lay dove's eggs, and there is never a rabbit in the litter of the wolf. A young fox has a keen nose that can sniff up and down the wind: yes – up and down the wind – and he may hunt as he sniffs. Has Dee'-nay sent the young fox to take that which belongs to the lion? The little bag belongs to Tso, and Tso will keep it."

Then he turned and, stepping noiselessly over to the great buffalo skull, caught hold of the nose and cautiously swung the head to one side. At the low sound made as the dry bone grated against the rock wall of the cave, he suddenly turned his head and looked down at Kay'-yah; but the closed eyes and deep breathing reassured him, and he turned again to his task. Quickly lifting out a small rock from a spot that had been covered by the skull, he reached into the hole thus uncovered, and brought out a small object that was hidden from Kay'-yah's view by the great hand that closed upon it. Moving around with his back to the watchful sleeper on the floor, the old man bent over the little object, mumbling joyously as he did so:

"You belong to Tso, and your Magic is for Tso. What does the young fox know of the magic sleep: of the power it gives to go; to see many things; many things? Old Two-horns keeps very still, and he will guard you safely from the young fox; yes, as safely as the hawk is safe from the sparrow."

At the old To-to'-me's mention of the Magic, Kay'-yah's heart beat so fast that he could scarcely retain his regular breathing. He felt as if he could not contain himself for joy at having so easily found where Tso had hidden the bag. He had mentioned the Magic, so the little bag *did* contain it after all.

Carefully restoring the coveted little pouch to its strange hiding-place, Tso replaced the stone, and after cautiously sliding the skull back to its accustomed position, he picked up his stout spear and, throwing his bow and arrow case over his shoulder, hobbled out of the cave. After giving him time enough to get around the curve on the ledge outside, Kay'-yah arose to his feet and quietly followed him, determined to learn how he got down from the shelf. As he neared the shoulder of rock around which the ledge curved, he paused for a moment to listen. He could hear nothing: and fearing that Tso might have stopped on the other side of the curve, and be listening to see if he were being followed, he waited in silence for a moment. Then he heard a low sound that seemed to come from far around the point and a little way beneath the shelf. Stepping quickly around the curve, he looked along the length of the ledge that now ran smoothly before him on the same level for some distance, and then seemed to end abruptly. The old To-to'-me was not in sight.

As he advanced along the shelf, he noticed that there were no other cliff dwellings, and there seemed to be no trail or passage of any kind by which a higher or lower level could be reached. A little farther on he came to a worn path that led to the outer edge of the shelf, where it ended at some great flat-topped rocks. Stepping out on these, he looked downward, and was surprised to see, some thirty feet below him, a small round pool of clear water whose placid surface made a perfect reflector for the bright blue of the morning sky. He sat down and looked over at the ledge in which the little basin lay like a polished jewel in its setting of red and yellow rock. There was no possible way down to it, as the rocks on which he sat overhung the pool, making a trail impossible, and he could see that no passage could be made on the steep wall that reached up to it from the country below. The little shelf with its pocket of water seemed completely isolated, so far as man and animals were concerned. No tracks were visible about the margin of the pool, but a number of small birds scolded and chattered about it as they flew up for their morning drink.

As Kay'-yah turned to get up, his eye caught a projecting piece of stout wood that had been driven horizontally into a crack between the rocks, and about it hung the loose coils of a long rope of buffalo hide like the worn one that he had seen hanging back in the cave. So here was where Tso got his supply of water; and doubtless it was here that the mysterious little people, who had once lived in the cliff dwellings at the other end of the ledge, had filled their water-jars in the long ago.

Kay'-yah walked slowly along, examining the countless footprints made by the old To-to'-me during his many trips to and from the cave. The tracks led on, then suddenly ceased as he came upon a section of hard rock where there was not sufficient earth on which to leave a trail. At one point, where the shelf narrowed down to a seemingly dangerous width, a pine log had been laid along the outer edge for protection, and kept its position by having one end securely anchored beneath a great flat-topped rock. He wondered how the old man could have brought so large a timber from the foothills up to so great a height, for the wood was not old enough to have been placed there by the little cliff people.

Still searching for some kind of a crevice or opening through which a passage might have been made, Kay'-yah went on until he came to the point where the shelf suddenly narrowed to its final ending in a mere projection scarcely wider than a man's foot. Puzzled by his failure, he examined the rocks beneath and the smooth walls that towered upward at his back; no possible opening of any kind was visible. Far down below he could see, here and there, the white lines of trails that wound in and out among the dark green trees and bushes of the foothills. Then stepping nearer the edge, he saw the outer margin of a trail that ran parallel with the shelf some fifty feet beneath. This must be a part of the trail used by Tso after he got down from the shelf. But how did he get down?

Baffled for the time being by the fact that he was unable to find the hidden passage, he retraced his steps toward the cave. He could, of course, sit down and watch the ledge until the old man came up from below; but he might not return for a day or more, and another plan now entered his mind, and he would doubtless have time to carry it out before Tso returned. Later, if he completed the task before the old man appeared, he would station himself at a point where he could not be seen, but from which he would be able to see the length of the shelf from the curve to its end.

Passing by the cave's entrance, he went on to the other end of the ledge, and after finding the entrance to the secret passage was soon feeling his way downward through the dark crack in the cliff that led to the ancient dwelling far below. It was difficult in the darkness to feel for the little niches with his feet, so the passage downward would require more time than would be necessary in the ascent, but it required less strength.

He decided that his final escape with the little bag must be through this passage if he found today, as he hoped he would, that the many To-to'-me trails that lay about the cliff ruin below him could be crossed with safety. Such knowledge could be gained only by daylight; and now that he knew, at last, where the bag was, he must be prepared to escape with it as soon as he had gained a little more strength for the journey and had learned the best way to return to the Nag'-a-pah camp.

As he descended step after step in the darkness, he realized why the upward climb on the night of his escape from the To-to'-mes had made so great a trial on his strength. At last he reached the wider opening that was immediately above the cliff dwelling, and could see the points of light that filtered up through the ceiling-poles. As he felt about for the movable section that covered the hole through which he had lifted himself on the night of his climb up the passage, his hand came in contact with a little deerskin bag. Even in the darkness its shape, and the two little silver beads were enough to identify it.

Puzzled beyond measure by the unexpected find, he slid the section of poles to one side and was soon standing in the light of the room below. Yes, there was no mistaking the familiar little pouch, and now he would know what it contained. Breaking the thong that loosely held the mouth of the bag, he shook its contents out into his hand. The carved ring of silver that might have delighted him at any other time, now only meant disappointment.

Had this ring been in the little bag when it had been taken from him by the To-to'-mes? He carefully examined the thick soft skin of the bag, and the worn marks on the lining left no doubt that the ring had lain within it for years. Then this little bag had never contained the Magic. That, of course, was in old Tso's possession, and probably had been ever since it had been stolen from the Nag'-a-pahs; but how did *he* get it? He seemed to know Dee-nay', and pretended to be his friend. Could he have used this friendship as an aid, and have stolen the Magic while on some secret visit? It was improbable that Dee-nay' would permit the old To-to'-me, even though he was an outcast, to enter Ah'-co. It seemed strange that, after all, the Magic should be in a little bag, for it was the question regarding the bag that so angered Tso. Strange, too, that it was by the merest accident that he had thus been led to the discovery that the Magic was in the old man's possession. Certainly the great Joho'-na-ai was guiding him on his mission.

Placing the ring back into the pouch, he tied it securely on the inside of his belt, and moved cautiously to the door of the cliff dwelling. After listening carefully for some time without hearing a sound, he looked out on the wide ledge that ran in front of the entrance. All was quiet, and as there was no one in sight, he dropped down on his hands and knees and crawled out to the edge of the shelf.

Looking below, he saw that the country beneath him was of barren hills with few trees or bushes large enough to afford any shelter if he were forced to elude a pursuer in the darkness of night. Trails seemed to run along every level. Off to the west rose the To-to'-me mesa, and the little stream that led out to it sparkled in the sunlight. To go westward, toward the Nag'-a-pah camp over the foothills was plainly impossible, as the great shoulder of the mountain that had hidden his view westward when he had stood in front of old Tso's cave, jutted out into the foothills and finally broke downward in flat vertical walls of rock that could not be passed except by dropping down to a point that would bring him too near the To-to'-me camp.

It was plain that if he was to get to the Nag'-a-pah country from where he now stood, he would have to go straight out into the desert and make a three days' journey over a long, circuitous route before he could get to the farther side of the To-to'-me mesa and on across the plains to his own camp. If he was pursued after he got into the desert, he might have to outrun his enemies and thus make a still greater circle before he could get to Ah'-co. He would need a three-days' supply of food for emergency, and water enough for a day at least, as it would require more than that time to get around to Mat-a-wee, the lake that lay near the head of the Nag'-a-pah canyon. Perhaps his best plan would be to take such food as he could from time to time and cache it in the secret passage: thus he would not deprive the old To-to'-me, nor arouse his suspicions.

As he leaned over, scanning the hills below, a party of To-to'-mes suddenly rounded a point on a trail some distance below. He jumped back instantly, but not before the quick eye of one of the men had seen him. A moment later he was in the cliff dwelling, and again seated in the upper passage with the section of poles secure beneath him. Here he waited a long time in silence, but he heard no sound of anyone approaching the entrance of the ruin. Doubtless the distance from the To-to'-mes up to the point where he had crouched on the rocks was so great that the man who had seen him had failed to note the particular ledge.

After waiting a little longer in silence, he arose and made his way up the passage to the now familiar shelf above. As he came to the last incline that led out of the entrance at the edge of the cliff, he cautiously raised his head to see if the old To-to'-me was in sight; but seeing that the trail was clear, he was about to step out of the passage when his eye caught a moving object in a clearing on top of the highest foothill far below. "A To-to'-me guarding one of the lower trails," thought Kay'-yah, as he quickly moved over to avoid being seen. Then he stepped out on the shelf and was soon in the cave.

Tso had not returned during his absence, as the spear and bow-case were still missing. Going to the curve in the ledge outside, Kay'-yah looked quickly along the shelf, to make sure that the old man was not in sight, then running back into the cave he swung the buffalo skull to one side and removed the stone from the hole containing the object of his long search. With heart beating high with excitement, he ran his hand into the opening and drew out a little bag of deerskin. It seemed too soft and round to contain anything like the little magic bear of turquoise. Opening the mouth that was held together by a draw-string of sinew, he hastily examined the contents. The pouch seemed to be filled with a kind of ground stone or earth. Pouring a little of it into his hand, he found it to be a reddish-brown powder that gave off a pungent odor like that from ground seed or bark. Disappointed by the unexpected discovery, he again put his hand into the hole but found it contained nothing more.

With a feeling of bewilderment and dismay he closed the little bag and restored it to its place. Then fitting the stone into the opening, he slid the buffalo head down over it. The great white skull seemed to grin down at him as if enjoying his disappointment.

Walking to the cave's entrance, he leaned against the stone doorway and tried to straighten out the perplexing tangle that now confronted him. All of his high hopes for immediate possession of the Magic were gone. Was it all a misunderstanding with the old To-to'-me, and was it this worthless brown powder that Tso had referred to as the Magic? Was it this bag behind the skull that he had supposed Kay'-yah wanted when he had inquired about the one he had lost the night of his arrival on the ledge?

He now remembered that as Tso had mumbled over the bag as he watched him from the floor in pretended sleep, he had said, "What can the young fox know of the magic sleep?" This brown powder was probably some kind of strong medicine used by medicine-men to make sleep. He decided that he would frankly ask the old man if he knew anything about the little blue bear, the great Magic of the Nag'-a-pahs. If Tso's anger had, as it now seemed, been aroused by the fear of losing the little bag of powder, it was probable that he knew nothing about the lost Magic.

Still puzzled by the unlooked-for discoveries that he seemed to be making at every turn, he walked out around the projection in the ledge, and crouched down where he could see the remaining length of the path that lay along the shelf. All was as silent as death. The whole mountain seemed to be wrapped in slumber. Small swarms of tiny gnats danced up and down in the bright sunshine, and a lone buzzard glided in great wide circles in the blue dome overhead. A wave of homesickness swept over Kay'-yah and he wished that he could walk into the familiar medicine lodge of Ah'-co and tell Dee-nay' of his many strange experiences, and of the many puzzling things that the wise old man could doubtless explain.

Then suddenly the silence was broken by the angry voice of a To-to'-me, who seemed to be just below the ledge, and the unmistakable voice of Tso replying to it. He leapt to his feet and ran along the ledge toward the point where the men seemed to be. Arriving above them, he stopped and leaned over the edge of the cliff as far as he dared without losing his balance. About fifty feet below him stood Tso facing a To-to'-me who stood with drawn bow, the arrow pointing at the old man's breast.

"Show me the trail! Show me the trail, or I will send you to the death!" commanded the warrior, the deadly calm in whose voice left no doubt that he meant what he said.

The old man was slowly backing up the trail; but he had been caught unawares, as no arrow was fitted to the bow that he held in his hand, and the man was too far away from him to permit him to make any use of his spear.

Jumping back, Kay'-yah found a stone about the size of his head, and stepping again to the edge of the shelf he took careful aim and drove the rock downward. As it crashed into the To-to'-me's arms it splintered the bow and arrow on the rocks beneath, and bounded out to the level below. An instant later the spear of the old man had done its work. Then, as Kay'-yah watched from above, he was surprised to see the old To-to'-me raise the foot that was fitted with the bear's paw, and with a scratching blow like that of a real bear, drive a deep mark across the breast of the lifeless warrior who lay on the rocks below him. Then picking up the body he carried it down to the edge of the next cliff beneath him and tossed it, as though it were a stick of wood, out into the depths below.

Realizing that in his present excited condition Tso might be very angry if he now stood and waited for him to come up, and thus be forced to disclose his secret of the hidden passage, Kay'-yah went back to the curve in the ledge and with body hidden behind the projection in the cliff, lay flat to the ground, with one eye still on the trail that led along the shelf.

He waited for a long time, and had about decided that the old To-to'-me must have gone back down his trail a little way, to make sure that no other spies were following him, when suddenly he felt as though he must be losing his reason as he gazed wide-eyed at the strange spectacle before him.

Slowly and silently the end of the great pine log that lay along the edge of the trail some distance from him, rose into the air, and then moved a little to one side. Then, from where he lay, it looked as though the whole end of the ledge were rising as the log began to lower again and the great flat-topped rock under which the tree was anchored tilted up at a sharp angle and slid inward toward the cliff. As the rock moved from its place he realized that it was the ingenious covering that had hidden the opening to the secret passage; and he moved backward out of sight just as the white head of old Tso arose above the ledge.

Figure 18

Tale of the Tribe, Relating the legends and magic by the oral tradition, Photo by Carl Moon

Chapter 9
The Magic Sleep

The arrows of Tso are straight and long;—
Woe to the foe at whom they are sped.—
For the medicine known to Tso is strong,
And the arrows are dipped in Witch-dyed red!

BELIEVING that the occurrence which had just taken place beneath the cliff might so excite the old man as temporarily to throw him from his mental balance, and into a condition in which he would not be accountable for his actions, Kay'-yah wisely decided to pretend, for the moment, that he had not taken any part in, nor even witnessed, the encounter with the To-to'-me spy. So as his aged host entered the cave he found him busily engaged in mending a thong on one of his moccasins. He did not look up until Tso had set his spear against the wall and had hung his bow and arrow case on its accustomed peg; then, as Kay'-yah saw that he still had something that looked like small game of some kind suspended by a thong from his shoulder, he quietly asked;

"Has good hunting come to your bow today?"

"So good a shot as Tso carries good hunting with him always," came the reply as the old man threw a large duck and some rabbits to the floor. "The squawking flat-bill flew high and fast but not so swift as the arrow that went up to meet him."

"I too can shoot," ventured Kay'-yah, "and would try my arm with the very good bow you have."

"My bows are for a strong arm and an eye that has judgment," replied the old man, "but you may try."

It was now evident that Tso was not excited; in fact, he seemed both calm and even happy. Stepping over to where it hung upon the wall, Kay'-yah drew the bow from its case and after selecting two arrows stepped out on the ledge, followed by his aged host.

He spent a moment admiring the arrows, as they were not only beautifully made but half of each shaft was stained a brilliant red. He smiled as the thought came to him – "The red arrows of the bear-witch!" – of which he had often heard. He fitted one to the string and drew it back and forth, delighted to find that his strength was sufficient to bend the strong elastic wood far enough to send the arrow the distance of a long bowshot. Far down the mountain side a crow sunned himself on a jutting crag, and far above the crow, a long bowshot from where they stood, a sparrow-hawk watched the hills below from the blackened limb of a dead bush.

"The hook-bill is too far for your arm," said the old man; but paying no heed to the remark, Kay'-yah drew the bow with all his strength and let the arrow fly. At the twang of the string the pointed missile flew on an errand that proved fatal for the hawk, who half spread his wings as if for flight, then tumbled limply into the rocks below.

At the splendid shot a grunt of approval escaped Tso, but he said:

"The boy with his first bow may have good luck with his first shot. The crow still sleeps on the rock and you have another arrow."

The last word had scarcely been spoken before the second shaft sped on its way to awaken the crow.

"The kaw has had his last sleep," said Kay'-yah simply, as the crow, pierced where he sat, now lay a black spot on the crag.

For a few moments after the last shot, which, owing to the crow's position below them, was far more difficult than the longer shot at the hawk, the old man stood in silence as the almost childish pride in his own skill with the bow struggled against giving Kay'-yah praise for the exceptional skill he had shown. Then without a word he hobbled back into the cave and brought out a bow that had been leaning against the wall, and handing it to Kay'-yah, said:

"The bows that are made by Tso send the arrows straight to the mark. This is yours. You shoot as though I might have taught you – and none shoot better than Tso."

Then in a more kindly voice than Kay'-yah had heard him use before, he continued:

"One who can unarm a To-to'-me dog with a rock, and can draw a good bow will not become a poor warrior."

Kay'-yah's face beamed with delight at finding himself in possession of the beautiful bow he had admired so much, but at the unexpected compliment and mention of the rock that had disarmed Tso's antagonist, he suddenly became too confused to make immediate reply. Finally he said:

"I am made glad by the gift, for my eyes have not seen a better bow."

"It will bring good hunting to you," remarked the old man, "for it has slain the buffalo, the bighorn, the black mountain-cat, the wolf, and has brought the eagle out of the clouds – but all by the hand of Tso."

"I hope it may do as well for me," replied Kay'-yah. "But," he added after a moment's reflection, "I would not draw it against the eagle, for it is the sacred bird of the Nag'-a-pahs."

"At the end of a day, just before the Sun-god went to sleep beyond the desert," said the old man, "the lion was hunting in the deep canyon near to the Nag'-a-pah camp, and he saw an eagle rise up from the canyon mouth and circle wide and high and higher, far beyond the bowshot of all men but Tso. Then I said to the arrow upon my bowstring, 'Go up swift as the arrow of light that is shot by the Thunder-god before he roars from the black storm-cloud, and bring down the big bird, that I may have his tail feathers for my prayer-sticks, his wing feathers for my arrows, and his sharp claws for strong medicine.' So I sent the arrow, and the eagle screamed as he tumbled down and down, but he fell to earth beyond a little hill and I ran to pick him up before darkness should come to hide him from my eyes. Beyond the hill stood a little Nag'-a-pah girl, and when I came to her the eagle lay dead at her feet. She was angry with great anger, like the cat that is caught in the hanging trap, and she shook her arms and hands at me and in To-to'-me language called me by new names that I would not like to keep."

The old man stopped to grin broadly and chuckled beneath his breath.

"She said the eagle belonged to her father," he continued. "And if I took it she would scratch the eyes from my head so I could see to shoot no more eagles."

As Tso lapsed into silence Kay'-yah asked:

"Did the little girl keep the eagle?"

"Yes," replied Tso. "I laughed at her, which made her the more angry, and I said to her, 'You may keep the eagle for strong medicine to keep the Shin-di and old To-to'-mes away.' Then she said, 'If it will keep a To-to'-me away it will keep the Shin-di away, for they are alike.'" Then after a moment's pause he continued, "But Tso has shot many, many eagles, for none can escape the arrow that goes from my bow."

As he finished the account he laughed his low laugh that somehow added to his extravagant boast.

As the two now returned to the cave, the old man searched among the bundle of skins that hung against the wall, and brought forth a bow-case of panther-skin, and remarked as he handed it to Kay'-yah:

"The bow should have a good place to sleep when it is not hunting."

As there were a number of good arrows in the quiver of the case, Kay'-yah felt the strong call of the hunter rise joyously within him as he slipped his bow into its place, and he felt elated with the thought that he was now armed once more without having to steal a weapon from his old benefactor, for whom a strong friendship was beginning to grow up in his heart. Without looking at Tso he remarked:

"Some day the Rain-boy may find a time when he can give gifts to Tso."

"The Lion has all things; he has need for nothing," said the old man, but his voice and the expression of his face betrayed the pleasure Kay'-yah's remark had given him. "The Lion saved the Rain-boy when he fell from the cliff. The Rain-boy drove the rock at the To-to'-me arrow that was aimed at the heart of the Lion. The Earth mother gives help to you through me that she might give help to me through you." Thus reminded of the To-to'-me spy he continued: "The dogs have followed Tso many times, and always they are sent to the long sleep with the mark of the bear-witch on their skin. The mark is strong medicine, and when the other To-to'-me dogs find the one that sleeps they have great fear and say, 'He is killed by the bear-witch!' It is always a long time before another dog finds the trail of Tso and dares to follow."

Then dropping his voice to a low tone, as if talking to himself, he continued:

"But the old Lion has left the time of his youth far back on the trail of other days, and his eyes do not always see with quickness the dog upon his track."

Waiting for some time after Tso had ceased speaking, Kay'-yah decided that the old man's present humor made it an opportune time to ask him the question that had been uppermost in his mind since his discovery of the bag behind the skull.

"Have you ever heard of the little bear of blue stone, the great Magic of the Nag'-a-pahs?" he boldly asked.

"No," replied Tso; "what should the Lion know of a blue bear? Let my ears hear what you have to tell of it."

"It has been lost to the Nag'-a-pahs for many seasons," said Kay'-yah; "and it is the little bear that Dee-nay' has sent me out to find."

The old man was silent for some time as he turned the matter over in his mind. "I found you without weapons when you fell over the cliff, but I now can see that you had no need of them if you hunt for a bear of stone. Then Dee-nay' has not sent you for the magic sleep?"

"I know nothing of the magic sleep," replied Kay'-yah; "but I must find the great Magic, the blue bear, and return it to my people."

"There is a way to find whatever is lost, and Tso may tell you of the way, sometime," he mumbled.

Then, as though he had been speaking of Dee-nay', he continued;

"Yes, the old eagle of the Nag'-a-pahs is a great medicine-man. If a bear should swallow down his throat all the witches of the mountain and spirits of the desert, he would yet have less wisdom in his stomach than is in the head of Dee-nay'. When Tso, the Lion fell down, down from the cliffs, down from fighting the dogs of Ta-pau'-wee, Dee-nay' found me in the hills when memory of all things had gone from my head, and he gave me the strong medicine of sleep, and food for strength. Then I showed him some of the blue sand for the sky painting, the painting of much magic for the medicine lodge, and Dee-nay' was glad with much happiness that he might have it, for none but Tso knows of the little sky-blue sand that is left in the mountain. When Dee-nay' left the Lion with food and weapons, summer came and camped in the hills and on the desert. Then the Earth mother led the wounded Lion to find the secret ledge, and brought him to the cave that has been his den. No one but the Lion knew of it until you fell from the mountain top with no weapons to fight the Lion, so the Lion knew you came from the Earth mother.

"Many, many suns after Dee-nay' had gone, and the summer had run away from the north winds that came roaring over the mountain, the Lion said within himself that he would go westward to the canyon of the Nag'-a-pahs that he might again see Dee-nay'. One night when the white powder of winter was over the face of the Earth mother, the Lion took a bag of the sky-blue sand and turned his face toward Ah'-co. In the early night as the Lion watched, two Nag'-a-pah men walked home from hunting, and their feet fell soft in the white powder along the wall near the canyon's mouth. One man was Dee-nay'; but the Lion made no sound, for he must see the Nag'-a-pah eagle alone. Then as the two walked on beyond Tso, three To-to'-me dogs jumped from the darkness of the rock shadows, and the man with Dee-nay' fell with a To-to'-me arrow in his back. Then the Lion growled with the loud growl of the bear and his arrow sent one dog, then another to his last sleep. The other To-to'-me ran with great fear in his heart. But Dee-nay' stood still as a stone on the mountain, for he knew the growl of the bear and was glad in his heart that Tso was there to shoot with great skill. Then he called to the Lion, 'I will give to you a bag of great magic, the magic sleep, and when the bag is empty come with it to the Nag'-a-pah shrine beneath the cliffs and leave it beneath the stone of the altar. When the next moon is new in the west you will come and find it filled beneath the Thunder-rock of Ah'-co.'

"Then Tso gave Dee-nay' the sky-blue sand he had brought, and Dee-nay' was made glad. With his hand on the shoulder of the Lion, he said, 'The gods give justice for justice. You have saved Dee-nay' from the long sleep, because you were given life and strength from the hand of Dee-nay'. The sky-blue sand comes to the Nag'-a-pahs and the bag of magic sleep goes to the home of Tso. So be it!' Then he was gone and the Lion found the two To-to'-me dogs lying in the white powder of the winter and he left the mark of the bear-witch upon them. When the Lion came again at night to the Nag'-a-pah shrine, he found the bag of magic sleep beneath the Thunder-rock. So it has been each time of the cold, when summer has gone, Tso takes the sky-blue sand and brings back the magic sleep."

At the end of Tso's long account, Kay'-yah felt a renewed fondness for this queer old man who had saved the life of Dee-nay' and proved himself to be a friend to be trusted. Then he told of his own experience as a captive in the To-to'-me camp: but when he came to the account of his fight with Wau-ko'-ma Tso suddenly rose with a growl in his throat, and with clenched hands repeated he again and again the name of Wau-ko'-ma. Then sitting down again, he frowned deeply, as if to regain some lost memory, and struck his forehead with his open hand several times as he spoke the name over and over again. Thus interrupted in his account, Kay'-yah stopped and tried to think of some way to aid the old man in his mental search for some forgotten event.

"Enough, Rain-boy!" commanded Tso at last. "Say no more the name Wau-ko'-ma; it makes the Lion's head to roar and he cannot think."

Changing the subject, Kay'-yah remarked:

"Since my people have lost their great Magic, much trouble has come upon us. Hunting in the canyon is good no more, as the upper waters have ceased to flow, so that the animals come no longer for their drink. The lake Mat-a-wee gives us but enough to drink and not the great waters as it did long ago. The little stream of Ah'-co is not large enough for our fields of grain, and the green fields at the desert's edge have turned to the brown and the dust of thirst. Many prayers have gone up from the medicine lodge and big ceremonies have been made to the god of the waters, but still he holds the water in his fist and but few drops come through for the Nag'-a-pahs."

The old man looked up with keen interest during Kay'-yah's account, and when he had finished he slowly nodded his head as he remarked:

"I know, I know, and the Lion can make the great water again to flow toward the Nag'-a-pahs."

"Do you mean there is a way to make the water to flow again down through our canyon? All the strong medicine of Dee-nay' has not been able to do that, and are you wiser than Dee-nay'?"

The old To-to'-me laughed his deep, quiet laugh.

"Dee-nay' knows all about great medicine, and Tso knows something too. It is not Magic that will make the waters to flow."

Then after a long silence he continued:

"When you have returned to Dee-nay', and there are none with you to hear, tell him the Lion has said that before many suns have risen and set much water will begin to flow down the stream of Ah'co."

"I will bear your message," said Kay'-yah; but in his heart he felt there was little hope of the fulfillment of the old man's promise.

"You have said that there is a way by which lost things are found," said Kay'-yah; "and as I must find that which is lost, I would have your counsel, for you have lived long and the Earth mother has taught you many things."

The old To-to'-me bowed his head on his hand and remained silent for a long time. Then, making wide gestures with his arms, as if to emphasize his remarks, he began:

"Between the great land of the Sky people above and the face of the Earth mother beneath, is Wah'-ma-ha, the finding spirit of the air. There is no place where the air spirit does not go; nothing he does not see; nothing he does not hear, and he knows where all the lost things hide from the eyes of men. When the wind, which is the strong breath of Wah'-ma-ha, blows over the face of the earth, he tells of many things. He tells of the cold before the winter comes; of warmth before the summer is here, and he tells us of the smell of rain from far away; the smell of the campfire and of food that is not seen, and gives to the nose of the animal brothers the smell of men while men are far off. With great medicine I will bring Wah'-ma-ha to you, that he may tell you where your lost Magic may be found."

Rising from the floor, he took from the wall the bags of powdered earth paint and colored sands, and after clearing a large space on the floor with an eagle-wing brush, he knelt down and began the outline of two ceremonial pictures. In less time than Kay'-yah would have believed it possible to do it, he had made a small, well-drawn painting of the earth and sky symbols. The sky god was of the powdered blue sands whose hiding-place was known only to Tso, and on its smooth surface the snow-white stars and constellations of pipe clay shone brilliantly. The earth goddess was of brown earth paint, and from the center toward the four cardinal points ran well-made sprigs of the green corn, the vine of the bean, the leaves of tobacco, and the wandering tendrils of the melon.

Rising from the floor, the old man moved the buffalo skull to one side, this time without making any attempt to hide his movements, and bringing forth the little bag, dropped a pinch of the coveted powder into a small earthen bowl, and after making a little fire of sticks he poured some water into the bowl and set it on the flames.

Figure 19
"He Stopped In Front Of Kay'-Yah And,
Shaking The Rattle And Prayer-Stick He Chanted His Song"

Kay'-yah watched the proceedings with mild interest. Such things were not new to him. As the friend and pupil of Dee-nay', he had often watched the old man prepare for strange ceremonies in the medicine lodge of Ah'-co. But something within him, something that he had never voiced to others, always spoke against the idea that any power or virtue could come of incantations, weird chants, and sand paintings. His morning prayers to the Great Spirit, Joho'-na-ai, always left him with the thought of one great power, and that all help for the earth children against evil spirits must come from Him who would teach them justice and bravery and honesty. So he thought indulgently of old Tso's serious performance, and decided it was best to permit him to have his own way. Within his heart he knew that if he was to find the lost Magic it must be by his own efforts and the guidance of Joho'-na-ai and not through the powers of the strange gods of the old man who stood before him.

After a short time Tso removed the bowl from the fire, and placing a small skin mat between the two sand paintings on the floor, motioned for Kay'-yah to be seated upon it. Then taking a ceremonial rattle in one hand and a feathered prayer-stick in the other, he stood above him and began a low weird song or chant, to which the slowly shaken rattle kept perfect time. The chant was of the mountain; of the desert; the clouds and the stars; of praise for the gods and a curse against the witches and ghosts of the famine and sickness; of drouth and raging storms.

After the song had run along monotonously for some time he stopped and, after testing the potion in the bowl and finding it cool enough to swallow, he held it to Kay'-yah's lips with the command to drink. When he had taken what seemed to be the required amount the bowl was again placed upon the floor and the ceremony continued. Now the old man began to hobble around and around the painted floor, continuing his weird song in a higher key as he bent his body low to the ground or rose straight with his great arms shaking above his head.

Suddenly he stopped in front of Kay'-yah and, shaking the rattle and prayer-stick just above his head, he chanted his song:

"Wah'-ma-ha, Wah'-ma-ha,
God of the night-wind,
God of the day-wind,
Come to my calling, blow in upon him:
Come with your knowing, quickly to tell him,
Tell of the place where the lost thing is hidden.
Come to his nostrils, into his breathing;
Carry the message that he may know it.
Wah'-ma-ha, Wah'-ma-ha,
Out of the cloud land,
Out of the desert,
Down from the mountain —
Up — through — the — c-a-n-y-o-n —"

The last words trailed out and grew faint in Kay'-yah's ears, and the voice of Tso seemed far away. The figure of the old man grew dim and small; quivered like an image of smoke in waves of heat, and disappeared.

He felt himself floating away somewhere; far beyond the mountain and the desert, and the floating and flying were so natural he thought how foolish for men to walk and run when flying was so much easier.

Then he seemed to hear the soft familiar steps of little feet on a mountain trail, and he looked up into the eyes of Sah'-ne. A sad smile was on her lovely face and she was saying something, something he could not quite hear. He leaned closer to her that he might catch her words. Then faintly they came to his ears:

"But I am To-to'-me – and you do not like that; you do not like that."

Figure 20
Navajo Medicine Man, Meguelito, Photo by Carl Moon

Figure 21
Native American cultures believe everyone has a birth totem that incorporates elements of their personality and individual characteristics.
Photo by Timothy Beckley."

Chapter 10
Sah'-Ne In The "Eagle's Nest"

The sun sinks low in the burning west;
O, the trail is steep from the rock to plain;
But the time has come for the final test;
The trail is steep from the rocky crest,
But leads toward home again.

THE trail to the To-to'-me camp seemed long to Sah'-ne, and the two men Dee-nay' had sent as guard were silent as shadows. She was glad when the high mesa on which Ta-pau'-wee was situated came into view, though the trail leading to its summit looked steep and she was very weary.

She spoke to the two men.

"Return now to Dee-nay'. From here I go alone. The trails may be guarded."

The men turned without a word and retraced their steps back in the direction from which they had come.

The sun was low in the west and threw the rock walls of the To-to'-me mesa into golden relief against the purple shadows of the mountain that rose beyond. Sah'-ne looked, and stood still. Her heart beat fast within her. There lay the place where she had been born; the home of her own people – and she came to it as a spy to steal its secrets! The thought was bitter, and yet why should she have love for a people of whom she had heard much evil and little good. The Nag'-a-pahs had been kindly when they had thought her one of themselves: and perhaps again, when she had proven where her heart lay, they would have smiles for her. And a new thought brought the blood to her cheeks – was Kay'-yah captive in that mesa town and would the gods give it into her hands to deliver him? But, if he were dead – if they had killed him as a spy – then she too would follow, if need be, the same trail. But first there was work to do. And she again started forward with her eyes lifted to her journey's end.

She did not see a man step out from the shadow of a large boulder on the trail in front of her and wait silently for her approach. She did not see him until she had almost reached him, and then she stood still with a sharp intake of breath. Another man stood close to the boulder, and she knew them for To-to'-mes. Fear flashed into her heart, but she closed her thought to it. Here was no place or time for fear. The man spoke before she had breathed twice;

"Why is a Nag'-a-pah woman on the trail of the To-to'-mes?" He spoke in poor Nag'-a-pah but she answered him in his own tongue. Her heart beat fast but her voice was steady with the words.

"I am no Nag'-a-pah. I am To-to'-me. Take me to Tag-a'-mo."

"Wau-ko'-ma is our chief," answered Ha-wal'-li, for it was he.

"But it is Tag-a'-mo I would see," said Sah'ne.

"Your words are strange for a captive. A captive follows at the word of him who has captured. Why do you say you are To-to'-me? You have the look of a Nag'-a-pah and have never been seen among my people." Ha-wal'-li's words were not without kindness but there was incredulity in his voice.

"I have proof," said Sah'-ne, "but my proof is for Dis'-din alone."

"Dis'-din!" And Ha-wal'-li now spoke with amazement. "Dis'-din! What know you of Dis'-din?"

Sah'-ne looked at him and there was a speechless pleading in her eyes.

"I am very weary – the trail is long from Ah'co. Take me to Dis'-din or to Tag-a'-mo and I will prove my words."

Ha-wal'-li stood for a moment in thought.

"If you speak true and are in truth To-to'-me I will take you to Tag-a'-mo. But we may not go by the main trail – the dogs will howl, for you have the look of a Nag'-a-pah – but there is another trail. Look you, Chaz'-pah," – he spoke to the other man – "guard this woman until I return."

And again he spoke to Sah'-ne:

"I will bring my sister and she will make you look To-to'-me. It will be better so."

Sah'-ne nodded gratefully, and Ha-wal'-li set off up the trail in a swinging run.

A great wave of homesickness rushed over Sah'ne that night, as she lay in a strange hogan on a couch of hides. All had gone well; she had been received by these people as one of themselves. The word she had spoken into Dis'-din's ear had proved beyond all doubt that she was the daughter of his sister, who had been wife to Gō'-me, the spy, and she had been welcomed into a family of cousins of whose existence she had never known before this day – Ha-wal'-li among them. She had explained easily and clearly why it was that she had, until now, remained with the Nag'-a-pahs, that she had thought herself one of them until the death of her father five summers before, and that since then she had been made very unhappy among them and had gradually thought more and more of her own people until she could no longer stay away from them.

She had been received with kindness and many questions by the girls who surrounded her, their eyes dwelling in wonder on her strange ornaments and unfamiliar garments. And she had been brought to this hogan with its soft skins and mats and many curious articles, and here, among her cousins, she was to have a home. It was all as she had wished, even better than she had really expected, and yet her heart ached within her. She had heard no word of Kay'-yah nor of the Magic, and an old hag, who sat outside of the hogan and stirred a pot, watched her with deep-sunken, suspicious eyes; eyes that burned into her consciousness and followed her and haunted her. Could the woman read her secret thoughts?

Sah'-ne lay with sleepless eyes staring up at the smoke-hole in the hogan roof until the stars grew pale and the dark blue of the sky gave place to purple and then to pink and her weary eyes closed in restless slumber as the sun rose.

She awoke to the sound of low voices, and rose on one elbow to see who the speakers were. It was broad daylight now and she could see clearly every object in the hogan, but there was no one there. The hide at the doorway blew slowly back and forth in a gentle wind, and it was from there the voices came. At first she gave little heed to the words, but soon was startled into close attention and rose from a sitting posture silently to her feet and crept toward the doorway. A woman's voice spoke and the words were in a low whine.

"A great chief will not take the words of an old woman, but I have lived long and seen much. It may not be as I have said, but a maid – a maid who is fair of face – can deceive the very gods and may well deceive such as Tag-a'-mo and Dis'-din."

"Hush!" said a man's voice. "The maid will hear."

"Not she!" continued the woman. "She sleeps as one dead and will not wake until the sun is many hands high."

"You say the girl is fair?" again spoke the man.

A high cackle, evidently meant for a laugh, came in reply.

"The very words can draw even Wau-ko'-ma. But wait – you shall see her for yourself."

Sah'-ne drew back hastily from the doorway and sank again on her couch of skins. Wau-ko'-ma, chief of the To-to'-mes, was standing without, and the other, she had no doubt, was the old hag whose eyes had haunted her. There was a throbbing in her brain; what could the words mean? Was she suspected? What had the old woman said before her ears had been awake to the voices? And were they now coming in? She sank as low as possible in the couch and drew the skins about her, but they did not enter. There were a few more low words which she did not catch and then silence – had they gone?

She lay for what seemed a long time on the skins, listening. At first there was no more sound, but presently she heard a crackling of burning sticks and a thin, old voice began to croon. A weird air it was and spoke of the desert just before the dawn, when the black, silent night fades into a gray ghost of itself and flies, moaning, away. The words came in a little while – words that were far apart like the mesquite bushes in the sand and called to one another across the spaces:

"O – ee – the wind blows cold;
O – ee – the night is old.
The shadows wake,
And the pinyons shake
In the grip of the night-wind bold.

O – ee – the dawn is near;

O — ee — my heart knows fear:
For the secrets of night
Are seen in the light
When the ghost of dawn is here."

The voice broke off in a loud cackle and repeated again:

"The secrets of the night – he – he – the secrets."

Sah'-ne rose from her couch and walked to the doorway; she drew aside the hide curtain and spoke to the old woman, who bent over a pot of steaming mixture.

"Where are my cousins?"

The old face looked up and the eyes were inscrutable.

"There is ceremony today at the place of the flat rock; they are there. You would not like such ceremony; our gods are not Nag'-a-pah gods and their ways are strange to you, but we have Magic." She cackled again. "Oh, yes, we have Magic." And her eyes grew dark and keen as she watched Sah'-ne's face.

Sah'-ne was troubled and knew not what to say; the suspicions of the old woman might be founded on mere guesswork, but how near they came to knowledge she could not tell. Her work must be done quickly if she was to escape with her life. She spoke again.

"I have heard that the To-to'-me Magic is strong – I am glad, for I am To-to'-me also."

The old eyes of the woman were shrewd and cold as she regarded Sah'-ne for a moment before she again spoke.

"The dawn-wind comes from the land of those who know, and has spoken to Chu'-nah," she said.

"Your words sound strange to me," said Sah'ne. "What is it that you know?"

The woman seemed to draw within herself as a turtle does, and answered shortly:

"More than I will tell."

"Enough!" said Sah'-ne, and her word was a command. All fear of this old crone had suddenly left her; what she knew or what she did not know mattered little, as she could prove nothing. "Speak more pleasantly to me or Dis'-din shall hear of your words; I am of his people and have given proof. The word was for Dis'-din and not for you." Sah'-ne spoke without anger though she had had sufficient cause for it.

The old woman dropped her head, and her voice was again the whine that Sah'-ne had heard on first awakening.

"I am an old woman; my words mean nothing. Do not speak to Dis'-din; my tongue shall say no more."

Sah'-ne walked away from the hogan without one backward glance for the eyes that still watched with unsatisfied suspicion. She spoke to her cousins that day of the old woman.

"Why does she stay about the hogan – her ways are not pleasant and her tongue is sharp."

One of the girls answered her with a light laugh;

"Oh, do not mind Chu'-nah. She is old and means but half of what she says. She has been nurse for each one of us and it would break her heart to be sent away from the hogan."

And Sah'-ne said no more.

Days passed and she now knew for a certainty that the Magic was not in the To-to'-me camp. She had heard of Kay'-yah's escape but thought him dead, though she knew guards were still placed on the many trails for his possible capture. She had seen Wau-ko'-ma many times, and his bold eyes haunted her even more than did those of the old woman who had not spoken again but whose enmity she felt. Of Wau-ko'-ma she had heard strange things, and when she had spoken of him to her cousin Dez'-pah, Dez'-pah had put her finger to her lips and looked cautiously about to be sure her words were not overheard.

"Speak that name with caution, Sah'-ne. There are strange things about to happen – so says our father, Dis'-din. Wau-ko'-ma is still, in name, chief of the To-to'-mes, but it is whispered that Tag-a'-mo has all but taken his place. I know not what it means, but we are told to keep our lips closed and our eyes and ears open."

She was now treated as one of the tribe by many and the sense of strangeness had worn away. She and Ha-wal'-li were on the most friendly terms and it was when she was in his presence that her sense of deception most hurt. She had learned all that she possibly could and felt that she could serve no purpose in remaining longer in Ta-pau'-wee; the time for her return to Ah'-co, if such return were possible, was at hand.

The dawn light crept into the hogan and Sah'-ne rose from her couch of skins and stepped lightly to the door. The others lay sleeping and she made no sound as she pushed aside the hide curtain and stepped out. The camp lay silent and she walked swiftly between the hogans, seeing not so much as a dog. At the edge of the mesa she gave one long look at the glorious scene below: the desert painted in the delicate hues that come before the sun, and with a swift glance behind her stepped onto the trail that led downward. There was a low laugh near by – a man's laugh that held in it a deep note of triumph, and she stepped hastily back, trying to conceal herself behind one of the large tumble-weed balls that lay near by. It was Wau-ko'-ma who strode up and looked over the top of the ineffectual hiding-place.

"I *thought* it was the little Nag'-a-pah bird who flew so silently," he said. "What a pity that the hawk was watching. I was told that you worshiped daily at the shrine of the Sun-god; but you are early today. See – he has not yet shown his face above the desert's rim."

"Joho'-na-ai is a great and good light-maker," said Sah'-ne, who was trembling from the surprise of this unwelcome encounter. "Do the To-to'-mes also worship at his shrine?" And she bit her lip at the admission she had made, for instantly there was a gleam in Wau-ko'-ma's eyes and quick came his words:

"The To-to'-mes? – Ah, then your gods are not the To-to'-me gods?"

Sah'-ne was silent and he looked down at her and smiled again, but his smile was not pleasant.

"Come, little bird," he said; "you are too fair to have an arrow in your heart. Sing for Wau-ko'-ma and the painted bars of your cage shall be bound with flowers."

The red flamed into her cheeks.

"Let me go to my hogan – I like not your words," she said.

He still stood over her, but the smile faded from his lips.

"A spy is a spy," he said, and his voice was now harsh. "I will give you until night to decide whether you will have smiles or frowns for Wau-ko'-ma. Today I trap the other Nag'-a-pah."

The blood left her cheeks and she looked up at him with frightened eyes.

"What mean you – is Kay'-yah then alive?"

He frowned as he answered:

"You know this dog? Yes, he is alive – but not for long. He is trapped like a fox in his hole, and no power can save him now from my arrows. Today we hunt him out."

Sah'-ne's face sank into her hands, but she was silent, her thoughts were whirling – what could she do – how keep Wau-ko'-ma here until Kay'-yah could be warned? —

"The hills are hot," she said. "Why hunt on such a day? There are cool hogans in camp and my hands have skill in preparing pleasant food." She looked up with a pitiful attempt at coquetry.

There was amusement in Wau-ko'-ma's face that quickly turned to anger.

"So you would save the Nag'-a-pah!" he said, and his face grew dark. "Tonight you shall have smiles for me or sleep the long sleep, as shall Kay'-yah, with an arrow in your heart – spies are not welcome in Ta-pau'-wee." His voice again changed to mock kindness. "Today Chu'-nah shall watch over the little bird and clip its wings."

Sah'-ne slipped back into the hogan like the caged bird she had been called and lay on the skins with her face in her hands. She knew well that the old hag, Chu'-nah, had been given instructions to keep close watch on her every action, and the gloating triumph in those old eyes stung her like the lash of a whip. She feared to go to Tag-a'-mo or Dis'-din for protection lest their suspicions be aroused. She must fight, but fight in secret and alone.

Her cousins were gay that morning and told her that they were all going to hunt pinyon-nuts in the foothills for the day and would not return until night, when there would be a moon. They were surprised at her refusal to go with them, but she thought that her chances for escape were far better away from them and decided not to leave Ta-pau'-wee.

Through the day she went about her usual tasks with a face which gave no indication of the emotions struggling within her and was asked no questions. She had seen the party, headed by Wau-ko'-ma, leave the camp and knew their cruel purpose, yet she could do nothing. It was now late evening and she stood on the edge of the mesa looking with burning eyes toward the mountain. Was Kay'-yah indeed there and alive, only waiting to be shot to death as the chief had threatened? And she could send no message of warning – nothing. She clenched her hands until they hurt, and all the time was conscious of the watchful eyes at her back – eyes that lost no gesture or movement that she made – eyes that said, as plainly as spoken words, "Your turn next, girl of the Nag'-a-pahs."

She turned fiercely on the old woman.

"Why do you watch me? Do you fear that I will jump from the mesa or injure myself?"

Chu'-nah mumbled something under her breath and pretended occupation with a jar she carried.

"I shall go for water," said Sah'-ne suddenly. "Follow, if you wish, but I shall go down the trail." And taking the jar from the old woman, she drew it to her shoulder and started swiftly down the trail.

Chu'-nah, taken completely off her guard, followed, protesting with every step. She spoke wildly and seemed not to care what her words revealed to Sah'-ne, for she feared to let the girl for a moment out of her sight; and Sah'-ne, unfortunately for Chu'-nah, had chosen a time when there was no one in sight on whom the woman could call for aid.

"It is Wau-ko'-ma's word that you do not go down the trail. If you go beyond my sight I shall give the alarm. There are guards on every trail. The place is steep for me – ai – ee – , the place is steep – " and she stumbled down the path like a witch who has lost her way.

Sah'-ne would have seen humor in the situation had not her mind been busy turning over some possible way of escape before the old woman could give the alarm. The sun had gone and the shadows lay dark in the hills: soon the moon would rise and she felt if she could once get away there would be many hiding-places among the boulders and stunted trees. She must get away before Wau-ko'-ma returned; he was much more to be dreaded than this old woman, who, after all, could not be very strong. She thought of the thong about her water-bottle, but of what use to bind the woman's hands if her mouth was free to cry the alarm. There was a shout in the camp – another, and another! The hunting party had returned.

Had they brought Kay'-yah – or had they left him – she shuddered. And then quick came the thought, "*Now* is the time to go!" And like a deer she sprang down the trail.

The shrill, agonized, "Ai – ee – , ai – ee – , Wau-ko'-ma – come – the Nag'-a-pah, the Nag'-a-pah!" of the old woman followed her but only gave wings to her feet. The cry seemed to go unheeded in the general commotion above. She ran straight down the trail; there was no time to choose a path among the rocks and trees to either side. The shouts of the camp and of the old woman came more and more faintly to her ears and finally died away altogether as she ran on with fast-beating heart but unfaltering speed.

Back on the mesa Chu'-nah, struggling back up the long trail, found her way through the village to Wau-ko'-ma's side.

"The girl has gone — " she gasped. "There – down the trail – toward Ah'-co."

Wau-ko'-ma gave a harsh exclamation and shook her roughly.

"You shall pay for this – you old witch!" he snarled, and threw her from him as he strode swiftly toward the trail.

"Chot'-zu, come!" he called, and as the other came close he spoke in a low voice.

"The Nag'-a-pah girl is gone – she must be brought back! Go – you, and head her off from above the canyon – I go the other way – she cannot escape from such a circle, and we will meet at the clearing this side of the pass. Come! – "

And both men ran swiftly down the trail.

Figure 22
The pottery maker, Nampeyo (painting pottery). (1904?-1910) Gelatin Print by Carl Moon

Chapter 11
"Be'-Ta-Atsin!"

The gods give strength to him who tries;
The tested wings are those that rise.

THE first faint glow of a rosy dawn shone through the cave's entrance as Kay'-yah opened his eyes on the morning after Tso's invocation to the god Wah'-ma-ha. His long night of heavy sleep had left his mind clear and active, and he arose from his bed with the keen joy of youth and strength singing in his heart. He remembered quite clearly all the details of Tso's weird ceremony that had taken place the night before, but now the sand paintings were gone and the cave's floor had its usual appearance. Tso was absent, but he had not been away long, as a little blaze still flickered through the charred sticks upon the fire-stone, and steam lazily rose from the bowls of food that sat on the floor about it.

Kay'-yah took the half-filled water-jar to the ledge outside, and after dashing its cool contents over his hands and face, refilled it at the pool and returned to eat his morning meal.

As he appeased his keen appetite with the crude though appetizing fare of the old To-to'-me, he thought over the events that had occurred since his arrival at the cave, and after forming and rejecting several plans for the immediate future he decided that he would take his leave of Tso just as soon as he learned the best way to go back to Ah'-co. It was not his intention to abandon his search for the Magic, but as he had learned that it was not in the possession of the To-to'-mes, he must now return for Dee-nay's counsel and advice before he could follow any future course of action.

Just as he was finishing, Tso entered and without a word threw his bow-case from his shoulder and stood his spear against the wall. Something in the old man's actions, and in the fact that he had returned so soon after starting on what had apparently been a hunting trip, told Kay'-yah that something unusual had occurred.

The explanation was not long in coming.

"The Lion will stay in his cave while the day is here," remarked Tso. "A pack of the To-to'-me dogs bark around the trails below and look up from the hills like chin-dogs that howl at the moon. So many of them have not hunted the Lion before, but they have not seen him, and shall not find him, for the hearts of the dogs fear the strong medicine of the bear-witch."

"It is me they seek this time," said Kay'-yah. "They had thought I had gone on the long sleep, or escaped to Ah'-co; but a few suns ago a To-to'-me saw me on the cliff, and my mind tells me they know that I am still in the mountain. They come to guard all trails that I may not escape them again."

To this the old man made no reply, but he stepped out on the ledge, followed by Kay'-yah, and rounding the point moved cautiously out to the edge of the cliff near the pool. There, through a wide crack in the rocks, he could look down into the country below with no danger of being seen. After peering downward for some time, he arose, saying as he did so:

"The dogs have made camp in the hills; their smoke rises from two fires, and they will stay by sunlight and starlight that they may starve the Lion from his den. They watch the lower trails and may come up to the cliffs below, but the trail of Tso goes from their sight. Come!" said he, as he motioned Kay'-yah to move along to another point on the edge of the shelf. "From there your eyes will see the wall of a house of the dead. The house is under the rocks on which we stand."

As Kay'-yah obeyed, he looked as directly below as he could, and was surprised to see the outer wall of a cliff dwelling immediately beneath him. Its top came up almost to the edge of the overhanging cliff.

"When the To-to'-me dogs look up from below," said the old man, "the house hides this part of the ledge. The end seems to be where the little shelf comes up that holds the pool. There is no way up to the pool, so the one who comes to find the ledge does not know where to go – and is blind to the Lion's trail."

"The gods of the little people of the cliffs gave them great wisdom," said Kay'-yah, and he thought of the other cliff dwelling from which he had climbed up to the secret opening far around at the other end of the ledge.

"Their gods gave them wisdom," remarked Tso, "but forgot to give them strong medicine against the Shin-di. The witches got them all – all, and sent them on the long sleep."

Then he slowly rocked back and forth as he chanted under his breath;

"Pale witch, black witch,
Strong is the magic:
Strong is the medicine
We weave about us.

Spawn of the spider:
Fang of the she-wolf:
Claw of the bat-wing:
Tooth of the snake:
Mingle thy magic
Well in the weaving.

Pale witch, black witch,
Back to the Shin-di!
Strong is the circle
Woven about us."

When he had finished his chant, Kay'-yah, still wondering about the trail that must be hidden near the house below them, asked:

"Does the house of the Na-ya-kaed' that is beneath us hide your trail?"

"The Lion's trail leads into the house of the dead," replied Tso, "and the To-to'-me dogs fear the house, for the sign of death is upon it and the traces of the bear-witch are about it. They do not know that the Lion's trail leads through the house, and another trail runs by it to a place more pleasing; but if the hearts of the dogs grew brave because of their number, and their wisdom grew enough to tell them the right way up to the ledge, they could not lift the great rock that Tso alone knows how to move."

Kay'-yah remembered his vision of the pine log as it rose into the air, moving the nicely balanced rock to one side, and it now came to his mind that the stout spear doubtless played its part as a lever when the old man came up from the trails below; but he said nothing. It was quite plain that Tso thought the To-to'-mes were after *him*, in spite of the fact that they could not know of his existence except as Doh, the bear-witch, whom they had never seen. Kay'-yah well knew whom the To-to'-mes were after, and that if they tried to get up to the ledge it would be with no thought of finding the dread man-bear.

As the two started back to the cave, he carefully thought the matter over, and deciding that it was no longer necessary to keep his knowledge of the other secret passage from his old friend, he remarked;

"At the other end of this ledge is a way down to the hills below. We may have strong need for its use if our food should all be eaten before the To-to'-mes leave the trails beneath this side of the cliffs. They would not believe that there is a way down at the place where I will show you, for the wall below it is very high and steep, and the passage is hidden within the cliff. Come with me," he continued as they arrived at the cave's entrance, "and I will show it to you."

He walked on toward the secret passage, with Tso looking wonderingly after him as though he suspected that his young companion had lost his reason, but he did not follow.

"Come!" said Kay'-yah. "What I say is true, as your own eyes shall tell you."

Then, with the old man hobbling somewhat reluctantly after him, he went on until he stepped into the passage that led down into the dark crevice below.

"It was through this passage that I came when you first found me. In the crack below are places for the hands and feet, made by the little people of the dead. The way leads down to one of their houses that is on a ledge far below, and from that house I climbed up here that I might escape the To-to'-mes who were on my trail."

To prove his words, Kay'-yah stepped into the dark crevice and climbed downward far enough to pass from the sight of the wondering old man who remained on the ledge above. When he had climbed out again, Tso looked at him incredulously as he slowly nodded his head.

"A way down may be there. I know the house of the dead that is far below us but the steps of the Na-ya-kaed' are not for the crooked feet of Tso. The feet of the little cliff people were small and straight." Then, as they started toward the cave, he continued: "A man climbs up without great trial where he climbs down with labor and great care, for the feet have no eyes for a new trail, and they are not sure of a way that lies in the darkness."

"This way is not a hard one," said Kay'-yah, wishing to assure the old man, "and I am sure you can go down it in safety, for I have been down the passage since I came up, and my feet found the steps without difficulty."

At the last remark Tso suddenly stopped.

"You have been to the hills below since you came up here?" he asked somewhat suspiciously.

"Yes," said Kay'-yah honestly. "I thought you had found the little bag I had lost when I first came here, and I had it in my mind to get it from you and to escape to my country by the way I came, as I thought the bag contained the Magic of the Nag'-a-pahs, but you did not have it, as I found it where I had lost it in the house of the Na-ya-kaed' far below."

Reaching into his belt he brought forth the little bag saying as he did so:

"See, it is here, and shall not be lost again."

At sight of the bag, the old man's face changed as though another being had stepped into his body. It was as if his half-clouded mind had been suddenly cleared of the confused impressions that had often thronged it and obscured his view of the past. Then a look of wonder came into his eyes, and like one who suddenly finds himself in the midst of unfamiliar surroundings, he gazed at his young friend as he would have looked at a stranger. With a growl of rage he grabbed the little bag with one hand as he clutched at Kay'-yah's throat with the other.

"Thief, thief!" he cried. "You stole it! Who are you? Where is the Yaz-yah? Speak! Or you shall never speak again."

Astounded by the insult and the unlooked-for actions of his supposed friend, Kay'-yah thrust the hand from his throat as the hot blood leaped to his face.

And now, as he gazed at Kay'-yah, a change more terrible than the first came over the old To-to'-me. As if frozen where he stood, his arms hanging helplessly at his sides, with mouth agape and eyes staring wildly from his ashen face, he looked as though some hidden terror had stricken his vitals with a mortal wound. The helpless jaws moved as though to speak, but no sound came from his throat. Then, as though he were wrenching himself free from some terrible spell that bound him, he suddenly turned and with great arms upraised, fled along the ledge shouting as he ran:

"Be'-ta-atsin, be'-ta-atsin, be'-ta-atsin!"

Dazed by the strange sight he had just witnessed, a spectacle that had driven all thought of anger from his heart, Kay'-yah followed Tso mechanically as the latter ran on around the point in the ledge to the passage that led below. As he reached the curve, and looked along the shelf beyond, he saw the old man frantically lift the end of the heavy log to swing the great rock from the opening. But he exerted too much strength, and the strong arms, as if acting without reason, and rendered still more powerful under the stress of excitement, forced the log upward and beyond its balancing point. The flat rock slid heavily inward, and the big timber, poising for a second on the edge of the opening, crashed downward through the passage below. A cloud of dust arose as the log plunged to the lower ledge, and the mountain walls echoed loudly with the booming noise as it crumbled the stone walls of the ancient dwelling beneath, then rolled outward and tumbled from level to level, loosening rocks and earth as it descended into the depths below.

Down through the cloud of dust the old man plunged, and as Kay'-yah ran to the opening he saw him a short distance below, hobbling over the pile of rocks that now remained where the protecting outer walls of the cliff dwelling had stood. A moment later the old To-to'-me passed out of sight as he sped along the trail, but he continued to shout and mumble to himself as he ran.

Wondering why the mere sight of the little bag should have caused Tso to act as he had, and knowing the danger that confronted the old man if he continued down the trail to any point near the watching To-to'-mes below, Kay'-yah ran to the crack between the rocks near the pool where he could get a wide view of the country beneath. He knew there must be a trail, perhaps more than one, that led northward around the mountain, and thus away from the party of To-to'-mes who were searching for him through the lower cliffs and foothills. Tso would, no doubt, take some secret trail that would skirt the mountain-side; but he had scarcely settled this point in his mind when he saw the old man running along an exposed bit of trail some distance below, and it now appeared that he intended to go directly down to the very hills on which the enemy were camped.

As his eyes searched the country immediately beneath him, he saw a dozen or more To-to'-me men, attracted by the loud noise of the falling log, running upward from a point in the hills just beneath the trail taken by old Tso; but as the rough ground of the mountain-side between them prevented them from seeing each other, he felt like shouting a warning to the old man; but on second thought he realized that such action would be useless. The threatening situation was clear to him. It was evident that Tso had totally lost his reason, and in his mad haste had accidentally, or it might have been intentionally, destroyed the hidden passage and laid its secret bare to all who might now approach the cliff. Worse still, the unarmed old man was running into the very clutches of his enemies.

Why had Tso acted as he had, and why the cry of "be'-ta-atsin," the words used by Tag-a'-mo the night of his captivity in the To-to'-me camp? These questions remained uppermost in his mind, but he could find no answer to them. He was half glad that Tso had taken the little bag with him, as it had caused him enough trouble, and he was tired of the many unanswerable questions concerning it that had arisen to baffle him.

As he watched the old man hobbling from level to level, now disappearing around some slight projection in the mountain-side, then appearing again on a lower section of the zig-zagging trail, he also watched the party of To-to'-mes who were steadily rising into higher ground and would surely meet him.

Although they were still far below, Kay'-yah's keen eyes could distinguish something of the features and build of the To-to'-me men, and he was not greatly surprised to see that they were led by Wau-ko'-ma. Would the To-to'-me chief take Tso captive and return with him to Ta-pau'-wee, or would he hold the old man under guard and continue upward in search for him? Then he suddenly remembered that probably no To-to'-me had seen Tso and lived to describe him to others, and it was not likely that Wau-ko'-ma and his men would associate their idea of Doh, the bear-witch, with the old man.

A moment later he saw the To-to'-mes stop as if in surprise as Tso, on rounding a point that had hidden him from their sight, met them on a level stretch of trail. Slowing his gait a little, the old man hobbled past them, waving one arm back toward the cliff and apparently shouting something to them as he ran. A second later his words came faintly up to Kay'-yah's ears: "He is up there, up there, up there!" For a moment Kay'-yah's heart grew bitter as he realized that Tso had betrayed him into Wau-ko'-ma's hands; but he waited to see what the latter would do. As if rendered speechless by the unexpected sight of a strange old man, having the appearance and tongue of one of their own tribe, the To-to'-mes made no effort to stop him as he hobbled on down the trail and passed out of Kay'-yah's sight around a point below. Then the To-to'-mes started quickly upward again, but had gone but a few steps when Wau-ko'-ma halted them, and after giving some hasty command to one of the men, in whose brutal face and figure Kay'-yah recognized Chot'-zu, the party continued more slowly upward.

At Wau-ko'-ma's word, Chot'-zu slipped back along the trail, fitting an arrow to his bow as he ran. When he had reached the point where Kay'-yah had last seen the fleeing figure of the old man, he carefully drew his bow and let the arrow fly. Kay'-yah could only guess at the probable result of the shot, but rage flared up within him as he witnessed the cowardly act that had been executed at the command of the treacherous young chief, and in spite of Tso's mad actions his former feeling of friendship for the old man returned, and thoughts of his many kindnesses made him long to avenge his death.

Rising quickly, he ran to the passage down which Tso had descended and tried to slide the great flat rock over the opening. He exerted every ounce of his strength, but to no purpose, as he could not move it. Then he climbed down the short passage of twisted steps into the cliff dwelling, now a pile of ruins, and looked about for a pole or piece of wood of some kind that could be used as a lever. There was not a stick of any kind in sight, as Tso had, doubtless long ago, removed all timber that might be used by an attacking enemy. He climbed back to the ledge, and after noting the distance the To-to'-mes would still have to climb before they could reach the passage, he ran on to the cave and threw his bow-case over his shoulder. Then he quickly made a package of dried meat and maize-cake and tied it to his belt. He looked about for a knife but could find none. A stone hammer lay beneath some skins and he thrust it into his girdle, as it might prove a useful weapon.

Then he ran to the secret passage up which he had climbed on the night of his escape from the To-to'-mes, and stepping down into the entrance he leaned over the edge of the cliff and scanned the hills below. In the little clearing on the hill, where he had seen the lone guard once before, now stood three men, and he drew quickly back as he saw they were all gazing up at the cliff. He had just stepped to the ledge again when a spent arrow arched upward in a graceful curve and dropped near his feet.

To go down the passage now was not to be thought of, for even if Wau-ko'-ma and his men were unable to find the upper opening, they would certainly camp in the cave, and the guards below not only knew that he was on the ledge, but they would guard well the shelf below on which the little cliff dwelling stood. If he entered the passage to hide, it would only be a question of time until he would be compelled to come out for water and food. He seemed to be caught like a rabbit in a trap, and as he fully realized the situation, he stopped and thought the matter over. Dee-nay' had often repeated to him an old admonition that now came to his mind: "Excitement goes blind in the presence of danger. Calm thoughts are eyes that may behold a way to safety."

Then he lifted his arms and calmly turned his face upward toward Joho'-na-ai, the Great Spirit, in whom he had always trusted, and his eye caught the rugged branches of the twisted pinyon-tree whose limbs overhung the edge of the cliff above. The light of hope leaped into his face as a possible way of escape came to his mind. Running with all speed to the rocks above the pool, he caught up the heavy coil of rope that hung over the peg, glancing down at the trails below as he did so. The To-to'-mes were but a little way below him, but the steep ascent caused them to climb far more slowly than when on the lower levels, and he knew they would move with the greatest caution when they came within bowshot of the ruined cliff dwelling. He might have time, but certainly none to spare.

Running back to the cave, he brought out the old rope of twisted hide, and taking the two to a point beneath the tree he tied them securely together, making one length that he saw would be long enough to reach from the ledge to the tree and back again. Taking the stone hammer from his belt, he tied one end of the stout leather cord to the head of the weapon, and after coiling the long strand into a loose coil at his feet, he made ready for the most important step in his plan. Stepping out from beneath the tree to a point that would make it possible for the stone hammer, when thrown, to pass over it and descend to the ledge again, he gripped the handle and, after taking careful aim, hurled it upward with sufficient force to drive it a little above the tree before its descent on the other side. He realized that his life might depend on the one throw, and his heart beat heavily with excitement and fear as the hammer arched over the tree, as he had intended it should, but lit on the edge of the upper cliff, with its handle projecting where he could just see it from below.

Catching the rope he gave it several short jerks, causing the weapon to slide nearer and nearer to the edge. One more sharp pull and it tumbled downward, bringing the slack end of the rope with it as the smooth twisted thongs slid over the strong limbs above.

A moment later Kay'-yah had twisted the two lengths together, either one of which was more than strong enough to support his weight, and as he untied the stone hammer and replaced it in his belt, he heard the triumphant shout of the To-to'-mes and knew they were coming up the last part of the trail and had discovered the now open passage at the other end of the ledge. Quickly taking the ends of the rope in his teeth, to make sure that his means of escape would be taken up with him, he was soon climbing hand over hand up the side of the bulging cliff to safety above. He climbed steadily, not daring to look up to see what distance lay between him and the top, as each pull made upon the rope in climbing brought down a shower of small dead twigs and bark, but at last his shoulder touched the tree, and just as he threw his arms over the limbs for the final pull that would draw him out of sight of his enemies, he heard a shout from below and knew he had been discovered.

A second later an arrow struck heavily as it ripped into the bow-case at his back and the arrows in the quiver rattled with the blow; then another flashed by him so close that he felt the wind from it on his face. Before a better aimed arrow could be shot he was out on the ledge, and had stepped from the sight of the angry To-to'-mes below. Pulling up the sagging loop of rope, he loosened it from the tree, and coiled it up on the ground at his feet.

With a happy heart he sat down on a rock to recover his breath, as the exertion of the climb was one to which he was not accustomed, and it required unusual strength. Then he removed his bowcase from his back to see to what extent it had been damaged by the To-to'-me arrow. Much to his surprise he found that the shaft had gone almost completely through the quiver and had splintered one of his own arrows in passing. He shrugged his shoulders as he thought of what might have happened to him if the deadly missile had been shot by a better marksman.

Then, rising quickly, as the thought came to him, he solemnly held his arms upraised to the afternoon sun, saying as he did so:

"Great Spirit, in the heart of the Earth child is thanks for the escape from his enemies. Let not my heart forget."

Pulling out the arrow, he tossed it over the cliff to his enemies beneath, to let them know how little damage it had done. He heard it strike the ledge below, but no sound from the men came back in reply. Doubtless Wau-ko'-ma and his men were inspecting the cave, preparatory to robbing it of everything of value, but he knew that some of his men would be stationed outside with drawn bows ready to let fly at him if he should attempt to look below.

Then he suddenly realized the danger of leaving the tree as it was, for Wau-ko'-ma would surely make an effort to follow him, and might even now be making a rope from the strong skins that were scattered about the cave. He must find some means by which the overhanging limbs could be broken off without exposing himself to the danger of shots from below.

As he looked over the wide slope about him, he saw that it was dotted with dwarf juniper and pinyon-trees, and gnarled sage-brush grew wherever it could find a footing between the rocks and boulders that had tumbled down from the low crumbling wall above. He might find enough dry wood with which to build a fire beneath the tree and could thus burn the limbs off, but that would require too long a time. The afternoon sun was not many hours above the horizon and he must make his way to the top of the mountain and, if possible, descend to the other side before darkness came. He knew that no man had ever found a way to its top, and it was for that reason the old men of the tribe had given the great flat plateau on its summit the name, "Bah-chi Din-och" (Shrine of the Gods).

From his present position it looked as though he might be able to reach the top without great difficulty, and as he realized the fact a thrill of excitement ran through him, as he knew he must be, even now, standing higher up on the mountain than any man had ever stood before.

As he contemplated this fact his eye caught a huge round boulder that stood some little distance above him and in an almost direct line with the tree. As he ran up to it he saw that it might be possible to roll it if the rocks and earth that supported it on the lower side could be removed. After breaking off a stout limb from a nearby tree he returned to the boulder, and using the limb as a digging tool, was soon removing the earth and stones from beneath its lower side. After long and patient effort he decided that a very hard push would start it on its way. He then gathered all the smaller rocks and stones that lay along the way between the boulder and the tree and laid them in a row on either side, to form a direct and uninterrupted path. This accomplished, he got above the great boulder and, bracing his feet against the side of the slope, and with shoulder to the rock, pushed with all his strength. Slowly the great stone rolled over, then, gathering momentum with each turn, it went plunging down the slope directly at the tree. A moment later a splintered stump remained where the pinyon had stood, and a sound like a mighty peal of thunder arose as the huge boulder crashed to the lower shelf and bounded out into the space below.

The continued rumble and more distant roar, as it dropped into the hills beneath, was mingled with the angry cries and shouts of the To-to'-mes, who were both frightened by the terrific noise of the falling rock and angered by the discovery that the tree had disappeared.

Picking up the coils of rope, he tied it to the back of his belt, thankful that he had thought to bring it up with him, for without it he knew he would have small chance of ever reaching the lower country. After throwing his bow-case over his shoulder, he waved a mock adieu to the cliff that now sheltered his baffled enemies, and started hopefully upward in search of a way over the mountain top, over the cloud-swept Shrine of the Gods.

Figure 23
Publisher of Lost Indian Magic Timothy Beckley is photographed in the Land of Enchantment by Charla Gene'

Chapter 12
Kay'-Yah Tests The Bow

A narrow trail; the shadowed night;
The open shelter of the sky;
The smell of sage; a hogan's light;
A far coyote's lonely cry.

QUA'-MA, the mountain that rears its mighty bulk from the foothills beside the To-to'-me mesa, is the highest of the range that stretches away to the northeast. Its lofty sides are girdled about with frowning cliffs, and above them steep terraces rise row upon row to the final support of its level summit. Scorning the rough winds and sands of the desert below, and the raging storms from above, it stands like a proud guardian over the lesser mountains and hills that trail out at its back. Its inaccessible top made Qua'-ma the mountain of mystery to all of the tribes of the vast desert region at its base. Accounts of the magic folk, mysterious witch-caves, and animal dens to be found on its forbidden crest had always had an important part in the stories told the To-to'-me and Nag'-a-pah children. None could say that the tales were untrue, as no one had ever been upon its summit, and Qua'-ma was just the kind of place where witches and fairy-folk would choose to live. When black storm-clouds obscured its top, the old men of Ta-pau'-wee would tell the little boys that the Shin-di was giving a dance to the witches, and that soon they would hear the beating of his big drum and then the clouds would tremble with fear and cry their tears down all over the earth.

From Ah'-co the little Nag'-a-pah children looked at the mysterious mountain through the blue haze of a greater distance, and though the distance caused the tales about it to be less fearsome, they were none the less weird and impressive. It was well known to them how Chun-gua, the headless wolf, always came out on the mountain-top to look for his head just as the new moon hung above Qua'-ma, as that was the only time in the month that he could see, but he could never find it, as the head could not call out to him because it had no body to give it breath to growl with, and the body could not call out to the head because it had no tongue or throat with which to make a noise.

The little Nag'-a-pah boys and girls were told that if they were ever very bad the witches might carry them off to the black caves that were high up on the mountain-sides, and the threat did more than all else to make them good and obedient children. Thus the fearsome mysteries of Qua'-ma were established in the minds of the little folk, and these impressions could not be altogether shaken off when manhood came.

As Kay'-yah worked his way upward over the rough slopes and steep terraces that lay between him and the lofty mesa above, the memory of many childhood tales of the mountain came to his mind, and through his thoughts ran the words of a little rhyme that had given him his first idea of its awe-inspiring mystery;

> *"On Qua'-ma's top a black cloud lies,*
> *Wau – mee, O – wau-ha-mee.*
> *The witch-winds wail; the bear-witch flies*
> *To tell the Shin-di – someone dies.*
> *Wau – mee, Wau-ha-mee."*

As the fearful impression this rhyme had made upon him as a little boy came to his mind, he permitted a slight shiver of the old fear to run through him just for the fun and mystery of it. Then suddenly he jumped as though he were shot, as a little ground squirrel whisked from the sage at his feet, and ran to the shelter of a nearby rock. He laughed aloud as he realized the foolishness of his thoughts – thoughts that should have no place in the head of a warrior.

Climbing steadily for some time, he came at last to a broken wall of rock scarcely higher than his head, and as he climbed over it the great level summit stretched evenly out before him. Standing erect on the wind-swept height, with the great earth of desert and hills stretching out far below, a feeling of exultation arose within him as he realized that, of all Earth children, he was the first to stand on the top of Qua'-ma, the Shrine of the Gods. The achievement gave him added confidence in himself, and he felt that he was more of a man and warrior than the inexperienced youth who had set out from the lodge of Dee-nay' to match his skill and wit against that of the To-to'-mes. Had he not matched his strength and skill against his enemies and, thus far, come off victorious in each encounter?

But boastfulness had little room in his character, and serious thoughts of the immediate past quickly gave place to a feeling of joy and freedom too strong for sober impressions, and with outstretched arms he ran westward toward the end of the mesa that lay nearest his beloved Ah'-co. The fresh, strong winds of the upper air flattened his hair back against his temples as he ran, and it seemed to him that he could almost fly out over the desert if he just spread his arms wide enough and ran fast enough. Blue-jays, rabbit-hawks, and black-birds flew noisily up from bush and sage as he passed, and chattered and scolded loudly at the sight of a man who was rudely invading their hitherto exclusive domain.

A strange excitement ran through Kay'-yah's veins as he leaped over sage and weeds in his path as each step brought him nearer home, and he could scarcely bring himself to stop as he reached the western end of the great flat top. Halting on the very edge of the plateau, he looked out over the wonderful scene that lay beneath him, and quickly searched for the spot where he believed the Nag'-a-pah camp must be situated. Then his eye caught the familiar twisting outline of the canyon that appeared, from where he stood, like a dark blue crack in the earth, and – yes, at its mouth lay Ah'-co, its cluster of tiny hogans barely visible in the dim distance. It seemed a long time since he had turned his back upon the Nag'-a-pah camp; his heart filled with thoughts of adventure and the recovery of the lost Magic. He had found the adventure, but the lost Magic seemed as far from recovery as it had ever been.

As he looked at the mountain-side immediately beneath him, he saw that he would be able to descend a long way before encountering the sheer walls of cliffs that had always proved an effectual barrier to all who had attempted to climb up from below, and that now might hold him prisoner on the mountaintop. Joho'-na-ai had led him through each difficult situation that had, thus far, confronted him, and he doubted not that the Great Spirit would aid him now.

He carefully studied the nature of the country over which he must pass before he could get safely out of the network of To-to'-me trails, many of which, he felt sure, would be guarded. As he scanned the smooth hills now flattened out almost like level country by the height from which he looked down upon them, he noticed a short canyon set squarely across the end of a ridge that ran for miles almost directly toward the Nag'-a-pah country. Then he remembered both the canyon and the ridge, as he had followed the northern slope of the latter when on his way to the To-to'-me mesa, and had had the good fortune to find a pass in the canyon wall that had permitted him to go down into it, and thus avoid the trails that he knew must lie on the To-to'-me side of the ridge.

As he looked out into the foothills for landmarks by which to guide his course when the lower ground was reached, he saw the snow-white body and twisted limbs of a dead tree standing on the top of a hill, and noted that the little canyon was but a short distance from it, and due west of the hill on which it stood. When he reached the country below, he would go directly to the little canyon if possible, for if he could get through the foothills nearest the mountain, where guards were most apt to be watching for him, and gain the canyon's shelter, he could elude his enemies, as the pass led into the open country north of the ridge. Thoughts of the strong bow and goodly supply of Tso's red arrows in the case at his back gave him a feeling of security and comfort, as he felt prepared to meet any foe who might cross his path.

The late afternoon sun hung low over the horizon, and he must find a way to the country below before darkness came. With a final look over the great desert world that lay below, he started rapidly downward, picking his way over the steep slopes that led to the more formidable walls of rock awaiting him far down the mountain-side. His descent was more rapid than his upward climb had been, and soon he found himself on the top of a wall that seemed both too high and too steep to descend. It being the uppermost of the three great cliffs that girdled the mountain, he felt sure that he would find a place where the floods from the plateau and slopes above had worn a passage, and after a short walk he found his judgment to be correct, as he came upon a break where the water had cut a deep gash in the wall, forming a passage to the next ledge beneath.

He felt that he had made considerable progress in his downward journey as he stood on the narrow shelf that topped the next great cliff below; and sitting down on the ledge, he looked into the depths beneath, scanning the walls as far as he could see in each direction. Only two cliffs now remained beneath him, but they were the two highest on the mountain-side. Far to his right he could see a crack in the cliff that now confronted him, and as he walked toward it he soon saw that he would have to go very carefully if he was to avoid a fall, as the sloping ledge was, in many places, too steep to pass over with any degree of safety.

At last he came to the point where he had seen the break, but he found it far less promising than it had appeared from a distance. The cut was both steep and very long, but it held out one small hope, for about half-way down it a stunted pinyon-tree clung with gnarled roots to the rocks and scant earth of the almost perpendicular slope. If he could get to the tree his rope would aid him in descending to the next shelf below it; but to climb down to it from where he stood was out of the question, as the cut was both too steep and too smooth to afford a footing of any kind, and there was nothing near him over which the rope could be hung.

Crawling on for a short distance beyond the break, he examined the wall immediately beneath, and found a little projection several feet below him large enough for a firm footing, and beneath it were two others that seemed to run back to a point that must be near the tree. If he could get down to the lower projection he might be able to work his way back toward the pinyon, and if successful the rest would be easy.

Removing his rope, stone hammer, and bow-case, so that nothing could hamper his movements where even the slightest extra weight, or false step, might cause him to fall, he let himself down to the first projection, and after cautiously lowering his body to the last footing, slowly worked his way back toward the little tree whose projecting branches he saw to be on a level with his head. But at the very end of the slight projection on which he stood, he found that he was still too far from his goal to be able to throw the rope over the tree successfully, as its small thick branches spread out toward him, making it impossible to get the rope over the stout trunk. One plan that might be followed came to his mind, but he would use it only as a last resort.

Climbing back to the ledge above, he walked on for some distance in search of another passage that would present fewer difficulties; but the farther he went, the less promising the wall became, and the shelf on which he walked was becoming narrower with each step. The sun was on the horizon now, and but little time would be left to him before darkness came making further descent impossible. The moon would rise later, but it is difficult to judge heights and depths accurately by moonlight and the black shadows would make climbing doubly dangerous.

Going back to the cut, he uncoiled the rope and doubled it so that the ends would be even, for if he were successful in reaching the next ledge below, he must be able to pull the rope down from the tree after his descent, as he would have still greater need of it when attempting the passage over the remaining cliff which he knew to be the highest of them all. Picking up the bow-case in one hand and the stone hammer in the other, he weighed them carefully. The bow-case was a little the heavier of the two. Removing a handful of arrows from the quiver, he weighed them again, and being satisfied that they were of about equal weight, he carefully stuck the extra arrows into his belt, and tied the bow-case to one end of the rope and the hammer to the other.

Figure 24
"He Extended His Right Hand As Far As Possible
Toward The Rope That Hung From The Tree"

Carefully lowering the end on which the hammer was tied, he let it slip down past one side of the tree, and when half of the rope was thus played out he lowered the bow-case until it passed the tree on the opposite side, and then let go. The weighted rope tightened firmly over the gnarled trunk as the hammer and bow-case slid downward to within a few feet of the lower shelf. With rope and weapons hanging far below him, his one way of getting down now lay in taking a chance he had hoped to avoid. Stepping over to the point where he had climbed down before, he lowered himself from one projection to another until the last footing was reached and again moved cautiously out toward the tree. Beneath him dropped the great vertical cliffs over which a slip or false move might cause him to plunge into the yawning depths below. Slowly and cautiously he moved out to the last inch of the little projection; then, with left hand clinging to a crack in the wall above him, and with every muscle tense for the trial that was to be put upon them, he extended his right hand as far as possible toward the rope that hung from the tree. He knew that both strands of the rope must be grasped at the same instant, and his position, flattened as he was against the wall, would make the intended leap an awkward one. Loosening his hold on the crack above, he lunged forward; and a second later was swinging back and forth in mid-air but holding firmly to the two strands of rope.

A few moments later he stood on the sloping ledge below, his heart pounding and limbs trembling with the strain that had been put upon them. The hardest part of his descent was over, in spite of the fact that the cliff that remained below was the highest on the mountain, for he could now use his rope in one long strand and he could see that its length would reach to the bottom of the wall. Up to this point he had been forced to take the rope with him, but he could now fasten one end securely to the ledge when making this last descent, as he would not need it after reaching the ground below.

Untying the hammer and bow-case from the rope, he pulled it down from the tree and sought a spot level enough to permit him to go to its outer edge and examine the cliff below. The sun had now dropped below the rim of the desert, but its fiery afterglow flooded the western sky and cast its vivid coloring over hills and mountain-side, turning rocks and trees into a blaze of red that slowly faded into copper and dull gold. Seated on the ledge Kay'-yah witnessed the wonderful color effects of the sunset with keen appreciation, and watched for a moment the hills below now darkening into deep purple where the mountain cast its great shadow across them.

"Great is the power, and great is the goodness of Joho'-na-ai," he reverently murmured under his breath, as he rose to prepare for the final step in his journey to freedom.

There were many narrow cracks in the rock ledge about him, and finding one that ran parallel with the edge of the cliff, he placed his hammer, handle downward, into it and found that it could be driven half way to the head. He then bound one end of the rope securely about it and with a large stone drove the hammer as deep into the crack as its stout handle would permit it to go. After making a meal of the bread and dried meat that he had wrapped in the piece of buckskin before departing from the cave, he bound the small piece of hide about the rope at the point where it would come in contact with the edge of the cliff to prevent its wearing through while he was making the descent. Making a final test of the strength of the hammer handle by pulling upon the rope with all his strength, he carefully lowered himself over the edge of the cliff and began his last downward climb to the hills below.

When his feet touched the firm earth he ran down the slope to the more level land, feeling as though he would like to shout for joy at being free once more; free from the seemingly endless walls and cliffs that had held him prisoner since the day old Tso had found him lying unconscious on the rocks near his cave. Soon he was among the trees and bushes of the hills, and turning his course westward made his way more slowly now, as twilight was rapidly fading into darkness, and the ground was rough with fallen rocks and tangled brush. He knew that he must be some distance from the point where the ridge led out toward the Nag'-a-pah country, as he had wandered a considerable distance around the side of the mountain while seeking his way down, but a little later the moon would be up and he would then be able to travel as rapidly as he wished.

After what seemed a long time, a pale light diffused the earth, and grew brighter as the sky to the eastward of the great mountain became more luminous. He could go a little faster now; but he had gone only a short distance when he came upon a well-marked trail, and a little farther on crossed a second one, causing him to move with greater caution. Then dropping to his hands and knees, he crawled forward, stopping every few feet to listen for the sounds of any guards that might be stationed in the near-by hills. The moon was not yet high enough for him to see any of the landmarks that he had selected to guide him on his way, but the evening stars gave him the points of the compass and he continued his course by them.

Suddenly a sound as of someone running through the brush far down to his left came to his ears, and he stopped, placing an arrow on the string of his bow, as he waited, but the sound died away, and as the light grew brighter he saw, some distance below him, a low hill; and on its summit the white body and twisted limbs of a dead juniper-tree stood boldly out against the dark sky. He smiled with pleasure as he recognized it as the landmark he had noted from the mountain-top, and knew that due west of him lay the friendly little canyon with the ridge beyond.

Crawling forward, he had just reached the tree when he heard the sound of a woman's voice a little way below him. The voice was low but tense with excitement, as if its owner were possessed of mingled fear and anger.

He leaped to his feet, and his heart stood still within him – the voice was like that of Sah'-ne. But even as he ran forward he realized that Sah'ne could only be in Ah'-co, and that the voice might merely be like hers. Torn by uncertainty, and realizing that he must not allow excitement to lead him into unwise actions that might cause him to fall again into the hands of his enemies, he stopped and crouched down in the sage to listen. As he did so, angry voices and the sound of a struggle as of two men fighting, came up from the spot where he had heard the woman's voice. He could now see that the men were in a small clump of bushes that stood on the edge of the smooth sage-covered slope that ran off toward the south. As he listened, uncertain just what he should do, he could hear the men struggling desperately. Men of the same tribe often quarreled, but they seldom fought except on extreme provocation. One of these men might be a Nag'-a-pah.

Figure 25
"Let An Arrow Fly At The Fleeing Figure That Was Now Running Swiftly"

Crouching low in the sage, he moved forward again, hoping to get near enough to see something of the combatants without being seen by them. As he drew nearer to them, one of the antagonists fell with an angry cry, and the other ran off up the slope toward the head of the canyon. Although he had come to within a short distance of them, neither of the men had seen him, so intent were they in the struggle. Then the fallen man half rose, calling out as he did so:

"By the gods! You shall pay for this, Chot'-zu!"

The mention of the name was enough to cause an instant change in Kay'-yah's actions. Paying no heed to the wounded man, whom he now knew to be To-to'-me, he changed his course to avoid the bushes, and dropping on one knee let an arrow fly at the fleeing figure that was now running swiftly some distance up the slope. With a loud cry the man leaped into the air and fell forward in the sage.

With the feeling that he had done his duty in avenging Tso, Kay'-yah rose to his feet, then quickly fitting another arrow to the string he turned back toward the bushes and the wounded man in whose voice he had recognized Ha-wal'-li.

"Ah!" exclaimed the latter in obvious surprise, as Kay'-yah approached him; and he made a quick move as though to recover his bow that lay on the ground a few feet from him, where it had doubtless fallen during the struggle.

"Hold – or you follow your friend Chot'-zu!" commanded Kay'-yah quietly. "Who was the woman and where is she? Speak quick!"

"Not so fast, Nag'-a-pah. She is safe enough, since you kill one that was after her and the other one has not yet come this far. Put down the bow. I will tell you what you have need to know."

"I am not caught twice by the same dogs," replied Kay'-yah, without lowering his bow. "Speak!"

Seeing that the man before him was in no mood to parley, Ha-wal'-li replied.

"The girl is from Ah'-co, and known to you, but is of my family and my people. I protect her as quickly as you. Wau-ko-'ma and Chot'-zu were both after her. Chot'-zu threatened me that the chief would be here soon. It was, no doubt, their plan to meet at this place. The girl was trying to escape from Chot'-zu, who knew not that I stood guard here. I caught him about the arms and held him until she escaped toward the canyon below us. As she ran away she said, 'I go to Ah'-co.' Why she goes to Ah'-co I know not."

Waiting to hear no more, Kay'-yah, without lowering his weapon, moved quickly over to where the To-to'-me's bow lay on the ground, and reaching out with his foot he kicked it still farther to one side, out of leaping distance of its owner; then picking it up, he turned to go.

"I believe there is truth in what you say. You have given her help, so I do not kill you, but you follow me or tell others of where I have gone at her risk as well as your own."

Taking his knife from his belt and laying it on his open hand, Ha-wal'-li stepped toward Kay'-yah:

"Here is proof that I know more of you than you of me. I was here to take you captive, but my heart is more in the safety of the girl. You have no knife, and Wau-ko'-ma may come too close for you to use the arrow. – Quick, for someone comes!"

At the unexpected kindness, Kay'-yah hesitated for a brief moment; then taking the proffered weapon he turned, saying as he did so:

"I understand. My thoughts are grateful – and my memory is long."

Diving into the brush and trees of the hillside, he ran swiftly down the steep approach that led to the little canyon, his heart pounding with mingled pain and joy at the thought of being so near to Sah'-ne. Sah'-ne at Ta-pau'-wee could mean only one thing, and the thought filled his heart with bitterness and a strange anger that seemed to be directed as much against himself as her. His one duty now was to save her from Wau-ko'-ma, and, he told himself, he would do that for any woman of Ah'-co. He now felt doubly glad that he had made an end of Chot'-zu, as the latter was on his way to the head of the canyon to intercept Sah'-ne when his arrow had laid him low.

On he ran down the hillside until fallen rock and low broken walls near the canyon's mouth brought him to a walk. Climbing over the few low ledges that blocked the way, he was soon running along in the dense shadow of the canyon's eastern wall. After some little distance he stopped and listened. The pounding in his heart seemed so loud he could hear little else, but after putting his ear to the ground he could hear the crunch of sand beneath swiftly running feet far ahead of him. The footfalls were too light to be those of a man. Springing to his feet, he ran forward with increased speed, and, after a few moments, stopped again.

"Sah'-ne!" he called in a low voice.

"Kay'-yah!" came the startled voice of Sah'-ne, as she stopped and leaned backward with outstretched arms against the canyon wall.

"Yes, – it is I," said Kah'-yah evenly, as he ran up to her. "We must be quick! Wau-ko'-ma hunts for you, and I must put you on the right way to Ah'-co before I deal with him. Come!" he commanded.

Sah'-ne was both too surprised and overjoyed to make reply, and she followed as he took the lead and ran back to a point where the canyon made a slight bend. Then, after stopping a moment to listen for the sound of any approaching feet, he motioned for her again to follow and darted swiftly across the bright patch of moonlight that covered the narrow canyon floor. A moment later they stood beneath the pass that led to the open country beyond the ridge.

"This is a break in the wall where we must climb," said Kay'-yah simply. "I will help you up. Keep to your right when you get to the top – follow the green star that is in the west."

Lifting her to a ledge a few feet above the canyon bed, he climbed up beside her; then stooping down he commanded her to step upon his shoulders. Holding to the rocks above, she obeyed; and as he rose she was able to step to a much higher level that led gradually upward. "From where you now stand you will be able to make your way to the top without my help. When you have traveled until you are weary, wait for me. I wait here until I know you have time to get far away from those who are after you, then I will follow. When you have thought it is time for me to come, listen for the call of the Dak bird."

"Your voice has the cold of anger in it," said Sah'-ne. "Is it not cause for happiness to be with a friend again?"

The unexpected question and the sweetness of the voice filled him with momentary confusion, and when he replied he spoke harshly to hide it.

"My friends do not visit Ta-pau'-wee," he said.

There was a teasing note in the low voice as she replied;

"That is strange, since they would but be doing what you have done."

And turning quickly she ran up the slope, leaving Kay'-yah to battle with the tumult of emotions that arose within him.

* * * * * *

A To-to'-me guard, stationed far up among the hills, attracted by the loud outcry of the ill-fated Chot'-zu, ran down toward the clearing from whence he was sure the sound had come, and would have passed by Ha-wal'-li without seeing him had not the latter called out to him.

"Where is he?" asked the man as he came up. "Where is the Nag'-a-pah?"

"I do not know," replied Ha-wal'-li. "There is a cut in my side. Help me to bind it up."

"Ah-e e e!" exclaimed the guard. "Always the Nag'-a-pah fights like a Shin-di, yet we have word from Tag-a'-mo not to do him harm."

"The cut is not deep and is not from the knife of the Nag'-a-pah," replied Ha-wal'-li. "The man who did it has paid the price of death."

"Ah-e e e!" exclaimed the man again. "Are Wau-ko'-ma's men on this side of the mountain?"

"Yes," said Ha-wal'-li, as the guard finished binding some soft earth over the wound; "and Wau-ko'-ma himself may soon come this way."

"What To-to'-me fights you with the knife?" bluntly asked the guard, whose curiosity was thoroughly aroused. Then he sprang to where he had laid his bow upon the ground, as the sound of someone coming through the sage-brush from down the slope came to their ears.

"Let me have your knife," said Ha-wal'-li. "I have no weapon."

The man obeyed, and the two stood silently waiting for the approaching figure, who seemed to move swiftly though with great caution. A few moments later the guard lowered his bow as Wau-ko'-ma approached them.

"Has Chot'-zu passed this way?" he asked as he stepped before them.

"Yes," said Ha-wal'-li. "He lies with an arrow in him in the sage yonder – a little way up the slope."

Wau-ko'-ma gave a slight start at the unexpected news, and his eyes caught the bandage on Ha-wal'-li's side. He made as though to speak, but changing his mind ran on up the slope in the direction indicated by Ha-wal'-li. At this unlooked-for revelation, the guard's jaw dropped with astonishment as he stared at his companion.

"This is trouble for us," he finally exclaimed, as the thoughts of dealing with the angry chief came to him.

"Hold your tongue, Chaz'-pah, you will learn more in a short time."

Scarcely had his words been spoken when Wau-ko'-ma came running back to them. In his hand he held a blood-stained arrow, and as the moonlight fell full upon him, both men were startled by the look of fear and suppressed excitement that shone in his face.

"Look!" he exclaimed. "The red arrow of the bear-witch! I pulled it from the body of Chot'-zu that I might know whose bow had sent it. Don't stare at me like babies! Speak! What do you know of this?"

"I know nothing about it," replied the guard. "For I did but come before you."

"You, Ha-wal'-li?" questioned Wau-ko'-ma, as he scowled at the man before him.

"The arrow that killed Chot'-zu was shot by the Nag'-a-pah," said Ha-wal'-li quietly; "and he has gone on to protect the girl Sah'-ne from any others who may attempt to capture her."

"The dog of a Nag'-a-pah shall not escape us again!" said Wau-ko'-ma between set teeth. "'Which way has he gone?"

Sensing the fact that the threat was but an idle boast to hide his fear, Ha-wal'-li replied:

"The Nag'-a-pah has gone with the girl to the mouth of the canyon below. He will wait for you there or in the pass, as he knows you seek her and will see that you find him instead."

"If you know that, why do you stand here like frightened rabbits? Do your cowardly hearts fear to go after him?"

"Our orders are from Tag-a'-mo," said Ha-wal'-li evenly. "He sent us to guard the trails in the hills. There are no trails in the canyon. Since you are under no man's order, and have no fear of the Nag'-a-pah, we know you will go down to the canyon to kill him."

With face turned in the direction taken by Sah'ne and Kay'-yah the young chief stood for a moment as if helpless rage and fear fought within him. He could not attack the two armed men before him, and all confidence that he could conquer Kay'-yah single-handed had gone from him.

Facing Ha-wal'-li and shaking his clenched hand in the air, he exclaimed:

"I shall make an end of this plot against me, and those who take orders from any but myself shall feel the heavy hand of Wau-ko'-ma!"

With this empty threat, made in an attempt to distract the attention of his hearers from the proof of his cowardice, he turned back in the direction of Ta-pau'-wee.

Chapter 13
The Place Of The White Rock

All trails lead back to home, at last;
The glowing fire, the friendly smiles;
The heart forgets the dangers past;
The weariness and lonely miles.

SAH'-NE now ran over rough country; before and about her, rocks and underbrush piled high in miniature mountains and foothills, and the ground was broken with many dry stream-beds. Mezquite, pinyon and cactus, assuming many fantastic shapes, reared themselves in every direction, and great balls of tumble-weed loomed gray in the moonlight and stirred with every breath of wind; and under the broken silver of the sage moved the animal life of the desert. The little hares that scurried in alarm at the sound of a human footstep; coyotes that slipped by like ghostly shadows in the distance, sending their clamorous cries into the night, and the silent, sliding ones that crept into the warm cracks of the rocks to avoid the cool night air and slept with every sense alert. Sah'-ne knew them all and feared not one, and her light feet made little of the roughness of her path. She went swiftly, and the words Kay'-yah had spoken kept pace in her thought with her swinging stride:

"Follow the ridge and the guidance of the green star," and, "Answer the call of the Dak bird."

For the rest she must choose her own trail and keep eyes and ears alert for possible enemies. The open desert she loved, and knew its every sound and aspect, and tonight her heart sang within her and her feet seemed to have wings. Was not Kay'-yah alive and free, and had he not spoken words to her? It was true that his eves had avoided hers and his voice was cold, but what was that to the fact that Wau-ko'-ma had failed in his boast and Kay'-yah had escaped?

A little hoot-owl sent forth his clear call from somewhere near at hand, and presently flitted from tree to tree, seeming to follow her in her flight. Sah'-ne smiled: perhaps Joho'-na-ai had sent one to guard her in the night, and the thought pleased her. The moon was now almost directly overhead and brilliant as it can be only in the clear altitudes of the Southwest. The shadows were not the dense, thick shadows of other lands but, purple-blue and clear and sharp, they lay like pools of still water out of which rose great rocks, ghostly white and creamy pink; queer, twisted trees and silvery clumps of sage; and over all the magic mantle of the moonlight.

Sah'-ne was not indifferent to the shimmering, white splendor about her, and the words of a song she had often heard in Ah'-co came to her mind, and half-unconsciously she hummed them under her breath:

"The Moon-god sends a spell of light;
A magic spell into the night;
Of silver dreams he softly weaves
On rocks and trees; on sage and leaves;
As to and fro the witch-winds go;
The witch-winds go, and softly blow.
The warrior's heart is bound in dreams;
In many dreams; in silver dreams.
The medicine is strong — is strong.
The Moon-god spell is long."

Did Kay'-yah feel the magic spell of the night, she wondered; surely he must, for everything was under it. The Star-brothers themselves did not seem cold and far away as usual, but were like countless camp-fires of those who had gone before; camp-fires that sparkled warm and friendly about the great father-fire of the night – the Moon-god himself. And the silence was not the silence of an empty hogan or great, cold spaces, but the soft hush that comes when all have spoken in the home and sit content about the fire busy with happy thoughts. The Earth mother had been at her tasks all day and now lay at rest, cooled by the breath of the night breeze and lulled into slumber by the soft night sounds. Sah'-ne almost held her breath, as if afraid to disturb the sleeping world, and then she would throw back her head and laugh to herself. "But it is not sleep," she whispered more than once, "it is rest; rest in the heart, and that is very different."

Presently she came to a twisted pinyon-tree, larger than those she had passed, and under it a flat stone invited her to rest.

"Here I will wait," she thought. "Kay'-yah will come soon."

And the little hoot-owl perched on a limb above her and called monotonously over and over again, until she answered him in playful mockery, many times.

It was not long before out of the shadows she had left behind came clearly the call of the Dak bird, the little brown Dak bird that nests in the fields of Ah'-co. Sah'-ne thrilled to the call, but some spirit of mischief held her silent. Again came the call, from nearer at hand; but still she did not answer and clung close to the shadow of the tree.

Kay'-yah came out into the moonlight a short distance away and stood looking about him. Again he called, and this time Sah'-ne could not repress a little laugh that rose to her lips. He looked about quickly and took a few steps toward the tree. He was frowning slightly and his words were cold as he spoke.

"You did not answer the call."

"Was that a Dak bird call?" she asked in pretended innocence. "A Dak bird is always *happy* and calls like *this* – " and there was such a thrill and laugh through the call she sent out into the night that Kay'-yah's face relaxed for a moment and he could not keep from smiling; but almost instantly the troubled look came back and he opened his lips to speak, but before the words could come Sah'-ne spoke again.

"Hush!" she whispered. "Words are not for now – listen!" And through the silence came a slight sound, unmistakable: someone was coming; someone whose swinging bow had struck lightly against a rock as he passed.

Quick as thought, Kay'-yah drew Sah'-ne down into a great clump of sage and put an arrow to the string of his bow, as they waited breathless for the approach of him who came. It was not long before a man came into view, a man who ran quickly and silently, stooping and crouching as he slipped from bush to tree, and peering and listening in every direction. He did not act as a man would who was hot on a trail, but seemed uncertain of what he followed, and at times looked up into the tree branches as if what he sought could be there.

Kay'-yah followed his every movement with his arrow taut on the string, but did not shoot, as that he would do only in self-defense or retribution. When the man was gone beyond sound of their movements, they rose from the sage and Sah'-ne whispered:

"It was for you he looked – it was the call he heard."

Kay'-yah put his finger to his lips.

"We must not talk now – come!"

And they picked their way through the sage, going as swiftly as the rough country would allow.

Kay'-yah stopped frequently to listen for possible pursuers and to study the country for the best trail. They had traveled for quite a while in silence when Sah'-ne spoke with a shade of timidity in her voice.

"Was there a fight in the pass?" she asked.

"There was no fight – no one came," answered Kay'-yah: and again there was silence for a while. Kay'-yah's thoughts were in a turmoil; not yet had he recovered from his astonishment and dismay at finding Sah'-ne near Ta-pau'-wee. One thought hammered at his brain: "A spy, a spy like her father!" And yet it was agony to harbor it. But, if a spy, why was she flying from the To-to'-mes and yet protected by a To-to'-me? He longed to ask her the answers to these questions, but a strange embarrassment and timidity very foreign to his nature held him silent. Finally, with great effort, he gathered his courage together and spoke, in a voice so low that she barely caught the words:

"Sah'-ne, why did you leave Ah'-co? The trail of the To-to'-mes is no place for a maiden of the Nag'-a-pahs."

She had paused as he spoke and now stood still but looked away from him.

"I have said I was To-to'-me," she answered, and did not see the deeper look of trouble that came into his face.

He in his turn looked away from her as he asked bitterly:

"Then why do you return to Ah'-co?"

"I *was* To-to'-me," she repeated, putting strong emphasis on the second word. "I was born To-to'-me, but until lately knew it not. My heart has always been Nag'-a-pah. Dee-nay' believed and trusted me." A deeper bitterness crept into her voice. "That is why he sent me to Ta-pau'-wee."

"*Dee-nay'* sent you!" There was incredulous amazement now in Kay'-yah's voice. "*Why* should he send you?"

She lifted her head a little at this.

"Dee-nay' is medicine chief of the Nag'-a-pahs; his word is above the word of all others; when it has gone forth it is not scattered on the wind for every ear to hear. If you are to know, Dee-nay' will tell you."

The tone of her voice no less than her words left Kay'-yah speechless. He gazed at her in the bright moonlight, and the look of amazement in his eyes brought a sudden change of mood to Sah'-ne; the corners of her mouth twitched, and lest he should see the amusement in her face she threw up her head and sniffed.

"I smell the camp-fires of Ah'-co!" she cried. "Come, let us go!"

Kay'-yah still looked at her, but the light came back to his eyes. He, also, threw back his head and laughed up at the moon.

"Then you are neither Nag'-a-pah nor To-to'-me but own sister to the fox if you can smell so far!" he laughed. "Yes, let us go. The Moon-god makes plain the way – look!"

There before them, clear-marked through the dusty sage, lay a narrow trail leading toward Ah'co. With joyous hearts they stepped into it and set off at a swinging trot toward the home country. They did not speak often after that, as the spell of silence seemed to be on all things, but once he asked if she were weary.

"Is the bird weary when he is nearing the nest?" she laughed back. "It may be, but he does not drop to earth. My feet have wings tonight. I shall rest in Ah'-co." And they went on.

The moon crept on toward the western horizon and the stars slipped out of sight, but still they ran on over the little trail through sage and mezquite, over sand and rock and shale: the dawn-wind blew in their faces, bringing a breath of the canyon coolness; and just as Joho'-na-ai sent a golden spear of light over the desert's eastern rim Kay'-yah called out:

"Here we will rest, Sah'-ne, and eat. This place is known to me and water is near."

She was not sorry to stop, and sank down under a juniper-tree with a little sigh of relief. She closed her eyes as she rested her head against the trunk of the tree, and must have dozed longer than she thought, for when she opened them again Kay'-yah was bending a few feet in front of her busy with fire-sticks and a little pile of brush, and beside him lay a rabbit, fresh slain. The fire caught quickly and the rabbit, clean-skinned, was soon sizzling over the blaze on the end of a sharpened stick. Kay'-yah looked up and caught the smiling expression of her eyes; he spoke quickly, as if afraid of his words and anxious to get rid of them.

"Joho'-na-ai has sent his light across the desert, and your eyes have caught its brightness."

She looked away, confused, and he rose from the fire, holding out to her the rabbit on its stick.

"Hold this," he said, "and I will go for water."

She looked about for a gourd or jar and then remembered.

"My water-jar lies at the foot of Ta-pau'-wee mesa," she laughed. "I shall come and drink."

"No," he answered gravely. "Not all water-jars are made of clay or woven reeds. The Earth mother has children in the desert and knows their needs. Wait here and rest, for you are weary and we still have far to go. – Look! The meat! – " he cried, and laughed to see her start and jerk the smoking rabbit from the flames.

"Before the tree shadow has shortened a hand's breadth I shall be back," he called, as he ran through the sage toward a little ravine near at hand. Presently he returned and in his hand was a stalk of cactus hollowed out and filled with water.

"It is not a gourd," he smiled, "but water is water. And I have brought other things. Here are pinyon nuts and ripe berries that were growing near the water. We shall fare well; the camp-fire of a great chief could not give us better, and I would rather sit with you than with a great chief," he ended bravely, and did not look at Sah'-ne, for he knew she was looking away from him.

They sat down to the desert meal together and laughed many times and talked much. They had many things to tell each other, and Sah'-ne listened in big-eyed wonder at the story of Kay'-yah's many escapes, while he, in turn, grew red with anger when she spoke of Wau-ko'-ma and his cruel words.

"It would have been well had my arrow found his heart from the rock ledge," he cried; "but I shall come back some day to his mesa town – my heart tells me I have not seen the last of Ta-pau'-wee or Wau-ko'-ma, its chief."

"What did the old man, Tso, mean by the strange words he called as he ran?" asked Sah'-ne.

"I know not; they were the words of one whose mind wanders. At times no man could speak more clearly than he, but at other times he was as a child; his thoughts would follow one thing and then another as a child does with blown feathers in the sunlight. Yet my heart grows sad at thought of him; I would that I could have stayed the arrow that slew him. The blood of the beast that paid for him was not enough. He was kind to me and my heart is warm for him."

They were silent for a while after this, and then Sah'-ne looked up with another question.

"And the Magic – you have found no sign of it?"

"The Magic remains hidden as before, only now we know that it is not with the To-to'-mes. But see the shadows shorten; if your weariness has grown less we will again take the trail; Ah'-co lies many horizons from here. Come, or night will again overtake us."

Sah'-ne rose swiftly and gladly; her youth would not tolerate the claims of weariness for long and the thought of the nearness of home restored her energy. They lost no time in finding the trail and were soon traveling at a fairly rapid rate of speed over the desert that was now glowing red and gold and orange in the full blaze of the sunlight. The heat of mid-summer had passed and the air was fresh with the autumn freshness; the jack-oak trees were beginning to turn and the tumble-weeds were a dusky red. Just after noon they entered the home canyon and the trail began to lead gradually downward. They quickened their steps as familiar landmarks, one after the other, began to appear, and Kay'-yah held his bow with an arrow on the string ready to shoot at any game that might come their way.

"*Now* can you smell the camp-fires?" called Sah'ne.

"No," answered Kay'-yah. "But stop, Sah'-ne; look!"

A great eagle rose from a nest in the side of the canyon and began slowly to circle upward. Sah'-ne stood still and watched the bird, but Kay'-yah, with pretended seriousness, drew back his bow and aimed straight at the eagle, watching Sah'-ne from the tail of his eye. After a moment her eyes left the eagle and came back to him, and when she saw the arrow she gave a cry and sprang toward him, clutching his arm. Her face went white and she was trembling violently.

"You would not shoot! You would not shoot!" she cried in a voice that sounded strange in her own ears.

Kay'-yah lowered the bow with his eyes on her face.

"I but jested, Sah'-ne. No, I would not shoot. But why do you tremble? What has caused you such fear?"

She grew more quiet, but her face was slow in gaining its normal expression.

"It is very bad medicine to shoot an eagle," she said, and her voice was still unsteady. "Once before I saw an arrow bring an eagle to the ground – once before."

"And what followed?" he asked curiously. "Was the evil omen true to its name?"

"It was the night your father died and mine," she answered simply. "The night the Magic was lost."

Kay'-yah's manner changed instantly and his intent interest was reflected in his face.

"Tell me," he said quietly. "We will sit here for a moment."

"It was nearly dark in the evening," began Sah'ne. "I had gone up toward the mouth of the canyon for pinyon nuts and was about to return home when I saw an eagle rise from Ah'-co. My father's eagle – he was keeper of the sacred eagle."

Kay'-yah nodded and she continued:

"I stood still and was watching the eagle soar high above my head when an arrow shot like black lightning straight toward him and down he came at my feet, falling like a god from the sky. My heart came to my throat, for the omen was bad, and fury burned in my blood for the one who had done this. It could be no Nag'-a-pah, and I looked toward the canyon from whence the arrow had come.'

"Tso!" breathed Kay'-yah; but the low exclamation passed unheard by Sah'-ne.

"An old man came out of the canyon, a To-to'-me he was. I know not what I said to him, for my heart was hot with fury. He asked for my eagle, but I would not let him have it, and at last he laughed at me and went back into the canyon shaking his head. It was dark then and I buried the eagle in the rocks to keep away the coyotes – he was too heavy to carry to Ah'-co – and I marked the place with a white stone, thinking to return the next day, that my father might see. But I did not return — " she broke off with a quick breath.

Kay'-yah was leaning forward.

"You are sure it was the sacred eagle?"

"Very sure," answered Sah'-ne. "I knew him well; we had tended him for many years, and also the red thong was on his leg."

Kay'-yah was silent a moment, and then:

"Could you find that place again?" he asked.

"The place in the rocks where I buried him?"

"Yes," he answered. "The place of the white rock."

She jumped up from her seat by the trail.

"Come!" she cried. "It is not far from here, and the way there is the way to Ah'-co."

They ran in silence now, but Kay'-yah felt an excitement stirring his blood; an excitement more than that caused by their near approach to Ah'-co. In his eager desire to go forward they seemed to crawl along the narrow trail. The sun was low now and the canyon shadows were again creeping up the walls, but those walls were growing farther and farther apart, and just as the sun rested on the horizon's rim they came out into the desert the home desert and Ah'-co lay before them, near at hand with the haze of many campfires hanging like a mantle over its familiar hogans.

Kay'-yah caught Sah'-ne's hand and his heart beat fast, his voice was husky as he spoke:

"I wish you were of the Nag'-a-pah, Sah'-ne," was all he said; but she turned away her face and her eyes grew wet.

"Yonder is the place of the white rock," she said in a small voice, and gently drew her hand away.

Figure 26
"He Drew It Out, Tight-Clasped In His Hand. . . .
Sah'-Ne Watched Him With Growing Amazement"

There was little to mark the spot, and the wear of five summers and winters had grayed the white stone to nearly the tone of the others lying about it, but Sah'-ne knew the place and pointed to the stone without hesitation. Kay'-yah knelt by it and began to lift away the little pile of which it was the top. He felt that his hands trembled, but Sah'ne did not see; she watched him curiously.

"Why do you open a place of rest?" she asked.

"Wait," he answered, and presently reached down into the shallow hole he had made and lifted out a mass of brown bones and what once had been feathers. He laid it carefully on the ground and straightened the dry bones as much as possible: the red bit of thong still bound the withered talon, and the great wing-bones were intact. He looked at it for a moment, and then with fast beating heart slipped a hand into the dusty mass under either wing. It seemed as if the blood stood still in his veins as his fingers closed on a little bag he felt under one wing. He drew it out, tight-clasped in his hand, and rose to his feet. His eyes gleamed, and Sah'-ne watched him with growing amazement. His expression was strange as he looked at her and spoke.

"The sacred eagle was trained to fly at the word of his master – that was known to us. He carried messages from the living to those gone before; but messages he carried also from the living to the living. I have heard it said that the sacred eagle was known to fly in the direction of Ta-pau'-wee; one message he did not carry to its journey's end – look!"

He opened his hand and showed the little bag lying there.

"What is it?" asked Sah'-ne simply; and Kay'-yah looked deep into her eyes, as if he would read her very soul. In that moment he cast from him forever any suspicion, any thought of her in connection with her father, the spy.

He reached for his knife and deftly severed the neck from the little skin bag, and shook out what it contained. In his hand, touched by the pink of the afterglow, lay a small, blue bear, roughly carved in turquoise. For a moment the two stood as if fashioned in stone, their eyes fastened on the little object he held in his hand. Then with a long-drawn breath Sah'-ne grasped his arm.

"Come!" she cried. "Oh, Joho'-na-ai has been good to us! Come!"

And like two children, hand in hand, they ran down the little slope toward the friendly campfires of Ah'-co.

Figure 27
The Dancing Lesson – A Taos boy learning the Corn Dance, Photo by Carl Moon

Figure 28
Publisher of Lost Indian Magic Timothy Beckley is photographed in the Land of Enchantment by Charla Gene'

Figure 29
Home from the Hunt, Taos Hunter, Photo by Carl Moon

Chapter 14
Tag-A'-Mo Speaks

Like a woven thread the story ran,
Weaving the lives and fates of men
Into a blanket of one, big plan:
Into the past and back again.

IT was dusk as Sah'-ne and Kay'-yah reached the camp, and many camp-fires were burning. Quick, questioning glances were thrown at them as they passed, and sharp exclamations came as first one, and then the other was recognized. The men rose from their places by the fires and took a few steps in their direction, while women looked up from the pots they were tending, brushed back the hair from their eyes, and broke into high-excited questionings. Dogs barked and sniffed at their heels and yelped joyously as they recognized old companions.

Kay'-yah lifted his hand in greeting to many familiar faces but did not check his pace, and Sah'ne, with smiling face but weary feet, kept at his side. Not yet did the women know what she had done; not yet would they accept her as one of themselves; but when Dee-nay' had spoken – ah, then could she come out and take her place, then would they know that she was no To-to'-me spy, but Nag'-a-pah, and heart and soul their sister – Nag'-a-pah in all but in blood, and her head drooped again at the thought and her eyes rested for a moment on Kay'-yah – *that* she could never change.

The medicine lodge was dark and silent and, as they pushed aside the hide and stepped within, Kay'-yah thought it empty: but a voice spoke quickly at his step.

"Kay'-yah, – my son, the gods have sent you back to Dee-nay'."

And with a breath the gray ashes were blown from the little fire that was all but dead, and the tiny flame leaped back into life. There was fire too in Dee-nay's eyes as he looked up and beckoned Kay'-yah and Sah'-ne near.

Kay'-yah could not speak; his throat seemed closed to sound; but he held out his open palm for Dee-nay' to see, in the light of the feeble blaze, the object that lay in his hand. And then a strange thing happened. The old man, who was known to all for his quiet dignity, leaped to his feet like a boy, and snatching the Magic from Kay'-yah's hand, placed it on the altar and sprinkled it with sacred pollen from a little bag that hung near. Then he stood in front of the altar, and raising his hands high above his head, broke into a strange chant. Kay'-yah and Sah'-ne, standing motionless and speechless, watched him and listened.

"Joho'-na-ai, the wise, the good,
Maker of the lives of men,
Back has come thy Talisman!
From the deepest heart of earth;
From the sacred blue of skies;
Back has come thy Talisman!
Down shall bow our enemies;
Green shall grow our harvest fields;
Back has come thy Talisman!
Strong again our bow and spear;
Strong the tribe of Nag'-a-pah.
Back has come thy Talisman!"

And ending as abruptly as he had begun, he stepped to the great drum and began to pound on it, at first slowly and softly, then more swiftly and loudly, until the great booming notes rolled out into the quiet camp, and at the call every Nag'-a-pah sprang to his feet and hastened to the medicine lodge.

And then began a night of feasting and dancing, singing and merrymaking such as never before had been known in Ah'-co; the camp went wild with joy. Now would return the prosperity and happiness of other days; no longer should they skulk about the desert in fear of other tribes, but boldly would they go out to conquer; again had the gods shown their smiling countenance, and all was well. The game would come back to its old haunts in the hills and desert, and the fields would spring into green at the call of rushing waters.

All this Dee-nay' told them at the door of the medicine lodge, and they believed – had it not been so before? And more than this he told them. Placing one hand on Kay'-yah's shoulder, he spoke to them:

"Old men of the Nag'-a-pah, listen! Young men of the Nag'-a-pah, also to you I speak, and to the women of our hogans – listen! Many years have I been chief counselor among you – you have come to me for words of wisdom; for advice and counsel and for aid to heal your sick. All these have I given you always – guided by a wisdom greater than my own – but not always may I be among you; not always will you find Dee-nay' when you come seeking him to the medicine lodge, and in that day you will seek another; one who has learned of the sacred mysteries; who has been taught the wise things of the elders, and who has been proven brave and worthy.

"It is the way of our tribe for the medicine chief to name him who shall come after – and him I name to you this night – Kay'-yah, who has been my pupil for these many seasons; who is, in all but blood, my son. It is he who will stand where I have stood in the medicine lodge – he who will be chief among you – when I am gone. If there be one among you who would raise his voice against him, speak now, while Dee-nay' may answer!"

No one spoke, and Kay'-yah stood red and hot with embarrassment, looking into the many faces raised to his. It was the custom, under such circumstances, for the honored man to speak to the people, and Kay'-yah knew what was expected of him, but it seemed for a moment as if his tongue would refuse to obey. Then some of the dignity of the old man who had fathered him descended to his shoulders and he spoke simply and without fear.

"The words of Dee-nay' are directed by the gods; when the time comes I shall obey and shall seek their counsel in all that I do."

And there was a murmur of approval among the crowd. Again Dee-nay' spoke, and drew Sah'-ne forward.

"And here is a daughter who has served her people well. It was Kay'-yah who returned to us our Magic; but Sah'-ne aided him and she has served us in ways unknown to you but known to me. She is a true daughter of the Nag'-a-pahs and worthy of the name – I, Dee-nay', have said it."

And he pushed her gently toward a group of women, who welcomed her with smiles and many pleasant words.

All night the people danced and the many fires glowed red. Kay'-yah had, many times, to repeat the story of his adventures, and small boys and little girls listened with open mouths in astonishment as he told of being on the summit of Qua'-ma – the mysterious Qua'-ma, the haunt of the fairy-folk; – and the women clustered close to Sah'-ne and heard in wonder her descriptions of life in Ta-pau'-wee. The two had forgotten their weariness, and the night wore on toward dawn with no thought of rest or sleep. Only when the fires began to lose their glow in the deeper red of the sky, and the voices of the singers to mingle with the calls of waking birds did Sah'-ne suddenly remember that she had not slept for two nights, and that she was very weary. She slipped away from the others and made her way to the familiar hogan where she had spent the greater part of her life. She threw herself on a soft pile of skins and was asleep almost before they had yielded to her weight.

She awoke suddenly in the early evening and lay listening; the drums had ceased – the people were calling with a new excitement in their voices. What did it mean? She rose quickly and made her way again to the crowded gathering-place – a little girl who had been sent for a jar of water told excitedly that the stream was growing broader as she watched; and in a very short time the village was empty, as every man, woman and child flocked down to the borders of the little stream, which grew into a river as the child had said, even as they watched with wondering eyes.

The girl who had first spoken waded out into the water and plunged her hands into the brown depths: she straightened up again with a shrill cry, and held a small object high for all to see.

"Look what I have found! Look what the waters have brought!"

It was a curiously wrought bracelet of bone in which were skillfully set turquoise and other bright stones, a little dulled by the water.

A woman pushed her way through the crowd and her voice was high and loud with excitement.

"The treasure! The treasure!" she cried. "The bracelet is a part of the treasure!"

Others took up her cry, crowding down into the water and groping with hands and naked feet in the little muddy stream which soon had more the appearance of marshland than river. Two or three more articles known to have been buried with their long lost treasure were found, but the bulk of it was not there.

"The water has washed it down!" someone cried. "Follow the stream up toward the canyon!"

And many men, women and children followed the advice, wading in the shallow water upstream, feeling carefully in the mud with hands and feet. And presently they were rewarded, for at one place, where the soft sandy bank had given way with the new rush of water, they came upon a bundle of rotting hide, and when picked up it dropped ornaments and articles of value: precious things made of carved bone and turquoise. The old men nodded with wise looks that said more plainly than words: "It is what should be expected – the Magic is working." While the younger men and women expressed their joy in shouts and renewed singing – their treasure was restored to them!

Kay'-yah, who was among them, felt his heart beat high with a new assurance as he remembered the promise of Tso that water should again flow down the canyon. Then surely the old man had escaped the arrow of Chot'-zu, and was alive and working in the interest of their friendship. The thought lifted an oppression that had lain heavier than he had been aware.

The sun shone red against the canyon walls, and the people of Ah'-co turned with joyous faces back toward home: but the strange happenings were not yet at an end, for as they turned toward the village a man at the rear of the crowd shouted;

"Quick, brothers! Your arms! Look! the enemy comes – from the canyon!"

And as they turned with startled faces, a large party of To-to'-mes emerged from the mouth of the canyon and came directly toward them; but at the appearance of panic among the Nag'-a-pahs, they stopped, laid down their arms and held, each man, his right hand above his head to signify that they came in peace. The people of Ah'-co stood still and waited for their approach with wonder in their hearts – strange things had happened since their Magic had been returned to its altar the night before, but this was the strangest of all – to see To-to'-mes approaching with signs of peace.

The approaching party was led by an old man, who towered above them and walked with the firm tread and dignified bearing of a born leader. As many of the Nag'-a-pahs recognized this man, with low murmuring of his name, Dee-nay' stepped forward and awaited his coming a few feet in front of his people. When they were within easy speaking distance of each other Tag-a'-mo – for it was he who led the To-to'-mes – stopped, and the two men stood for a moment gravely regarding each other in silence. Dee-nay' was the first to speak.

"You come in peace, Tag-a'-mo?" he questioned.

"I come in peace, Dee-nay'."

They were silent for a moment, and then Dee-nay' again spoke.

"The years have then rolled back – that is strange – it has been long since To-to'-me has looked upon Nag'-a-pah in peace."

"The fault has not been with me, Dee-nay', but with another – my heart has never changed toward you; – and – if the old days come again, then am I glad."

Intent and eager stood the Nag'-a-pahs, watching with curious eyes these men they had so long regarded as deadly enemies, who now returned their glances with friendly looks and a curiosity as intent as their own.

True to his race, Tag-a'-mo did not at once explain the purpose of his mission, but waited for the friendly bearing of his men to impress the Nag'-a-pahs and to give them time to regain their assurance. He stood quietly, at perfect ease, and his eyes dwelt on the swelling stream that now overran its banks. He waved his arm toward the water.

"The rains have not been heavy, yet the waters rise," he said, and his eyes had a strange gleam in them as he looked at Dee-nay'.

"Our Magic again rests on its ancient altar," said Dee-nay' a trifle stiffly.

A slight smile came to Tag-a'-mo's lips.

"The magic that loosed the waters dwells at the other end of the stream, brother."

"Is it so?" said Dee-nay'. "And was it to tell me this that you come to Ah'-co?"

Tag-a'-mo again grew grave.

"I come seeking the chief of my people," he said, and folded his arms quietly.

Dee-nay's manner grew cold, and he spoke shortly.

"Wau-ko'-ma is not here. Our hearts are, as you know, not warm for Wau-ko'-ma."

"It is not Wau-ko'-ma that I seek – my words shall be clear to you when I have spoken. Wau-ko'-ma is no longer chief of the To-to'-mes – it is of another I speak – the true chief of my people, he who was called Al-che-say' by his mother, but who is called by another name among your people."

"Your words have little meaning for me," again spoke Dee-nay'. "We have no such one among us – I know not of whom you speak."

Tag-a'-mo raised his head, and his keen eyes searched among the crowd of eager questioning faces that stood some little distance behind Dee-nay'. Slowly and deliberately he raised one arm and pointed toward a figure standing alone to one side of the crowd.

"He stands yonder," he said; and all eyes, following the direction of the pointing finger, turned toward Kay'-yah.

Figure 30
1904 Gelatin Print Photo by Carl Moon

Chapter 15
The Chin-Dog Howls

Pathless as the sea; no way marked down;
The desert sand no trail uncovered keeps.
Here many a hapless traveler death has found,
And mid the desolate wastes forgotten sleeps.

DEE-NAY' looked at Kay'-yah and back again at Tag-a'-mo.

"Make clear your words," he said briefly; "I like not mysteries."

Kay'-yah stood as if carved in stone. Had his ears deceived him? What was the meaning of the strange words spoken by Tag-a'-mo? His eyes sought Sah'-ne, who stood pale and still some distance away, with her dark eyes fixed on Tag-a'-mo's face. His heart beat fast as he listened in tense expectancy for the words of the To-to'-me, who now spoke slowly and with great deliberation.

"My heart is for actions more than for words, yet words are needed here, and the telling may not be made brief – for it holds the lives of men." And he folded his arms slowly and looked calmly into the many questioning faces turned toward him.

Few of the Nag'-a-pahs understood his words, but they realized from the attitude of Dee-nay' and Kay'-yah that matters of great importance were being discussed and they eagerly awaited the moment when Dee-nay' would speak to them in their own tongue; but Tag-a'-mo anticipated this expectancy and his next words, and all that followed, were spoken in clear-flowing Nag'-a-pah which was understood by most of the men who were with him.

"Many years ago," he began, "a son came to the hogan of Tap-a-wan', greatest of all To-to'-me chiefs – he who was known as 'Eagle Wings' because of the white wing-mark that shone on his cheek when in anger. Great was the joy at the coming of this son – for it was feared that another would rule at the death of Eagle Wings, and in my tribe the son rules when the father is gone. Not long after this son was born Tap-a-wan' was killed in battle, and his wife died also, of grief at his death; but before she died she placed about the neck of Al-che-say', her young son, a little bag containing the hereditary ring of all the To-to'-me chiefs. He was at that time under two years of age."

Dee-nay' stood like a tall tree, motionless, his white head glistening in the late sunlight, and his burning eyes fixed on Tag-a'-mo's face. Nag'-a-pahs and To-to'-mes alike seemed to hold their breath, but the eager expectancy of the crowd had the effect only of making Tag-a'-mo more deliberate, more calm. He stood silent for a moment before continuing his strange narrative strange in what it promised to reveal.

"There lived, at this time, a sister to Tap-a-wan', whose husband was dead, a sister and her son Wau-ko'-ma. It was he whose rule the people had feared before the birth of Al-che-say', for Wau-ko'-ma, though young, was then as he is now – my words need say no more, for Wau-ko'-ma is known to you. This sister came to the hogan where Al-che-say' was being tended and said she would take the care of him – and there was no one who could turn her away. She took the child and tended him with what seemed kindness – she and an old nurse named Lee'-tah who had been her nurse in childhood, and the nurse of the child also. But very soon those who passed heard wailing in the hogan and they were not permitted to enter, as Na-kee', the mother of Wau-ko'-ma, said that Al-che-say' was very ill with the spotted sickness and that it was death for any to enter. Prayers were made for him, and many dances and ceremonials in the medicine lodge – and day and night the chant of the medicine men rose to the skies but it was in vain for on the third day Na-kee' came to the door of the hogan with her hair loose about her face and the ashes of mourning on her head. She said that the child Al-che-say' was dead and, as you know, one who looks upon the dead, stricken with this sickness, dies of the same disease: – so none dared enter there and, as is the custom of our people, the hogan, with all it contained, was burned to the ground. With the little chief dead, Wau-ko'-ma was made ruler, much against the desire of the people, but the ancient law of heredity must be obeyed – and from then until this day he has ruled the To-to'-mes with an evil hand. Now – it has become known that Al-che-say', son of Tap-a-wan', did not die of the spotted sickness – these many years ago."

Tag-a'-mo again ceased speaking for a short space. There was a murmur among the crowd, as of the wind among leaves, but no one questioned him, and after a moment he again lifted his head, and his deep voice could be heard by everyone present, even to the farthest Nag'-a-pah.

"The chief of the To-to'-mes did not die as a child, but my words shall tell you how he lived – not as it came to me shall I tell you, but as it happened at that time. Listen, Dee-nay' and all you Nag'-a-pahs! The woman Na-kee', mother of Wau-ko'-ma, had desired always that her son should rule, and it was grief to her that a son was born to Tap-a-wan' – but when the gods put that son in her power her joy was great. But the gods show anger to one who would take the life of a chief, and she feared to kill Al-che-say'. One night, when there was no moon, she put the child into the arms of Lee'-tah, the old nurse. 'Take the child into the hills,' she said, 'where there are bears and great cats; place him upon the ground and watch from some safe place until you can return and tell me that Wau-ko'-ma is chief of the To-to'-mes. Take food and do not return while the child lives – his blood will then be upon the beasts, and not with us.'

"The woman Lee'-tah took the child, for she knew that if she did not obey her life should pay, and another would go in her stead. She crept out of Ta-pau'-wee and thought that no one saw her go; – but one followed – a medicine-man of the tribe – by name Tso."

Kay'-yah gave a low exclamation, but it passed unheeded by the others.

"Tso followed, and when he saw the burden that the woman carried he questioned her: for they were friends. With fear in her heart, the woman told him of her errand, and after some thought he spoke to her. 'The child must be saved, but his life would not be safe if he returned to Ta-pau'-wee – the followers of Na-kee' are many; I have a plan that is better – for a time at least. He shall be placed with good people who shall love him as their own, and when he is old enough he will return to his own people and claim what is rightfully his. I will make known to Tag-a'-mo and others what I have done, and we will watch his welfare and tell him when the time shall come. Wait here in a safe place on the mountain until I return, and Na-kee' will believe that you have done as she commanded.'

"He took the child and journeyed with him to Ah'-co, for he had heard of two there who greatly desired a son which had not been granted them by the gods. As he carried the child he noticed about its neck a little bag suspended by a thong; a bag that he himself, skilled in such things, had made and presented to Tap-a-wan' the chief. He was glad the bag was there, for the child would need the strong protection of the medicine he did not doubt that it contained.

"Al-che-say' he left just within the doorway of the hogan of Qua-hi'-da, the Nag'-a-pah."

There were sharp exclamations at this strange information, and quick questioning glances were thrown at Kay'-yah; but Tag-a'-mo continued:

"About his neck remained the little bag placed there by his mother before she died, and that little bag – contained the hereditary ring of all the To-to'-me chiefs."

"Umph!" exclaimed Dee-nay', and the exclamation expressed much.

The blood in Kay'-yah's veins seemed turned to fire, and a strange mist swam before his eyes; but Tag-a'-mo, his glance passing far over the heads of those before him, spoke calmly on:

"Tso returned quickly to where the woman Lee'-tah awaited him on the mountain. Three days had he been gone, and her heart had almost failed her as she watched for his return; but others also watched her, sent by Na-kee', who wished all trace of her crime destroyed, and as they saw a man speak with Lee'-tah, Wau-ko'-ma and two warriors sprang from the rocks and, after a short fight, threw first Tso and then the woman over the edge of the cliff on which they stood. Far down into the canyon they fell, struck the rocks and lay still.

"The woman was dead and the men returned to tell Na-kee' what they had done. Tso they also thought dead, and he remained for long as one in the last sleep. But he was not dead, and one came who found him there and brought the life back to his broken body."

Dee-nay' nodded slowly and a warm light came into his eyes.

"But the mind of Tso was as the mind of a little child from that time; he remembered not that he was To-to'-me, nor that he had lived among men, and the people of Ta-pau'-wee saw him no more. He made his home among the rocks and his only friends were the beasts and birds; until, in the course of time, one came to him, wounded and weary, and on the cheek of the stranger he recognized the mark of eagle wings, the mark that had been on the face of Tap-a-wan', and the sight awakened that part of his mind that had slept.

"He came to me but two suns ago, and it was from him I learned the greater part of what I have spoken. And now is it clear to you, Dee-nay', who it is that I seek?"

Dee-nay' answered in a low voice, speaking slowly, and as he spoke he turned toward Kay'-yah and the expression in his eyes was hard to read.

"It is clear but very strange. Kay'-yah, come! It is as a son that I have always regarded thee, and now I know not what words to speak. It must be as Tag-a'-mo has said and you are Al-che-say' – chief of the To-to'-mes – yet I doubt not that your heart remains with us of the Nag'-a-pah also. I have said that you shall be chief when I am gone – and the word of Dee-nay' has never returned to his mouth. That being so – then you shall be chief of both To-to'-mes and Nag'-a-pahs." His eyes flashed as he again turned to Tag-a'-mo. "It is thus that the gods fulfill old prophecies, Tag-a'-mo; it is thus that we planned many years ago, you and I, when the dream showed little chance of coming true. It is thus the Magic works!"

At the mention of the Magic, Tag-a'-mo looked thoughtful.

"Many years Wau-ko'-ma planned to steal the Magic of the Nag'-a-pahs, and at one time was very confident that he had secured it, as word came from Gō'-me, who lived among your people, that another day would bring the Magic to Ta-pau'-wee; but it did not come, and great was our surprise to hear that it had been lost from Ah'-co."

Kay'-yah, who had been standing silently by Dee-nay', now spoke for the first time.

"There is reason in what Gō'-me said. The sacred eagle of Ah'-co had been trained to carry messages to Ta-pau'-wee – as it may be that you know, Tag-a'-mo. It was to have carried the Magic also, but was shot by Tso, of whom you have spoken, and buried in the rocks by Sah'-ne – a daughter of your people — "

He stopped short: a new thought had entered his mind and the blood rose to his face. He turned slowly and looked back into the crowd to where Sah'-ne stood – her cheeks burning and her eyes shining. They were of one blood, he and she.

Tag-a'-mo spoke, very gravely now. "Al-che-say', born chief of my people, I come to ask that you take your place as ruler of the To-to'-mes – even as was your father before you. It is the wish of your people that you return to Ta-pau'-wee; they have many reasons for wishing that you come. They desire to show you kindness for the way in which you were so lately treated there – when they thought you an enemy and a spy – and also their hearts are weary of wrong and lawless ruling. I, Tag-a'-mo, have been sent to ask that you will come. What is the answer that I take back?"

Kay'-yah hesitated, and there was trouble in his face as he spoke.

"What of Wau-ko'-ma?" he asked.

There was a sudden commotion among the To-to'-mes as another small party emerged from the canyon. Tag-a'-mo turned his head in their direction.

"Wau-ko'-ma is here," he said.

A wave of suppressed excitement swept over the crowd as the second party of To-to'-mes came toward them; but any suspicion or uneasiness that may have been among the Nag'-a-pahs was silenced when it was seen that, with the exception of the two men who walked ahead on either side of Wau-ko'-ma all were unarmed. When they neared the edge of the crowd the voice of Dee-nay' broke the tense silence. Taking Kay'-yah by the arm, he stepped to the side of Tag-a'-mo, and with a wide gesture that included all about him he said:

"Come, brothers! The shadows of the canyon grow long; we will go to the better shelter of Ah'-co.'

And without seeming to be conscious of it, To-to'-mes and Nag'-a-pahs mingled as though of one tribe as they accompanied the new chief and the old medicine-men to the Nag'-a-pah camp, the guards with Wau-ko'-ma bringing up the rear.

Halting in the wide level space before the medicine lodge, the great gathering formed a circle and waited for what was to follow. As the people grew silent, a commotion arose at a point in the edge of the crowd, and a moment later a white-haired old man forced his way through the circle and hobbled across the open space toward Kay'-yah.

"Al-che-say'! Al-che-say'!" he called out. Then, as he came nearer he held something out in his hand, and a broad smile lighted his face as he exclaimed; "Here, Rain-boy, – the ring is yours, and the bag is mine, but I give you both!"

"Tso!" exclaimed Kay'-yah, as he stepped quickly out to meet the old man; and his voice failed him as he took the ring, and clasped the hand that held it out to him.

It was Tso, and apparently very much alive; but the look of mental weakness had almost gone from his face, and a keen light played in the old eyes. Dee-nay' also stepped up, and, much to the surprise of the crowd, held out his hand, saying as he did so;

"Kay'-yah brought me the message from the Lion, and much water again flows down the canyon toward Ah'-co, as you have said. I must learn of you a magic greater than my own."

Holding out his long arms, Tso smiled broadly as he replied:

"These are the magic. They dug away the rocks and earth where the dog Wau-ko'-ma and his men had turned the waters of Mat-a-wee away from your canyon."

Many questions were asked and answered as the three turned back to where Tag-a'-mo stood, and the expression on the face of the old To-to'-me medicine-man showed plainly that he had already known all that Tso had spoken. He now raised a hand as a signal and the men who guarded Wau-ko'-ma brought him forward into the center of the circle.

All remained silent as the deposed chief, now captive of his own people, was brought before them. No trace of the struggle and violent anger that must have ensued when he was made a prisoner now remained on the features or in the bearing of Wau-ko'-ma, but a fixed, sullen expression, that held the brutal face, thinly masked the inner desire for deadly retaliation against all those about him. Something of that inner hatred was clearly visible to Tag-a'-mo, and as he thought of the treachery Wau-ko'-ma had revealed in his secret dealings with the vicious tribe of desert pirates, he was glad that his days of evil were soon to be brought to an end.

With arms bound to his back, he stood motionless, with a poorly assumed air of indifference, where his guards had placed him; and into Kay'-yah's mind flashed the picture of the crowd that had gathered about *him* as he had stood bound before Wau-ko'-ma on the night of his captivity in the To-to'-me camp. Again he could hear the low exclamation of Tag-a'-mo as he had looked so intently at him, "Be'-ta-atsin, be'-ta-atsin." *That* mystery was solved now: and he now knew why the old medicine-man had sworn before the To-to'-me people that he should not be put to death before given trial, and why the treacherous Wau-ko'-ma had been so determined that he must be killed at once. Then, too, the strange actions of Tso were thus explained, as he also must have seen the birthmark on his face; and the unexpected revelation had thrown his defective mind into a temporary fit of madness.

The crowd, whose attention was divided between Kay'-yah and the deposed chief, was suddenly moved with excitement as the former walked up and stood with folded arms before Wau-ko'-ma. Something in the pose and bearing of Kay'-yah caused the group of old To-to'-me men, who stood about Tag-a'-mo, to break into low murmurs that expressed their strong emotion, and then, "The son of Tap-a-wan'! The image of Eagle Wings!" burst from one mouth, then another, as the strong likeness between the old chief and his son became so apparent to them.

The blood of a long line of wise and powerful chiefs flowed in the veins of Kay'-yah. The startling events and revelations that had just transpired had lifted him at a single bound from youth to the full stature of manhood, and he took his place as the leader of his people with an ease that brought surprise even to the heart of Dee-nay'.

A death-like silence fell on the crowd as, looking squarely into the shifting eyes of the captive before him, Kay'-yah spoke.

"Wau-ko'-ma, the gods give justice for justice among all Earth children. You and I have changed places – and as your chief, it is I who now pass judgment upon you."

While he was thus speaking, Tso, with arms half bent, and with hands clenched, pulled away from the hand of Tag-a'-mo, who tried to stop him, and moved stealthily out into the open space and up behind Kay'-yah, his eyes blazing as he waited with tense expectancy for the word that would give the death sentence to his hated enemy.

Turning his face to where Dee-nay' and Tag-a'-mo stood, Kay'-yah asked:

"Is it not so that, among our people, the word of a rightful chief is above all others?"

"It is so," said Tag-a'-mo: and all of the men of the crowd nodded approvingly.

"If my first act as your chief – in sight of the Great Spirit of us all – should bring the blood of one of my tribe upon our hands, it would be an ill omen that must cast its evil spell upon all."

The crowd moved uneasily, but became quiet again as he continued:

"Thus, my people, – and you are all my people – it is my will that my first act shall be one of justice – and justice without the shedding of blood."

Then raising his voice so none could fail to hear, he exclaimed:

"Wau-ko'-ma, as a murderer and an outcast in the eyes of all Nag'-a-pah and To-to'-me people, I shall send you as a wanderer, without weapons for further treachery, to turn your face forever away from the homes of real men and warriors with whom you are unworthy to live."

Scarcely had his last words been spoken, before Tso clutched his arm and shouted:

"No! No! The dog must *die!* If you let him go he will bring greater trouble on us, for he will go to the — "

His words were cut short as Kay'-yah pushed him backward, and the great hand of Tag-a'-mo closed over his mouth as he was forced back into the crowd.

A murmur ran through the throng, a murmur that seemed to express half-hearted approval of the young chief's decision: but fear of the suggested ill omen outweighed the desire for revenge, and within his heart each felt the wisdom of Kay'-yah's action.

Commanding the guards to loose Wau-ko'-ma's bonds, he motioned to the people on the side of the crowd nearest the desert to make an opening in the circle; then, pointing toward it and addressing the captive, he said:

"Go!"

With a sneer upon his face, but with slouching figure no longer held erect, Wau-ko'-ma walked away, and after passing the last hogan of the village, turned into the open desert.

As he faced the people again, Kay'-yah held up his hand for silence.

"My people, I have said to the people of Ah'-co, and now say to you all, that I will seek the will of the Great Spirit in all things – that wisdom may guide my actions toward you. You have, with justice, desired the death of that man, and so might I, with greater cause than any of you, desire it also; but I believe it is the will of the gods that I should do as I have done. And now let our thoughts turn to rejoicing that the days of peace and old friendship among us have come again, and that in heart we are all one people."

Loud shouts of joyous approval arose from the crowd that now began to gather about Dee-nay' and Tag-a'-mo, who, they knew, would tell them of plans for the days of feasting and dancing that would soon be held in both villages.

Figure 31
"And The Song Was The To-To'-Me Death Chant"

Taking advantage of the excitement of the crowd, Kay'-yah went in search of Tso, as he wished to explain to him why he had been compelled to ignore his advice to make an end of Wau-ko'-ma, but the old man was not with Dee-nay' or Tag-a'-mo, who said that he had disappeared in the crowd on the side near the medicine lodge. Feeling that his old friend had not been treated with the kindness and consideration due him, he searched among the people near the lodge, then went into the big hogan itself, but found it empty. With a vague impression that all was not right, he stepped upon a block of wood that stood just outside the doorway, and scanned the crowd; but Tso was not among the people. Again he stepped into the lodge and looked at the wall beside the door where he had hung his bow-case the night of his return. It was gone. His suspicions now thoroughly aroused, he slipped quickly out and around to the rear of the lodge and, unnoticed by the crowd, ran swiftly along back of the hogans until he came to the point where Wau-ko'-ma had left the village. Coming upon an excited group of little boys, he asked them if they had seen a crippled old man pass that way.

"Yes," replied one of the boys; "and he mumbled strange talk as he passed, and he went into the desert where the bad man went."

"Which way did he go? Speak quick!" commanded Kay'-yah.

"Around the ridge of rock yonder to the west," said the oldest boy.

Fearing he might be too late, but determined that his command regarding Wau-ko'-ma must be obeyed, Kay'-yah ran swiftly in the direction given him by the little boys. He knew that a thirst for a just revenge, and the deadly accuracy of Tso's marksmanship, might easily bring to naught his intended act of mercy, and that he alone could hope to appeal to the old man's reason.

As he rounded the last point of high ground that hid the view of the desert to the west, he saw, far ahead of him, the old To-to'-me standing like a statue against the dying light of the sunset sky. As he ran forward, the old man, with his face turned toward the west, and all unmindful of his young friend's approach, raised his arms triumphantly above his head; and Kay'-yah realized that he had come too late, as over the silence of the desert came the weird cadence of Tso's deep voice as he sang – and the song was the To-to'-me death chant.

"Howl ye, howl for the fallen foe:
Ah-ki-dah', – ah-ee-ah-ee,
In the long and silent sleep laid low,
Ah-ki-dah', – ah-ee.

Strong the warrior's bow and spear:
Ah-ki-dah', – ah-ee-ah-ee,
The ghost foe howls, he quakes with fear,
Ah-ki-dah', – ah-ee.

Up through the wind his spirit flies:
The death-birds circle wide the skies:
With beak and claw the silent fowls
Drop down, drop down: the chin-dog howls
Ah-ki-dah', – ah-ee-ee-e e.

Lost Indian Magic

Own This Beautiful Legendary Native North American Jewelry

====================

Become ONE With The Elements Of Earth, Water, Air And Fire WHEN YOU WEAR THIS BEAUTIFUL INDIAN MEDICINE WHEEL PENDANT AND CHARM

The Medicine Wheel, which is symbolized by a cross within a circle, is a powerful ceremonial tool . The Power of the Four Directions is implied whenever a wheel or circle is drawn. Since traditional Native American cultures view life as a continuous cycle, life mirrors the cycling of the seasons, the daily rising of the sun, and the phases of the moon. They also hold the view that all things are interrelated. The Medicine Wheel incorporates the Powers of the Four Directions and the interrelatedness of all things.

Ours is a large native paths pendant set in a sterling silver wheel with 8mm stones.
Amber – East Obsidian - West
Pearl (North) Carnelians (South)

( ) Order your Indian Medicine Wheel Pendant And Charm for Just $89.95 + $5 S/H

Inner Light, Box 753, New Brunswick, NJ 08903

732-602-3407 · PayPal: MrUFO8@hotmail.com

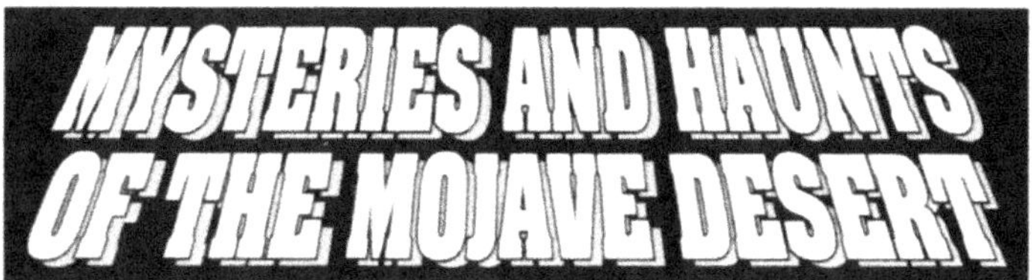

WHEN YOU RUN OUT OF WATER AND THERE IS NO SHADE AND THE TEMPERATURE IS OVER 125 DEGREES, YOU CAN BEGIN TO HALLUCINATE!

Join the ultimate road trip and help solve the riddles of California's Mojave Desert and Death Valley!

· Journey down Charles Manson's "Hole" said to lead to the Hollow Earth!

· Witness the landing of a UFO at Edwards Air Force Base, verified by an American Astronaut!

· Be petrified by the 12-foot levitating clown and find some gold, thanks to the teleporting leprechaun!

· Hunt for ghosts in the Death Valley Opera House!

· Attend Mae West's first seance!

· Keep your distance from the Albino Bigfoot running loose!

· Unravel the puzzle of the lost Viking ships in the desert!

www.RoadsideMonster.com

HERE ARE CHILLING TALES of abandoned mines, mysterious creatures, deranged killers, haunting, spook lights, space ships from faraway worlds, phantom stagecoaches, and many others strange tales and urban legends that will shiver your bones!

Contains the complete text of George Van Tassel's, ***"I Rode In A Flying Saucer!"***

Order DEATH VALLEY - SECRETS OF THE MOJAVE.
$20.00 + $5.00 S/H BONUS DVD included!
Global Communications
Box 753, New Brunswick, NJ 08903

www.ingramcontent.com/pod-product-compliance
Lightning Source LLC
LaVergne TN
LVHW061244100826
845148LV00008B/1022

9781606110850